Land-Value Taxation

LAND-VALUE TAXATION

The Equitable and Efficient Source of Public Finance

edited by
Kenneth C. Wenzer

Routledge
Taylor & Francis Group
LONDON AND NEW YORK

First published 1999 by M.E. Sharpe

Published 2015 by Routledge
2 Park Square, Milton Park, Abingdon, Oxon OX14 4RN
711 Third Avenue, New York, NY 10017, USA

Routledge is an imprint of the Taylor & Francis Group, an informa business

Library of Congress Cataloging-in-Publication Data

Land-value taxation : the equitable and efficient source
of public finance / Kenneth C. Wenzer, editor
p. cm.
Includes bibliographical references and indexes
ISBN 0-7656-0448-5 (hardcover : alk.paper)
ISBN 0-7656-0449-3 (pbk. : alk. paper)
1. Single tax. 2. Land value taxation. 3. Real property tax.
4. Real property and taxation. 5. Land use—Effect of taxation on.
6. Finance, Public. I. Wenzer, Kenneth C., 1950– .
HD1313.L33 1999
336.22—dc21 98–55374
CIP

ISBN 13: 9780765604491 (pbk)
ISBN 13: 9780765604484 (hbk)

To the Veterinary Staff of the Washington Animal Rescue League:
For Their Love and Compassion Extended to My Family

Table of Contents

Preface

This collection of essays examines the merits of land-value taxation. It distinguishes between two types of property tax, that on land and the other on improvements. The contributors, with their differing backgrounds, present the meaning and workings of the land-value tax from a variety of standpoints. They concur that it encourages optimal land use, fosters employment, helps prevent urban sprawl, and complements the free enterprise system. Taxing improvements, the authors agree, is a detriment to these goals, contributes to inflation, and complicates the tax system in general. To the essays on economics are added pieces on ethical, historical, and other aspects of land-value taxation. This anthology offers the scholar and the layman a well-rounded body of literature on its subject.

Within the Georgist heritage a great variety of interpretations, some of them conflicting, have taken form. That is a tribute to the richness and suggestiveness of the idea itself, especially in the form its eloquent champion Henry George presented it.

George himself, for example, wrote with passion of the sufferings of the poor under a system in which the value of land held by the wealthy went monopolized and virtually untaxed. Orthodox adherents of land-value taxation who are of George's inclination would therefore concentrate on taking for the public good that unearned value. They will insist on confining all taxation to that on land value—the single tax, it is called in its classical form. Such a tax was perceived essentially as a means of leveling unjust differences in privilege and collecting a revenue for the common benefit. In a conversation with the editor, Mason Gaffney observed:

> George's primary goal was to untax labor. With that in mind, he would regard as most inadequate any proposal to modify existing property taxation at the local level. That property taxation now takes only a small

> fraction. George would put a greater emphasis on untaxing labor by abolishing the payroll tax and those parts of the personal income tax that would fall on wage and salary income. He would also deplore any movement to raise so-called consumer taxes at the expense of property taxes. Merely to adjust the local property tax at the current low levels is a travesty of George's grand scheme and vision.

Some would regard as a triumph a gradual shift of taxation from improvements to land within the existing tax structure. The orthodox would maintain that such an approach does not attack George's basic premise that the inherent evil of civilization is private property in land and whisks under the almighty dollar his social and economic appeal for justice. Other recent advocates, whether supporters of the pure single-tax system or of the two-rate offshoot, also suggest ways in which the land tax will encourage good forms of behavior and the possibility of other benefits to present-day society.

Still others maintain it is unjust to impose any levy whatever on wealth other than land, including the kinds that fall to the well-off. This argument fails to acknowledge that all wealth brings privilege and contradicts equality, both economic and moral. Land taxers of George's gentle temperament would find that view as tantamount to shrinking his broader philosophy of reverence for the land, respect for work as ennobling in itself regardless of its income, and abhorrence of poverty. In the end, any kind of selfishly inspired and undistributed wealth is antagonistic to George's vision of a perfected world.

All this is to say that the concept of land-value taxation is less a coherent ideology than a fruitful beginning to discussion of both the moralities and the practical goods of social conduct and policy. It would therefore be imperative to distinguish among persuasions within the movement. It is to be hoped that the diversity of concerns and viewpoints in this collection will give some indication of the breadth of that possible dialogue.

Such an endeavor would be important, for over the years, as governments around the globe have sought additional funding to keep up with their increased responsibilities and demands, taxation has become more complex. As the level of taxation as a percentage of the GDP has risen, so too has the incentive for those who would otherwise be heavily taxed to find ways of escaping the burden, spawning a lucrative tax consultancy industry. A growing corpus of legislation keeps trying to plug up the loopholes. Also necessary is a larger tax bureaucracy with intrusive powers to cope with the paperwork and other chores. At least in the United States, the taxpayer has to turn into an accountant to maintain himself above water, and his civil liberties are curtailed. The demand is for a simplification of the tax system that would be easy to implement and understand. Land-valuation taxation, especially in its purest form—the single tax—is a necessary and easily obtainable first step.

An editor is only as worthy as the contributors with whom he associates. I have been fortunate in mine. In my graduate programs my mentors took for granted that history is the most important of all fields. After working with both academicians and laymen who are in other specializations, I have developed a deeper appreciation for their disciplines and backgrounds. I hope that they will view a historian kindly, as I have learned to perceive the work of scholars in the social sciences. All works, including reprints, have been edited without change in content. To Mrs. William Vickrey for her permission to use her late husband's works, I extend special thanks. I owe gratitude to Nicolaus Tideman for making me aware of these essays by the Nobel laureate and also those of Harry Gunnison Brown and Mason Gaffney. My friend and colleague Jack Schwartzman was slated to submit a piece, but an untimely personal misfortune intervened, which was happily surmounted. He, too, must be thanked for his intellectual companionship and, of course, repartee. My friend Thomas West has been of inestimable help. Sean Culhane's good cheer and belief in my work have, as usual, been nonpareil. The Lincoln Institute of Land Policy, the Center for the Study of Economics, and the Robert Schalkenbach Foundation should be mentioned for their timely financial support. Theodore Gwartney, Anthony Werner, Nan Braman, Sonny Rivera, Mark Sullivan, Joan Youngman, Joshua Vincent, and Sharon Fineman have given noteworthy help. Two librarians at the University of Maryland, Lily Griner and Patricia Herron, as usual, have been of immeasurable assistance. For making me a more aware person, and this book an effort toward the making of a more just world in harmony with the flora and fauna, I am grateful to all these people.

During the work on this book my beloved friends Clio, my dog, and cat, Raisonique, passed away. A hope for the preservation of the forests and river paths that have held so much meaning for Clio and me has enabled me to go on. And those cherished moments with Raisonique scampering around me will never be forgotten. My cat, Oliver, has been a continual source of joy.

Land-Value Taxation

1

Kenneth C. Wenzer

Some Reasons That Americans Do Not Listen to Henry George

Henry George, founding his reformist program in an ethical more than a technical spirit of renovation, looked to a world of prosperity informed by conscience, morality, and social justice. For the past century small numbers of people have advocated his ideas and his criticism of an iniquitous economic system. Supporters of the single tax are few. Much of the American political vocabulary speaks of little beyond material gain, and not of the whole but of *my* prosperity. Why have George's countrymen been so uninterested in any social vision larger than their own consumeristic private livelihood and comfort? The motive may be no more complicated than selfishness. But beliefs publicly stated and widely held reinforce this attitude.[1]

During the appropriately named Gilded Age in which Henry George preached, industrial growth and a market economy triumphed, announcing in the iron rail and the telegraph the conquest of time and space. The United States had become a great power, the first modern country outside Europe to do so. By 1920, she was the greatest industrial nation in the world. Wealth, or if not wealth a comfortable subsistence, seemed to be within the reach of everyone.

In 1920, Clarence Day wrote *Life With Father,* a romanticized account of his own boyhood in that time of comfortable middle-class naïveté. While growing up, Day recounts, he was living on a generous paternal stipend. It seems, however, that the young man managed to overspend this largesse. One day a creditor came knocking on his door. The visitor took exception to Clarence's indignation and threat of withholding his business.

> He said he was sorry to hear it. But he didn't sound very sorry. Times were bad, he explained, and he had to have money. I didn't believe him. Looking back, I realize that the long depression of the nineties had started and banks were beginning to close, but I knew nothing about this at the time. I was preoccupied with my own troubles.[2]

What blinded Day and his peers of the upper and middle classes was not the gleam of gold, but the patina of a baser alloy. And beyond the polished coldness of steel and glass, the smoking chimneys of factories were covering the lush farmlands with their pollutants. A corporate hegemony increasingly monopolizing land and industry created a new series of social relations and dislocations, including cycles of business depression and numerous violent strikes. Henry George sought to redirect these tortuous and potentially revolutionary changes into channels that flowed along the waters of American tradition.

Capitalist industrialism and its ethos, although beneficial to the urban well-to-do, threatened the small, bucolic communities that still regarded themselves as the custodians of American ways and virtues. The various new forms of labor and immigration, along with the shift toward a more complex urban society, seemed alien to those values. The strikes of 1877, punctuated with labor violence, awakened paranoia in the settled classes, as did the specter of the Paris Commune, the Haymarket Riot, and later the Bolshevik coup d'état.

It is to be expected that the major beneficiaries of land and industrial monopoly would fear radical reform. But the hinterland also feared or ignored ideas that came out of the new economic and technological conditions, even ideas that claimed to fulfill the vision of the colonial forefathers.

And that fear contributed to a paradox: Even as many Americans recoiled from the massive material and social degradation of the era, they aligned themselves with the major beliefs of capitalist industrialism, repelled at the possibility that some political order seemingly even more foreign to the American past would come to replace it.

Capitalism, then, had two apparent opposite forces working for it: While prosperity was beguiling the Clarence Days, the very newness of an industrializing nation was making others dread whatever politics seemed to be of its turbulent spirit. Besides, traditionalists too could take pride in technological innovation as an expression of primal American virtue. Out of all these factors came an ideational and mythic structure rejecting class consciousness or notions of a communality of purpose outside the acquisition of money. It was a mentality capable of swallowing up dissent and regurgitating it into an innocuous substance that most people would accept as sustenance. And it is because of that mentality that only a small number of people took seriously the ideas of Henry George, who extolled the American belief in the virtue of labor.

The labor of man is conscious and purposeful; what any other animal does is instinctual. Anything that man creates is an extension of himself. It is this willed act of mental or physical creation that defines the worker as human. An artisan, a machinist, or an engineer making use of God's own handiwork for socially useful purposes or for sheer pleasure is fully human. Inertia leads to destruction of the individual spirit and a free community. These beliefs formed an intrinsic part of George's morality and political economy.

With industrial capitalism came methods of production that threatened the act of independent workmanship: standardization, speeding up, and the reduction of workers to attendants of the machine. Beyond these components of production itself was an accumulation of capital that resulted in monopolization of land and industry and of services that have their roots in the land. Industrial monopoly was as deadly and counterproductive as land monopoly for the healthy growth of an equitable social organism, for it institutionalized the separation of man from the materials of his work and therefore from the work itself: his thinking, his acting, his integrity, his self-respect. Under capitalism in its present form, anyone who was not a craftsman or a farmer had to sell his labor power to another individual in exchange for money to buy the necessities of life. He then became alienated from his creation and was dependent upon the whims of others. During the period George lived, this alienation progressed more rapidly than at any other time in history since the breakdown of the craft heritage. Marx and Engels as well as Lenin would have agreed. What they could not foresee was that, at least in the United States, the development of labor would lead not to revolution but to a further tightening of capitalist control over workers deprived of self-identity in work, thus making them more open to identification with property, luxury, and the act of consumption.

The scientific management fostered by Frederick W. Taylor became symbolic, against some of his more humane intentions, of a capitalist effort (ironically extolled by Lenin) to rip out all humanity from the work process. To factory owners, Taylorism became premised on coldly calculating how to foster the least amount of physical movement, emotional needs, and mental exertion of the human being for the greatest productive output—a means of controlling an alienated work force and its milieus by attempting to reduce the laborers' human identity through the disassociation of the labor process from their hands. Thought and skill gave way to mindless repetition with more regulation and control. After describing the "obsessive-compulsive personality" of Taylor, one writer explains: "These traits fitted him perfectly for his role as the prophet of modern capitalist management, since that which is neurotic in the individual is, in capitalism, normal and socially desirable for the functioning of society."[3]

Henry Ford did not officially adopt Taylorism. But the conveyor-belt assembly line at his Highland Park plant presents the most physically symbolic manifestation of industrialist subjugation and degradation of the worker into an automaton. Here was a conscious adoption of Ford's own variant of a paternalistic and prussianized "scientific management." It represents a progression from craftsmanship to managerial dictation of repetitive, Pavlovian operations. The assembly line in the possession of capitalists threatened to complete the transfer of all human skills to an inanimate machine—the total transformation of the worker into a factor for the expansion of capital and a component in statistical formulas.

Although the Ford worker did eventually more or less acquiesce and accept the five-dollar plan (a very high wage before World War I), the assembly line served as a prototype for the stifling of working-class consciousness in the United States. Deprived of identity in employment, the worker was thrown back upon a form of identity that has always had the approval of American society: the ownership of tangible or monied property.

The gospel of standardization, speed, dehumanization, and control as basic methodology was adopted in industries outside the factory system, and throughout society. So potent and tempting were the reality and the image of efficiency that shop methods reached out into the world of consumerism and human relations, much as fascism would do at the same time.

During the earlier days of the department store from the 1890s until the 1930s, the saleswoman plied a craft. She was independent, proud of her ability to display and describe the wares entrusted to her. This system suggests the subcontracting arrangements between a manufacturer and an independent craftsman before the onslaught of capitalist mechanization, reminiscent of the early stages of a capitalist mode of production involving little alienation and control. Cohesiveness and proximity among the saleswomen enabled them to discard personal antagonism and to work collectively when necessary.

Subliminal forces of dictated efficiency, or Taylorism and Fordism, appeared, however, in the guise of modern, more expeditious means of selling that were introduced into the department store. Managers became resentful of the work culture of the saleswomen. They attacked the floor bonding and arrogated to themselves the process that had given the saleswoman self-identity. They instituted new modes of product presentation, reduction of the sales force, and lessening of decision making. Saleswomen resisted these efforts to cheapen themselves. They were, in fact, far more successful in fighting for their rights than were the factory workers. They maintained a modicum of dignity, refusing to sever their work from their intelligence. In the end, management began turning to the final elimination of their intelligence: It instituted self-service.

Taylorism and Fordism also filtered into society itself and were employed on the daily level of existence. Control, speed, standardization, and efficiency took over American tastes and created a suburban neuroticism that has palsied the independent spirit not only of the saleswomen of a bygone era and the working class, but of people in general. Artisanal and selling skills and the small mom-and-pop shops, for instance, have fallen victim to new modes of buying. Day-to-day life has become a revved-up assembly line. People think that they have harnessed wondrous inventions like the automobile and the computer, but it is individual integrity and independence that have been yoked: We have become slaves to this new religion which is killing our instincts for any social betterment.

For all the dread of radicalism, however, an initial reaction to the changes wrought by capitalist industrialization was reformist, and some of it was truly radical. Some of the reformist impulse took the direction that historians, with some disagreement call Progressivism. Sincere in their concern for social ills, most progressives were committed to capitalism in much of its prevailing character. Protecting American society from the wanton violence of protesting workers required whatever reforms might prudently soften it, and those had to come, as far as possible, from the top and not the bottom. It took quite a turnabout in the thinking of middle- and upper-class leaders to accept in the new industrial context even reforms so carefully managed. During the Progressive Era, the government began to be looked upon as an instrument for containing disorder and restoring sanity. Reform by a newly defined middle class could satisfy both small-town Americans and the urban privileged. It might make human sense out of a world turned impersonal. The beneficent workings of reform could master the cold technology of industrialism. American society would continue with its industrial capitalist destiny while maintaining much of its old virtuous and neighborly character.

Other critics of society went beyond the concerned but tempering strategies of mainline progressives, and did so with a degree of popular support. Socialism, today a forbidden persuasion within American politics, for a few years before our entrance into World War I and even briefly afterward enjoyed a small but credible presence. Robert La Follette's presidential effort of 1924, collecting 5 million votes, united socialists with progressive Republicans.

More centrist than the socialists, Henry George could see virtue in a restructured, ethically inspired market economy. Unlike them, he could speak with ease in the moral vocabulary of traditional Americans. And unlike the few diehard opponents of industrialism itself, he could praise the imaginative and craftlike virtues that went into the best efforts of modern technology. But like all the other critics, he threatened the land and industrial monopolists who stood between the worker and the product, the innovative entrepreneur and the rightfully earned property.

As late as the country's engagement in World War I, reformers were seeking to retrofit square-pegged people into prestamped rounded holes. The anti-German and other hysterical hatreds of the war period aided the course of Americanism, creating an orthodox consensus repressively imposed by the government and the mob alike. The threat of a Red deluge deepened the fear of radicalism. The nation, including whatever ethnic communities could be Americanized, was learning to think like a continental village, turning its back on intellectual and moral outsiders. The besieged hinterland, it seems, had at last captured the industrial city. The Eighteenth Amendment, combining progressive reformism with a traditionalist morality, was the symbol of its victory.

But its triumph required a hidden surrender on its part. The inequality of wealth that Americans had always accepted, now all the more strongly in their abhorrence of anything suggestive of socialism or deep-rooted reform, had come to mean an industrial hierarchy such as the hinterland and a portion of the middle urban classes had once perceived as itself alien to the American ethos. The unstated new formula went something like this: egalitarian democracy means private acquisition, which means inequality of wealth, which means a legitimated hierarchy of privilege, which is good. That reasoning could suit well the interests of anyone. All that was needed for the equation to become nearly invulnerable was a belief in the unlimited possibility of a social and economic mobility such as Horatio Alger imagined.

Even in creating the illusion of a homogenized unity and equality, capitalist industrialism fostered disunity among the working masses and stifled any conscious seeking for major economic and social change. The ongoing social labor process has produced stratification of jobs and identity within the working classes. Unions and management, moreover, have preserved sexual, ethnic, and racial division of tasks. Failing to shape a common consciousness, workers have had little alternative to seeking private gain within the present system, and so to giving it all their loyalty.

Also contributing to the rejection of any kind of major change is the general prosperity of this consumer-mesmerized country, the relative accessibility of a home, a comfortable income, and the luxury of free time. The contrast between all this and the massively encrusted systems of class and privilege in the Old World made it easy for immigrant workers to perceive themselves as part of an essentially middle-class American population. In the United States, the myth of worldly gain—"myth" in the sense not so much of untruth (which it only partly is) but of a story that orders events and values into a symbolic whole—has been an ongoing major motivating force. It is one reason why in this country medicine, entertainment, and sports are more revered than scholarship. That Samuel Gompers, a former

Georgist and socialist, turned to a "pure and simple unionism" confining itself to immediate economic objectives to the exclusion of all other reforms, and in so doing became the most successful leader of the American working classes, tells volumes about American society and culture. It is not the system that has to be addressed, but how it is to be carved up. Even during the embattled 1930s, for instance, most union leaders could believe that a contract could be so devised as to embody equality between labor and management.

The nature of American politics also puts limits on any major reform. The system of checks and balances among the executive, judicial, and legislative branches gives the appearance of a harmonious republican polity. The deathless two-party political structure diffuses potential political radicalism and labor militancy into carefully limited programs, devoid of any fundamental ideological content.

Further, to understand the mind of Americans, go back to World War I. All that was or could be good and pure in life and close to God and earth gave way to the four-year carnage that was no-man's-land and brought a cold mechanistic Bolshevism, and soon after a genocide. It contradicted the hope that a new time of peace was awakening; it horrified the religious, especially many Christians. It also revealed that this country, which Americans had believed in with a patriot's gullible heart, was no longer an innocent among the corrupt. The United States was now the most powerful country in the world. The forces of materialism, meanwhile, were erupting in great cities that threw their arrogant shadow over the simple countryside. The fundamental truths of religion and morality were under siege. A sense of alienation tinged with xenophobia reigned in the country. Many Americans had undergone a more profound experience of spirituality: their religion, at any rate, was acquiring a more intense expression. People must have a firmer belief in God, they felt, and morality was seen as an outward manifestation of that faith. Anything that jeopardized that communion was immoral. It was therefore the duty of every Christian to defend the faith.

At the core of the new secularism was the terrifying Darwinian theory of evolution with its projection of a simian prehuman ancestry. In this new war the battle lines were not over a patch of land: they were for God's loving divinity, the souls of people, the Mosaic account of creation, a special destiny of man, and the imminent universal brotherhood. Without biblical miracles the world would be devoid of meaning, and immortality called into question. Evolutionists were most assuredly infidels. Rather than perceive the evolution of living organisms as an expression of divine creativity, frightened Christians pulled further into social fortresses safe from all threat of change, including the social reform that American Christianity had earlier embraced.

In the short run, George has lost out. Blue- and white-collar workers alike, deprived of full autonomy in work and beguiled by the rich and pleasant goods that industrialism itself, capitalist or not, can produce, have surrendered to consumerism and keeping up with the Joneses. So have the poor and the marginalized, who clutch at whatever consumer goods may give them a substitute for pride and public respect. As for the victims of American imperialism abroad, held in poverty by our client regimes, or mentally wrecked by the tortures of our client police, or killed by our client armies: They were never asked. And for those locked in a religious parochialism who identify their belief structure with this corporate-industrial Americanism, rejection of reform is preordained.

The voice of George, which warned against land and corporate monopoly with its godless morality and the power it entails, has been muted. We have lost our individuality, for most people are incapable of making decisions, and we seek identity in cultural group perceptions, replete with an impatience and laziness—the forestallers of any concern for others and the catalysts of greed. A corporate-monopolistic, military, and state complex (there are blurred distinctions among these) identifies itself with the goals, different faiths, and myths of our society. It tells us how to think, what to teach, what to believe, what to buy and at what price, all at the expense of innocent animals unnecessarily tortured for science and human lives blown up overseas for economic gain.

Henry George forewarned us. The barbarians are still rampant in the streets; poverty and war that enrich the few make for domestic tension, and foreign fighting fuels the monopolistic-corporate structure. If there is hope, it will come from people with the ability to compound the best in modern technology and free enterprise with the best in traditional values.

Notes

1. These works were consulted for this introductory essay: Susan Benson, "'The Customers Ain't God': The Work Culture of Department-Store Saleswomen, 1890–1940," in *Working-Class America: Essays on Labor, Community,*

and American Society, M.H. Frisch and D.J. Walkowitz, eds. (Urbana: University of Illinois Press, 1983), 185–211; Harry Braverman, *Labor and Monopoly Capital: The Degradation of Work in the Twentieth Century* (New York: Monthly Review Press, 1974); Mike Davis, *Prisoners of the American Dream* (London: New Left Books, 1986); Elizabeth Ewen, *Immigrant Women in the Land of Dollars* (New York: Monthly Review Press, 1985); John K. Galbraith, *The New Industrial State* (New York: New American Library, 1967); David M. Gordon, et al., *Segmented Work, Divided Workers* (Cambridge: Cambridge University Press, 1987); John M. Laslett, "Samuel Gompers and the Rise of American Business Unionism," in *Labor Leaders in America,* Melvyn Dubofsky and Warren Van Tine, eds. (Urbana: University of Illinois Press, 1987), 62–88; Stephen Meyer III, *The Five Dollar Day* (Albany: State University of New York Press, 1981); Ronald W. Schatz, *The Electrical Workers* (Urbana: University of Illinois Press, 1983); Alan Trachtenberg, *The Incorporation of America* (New York: Hill & Wang, 1982); and Robert Wiebe, *The Search for Order, 1877–1920* (New York: Hill & Wang, 1967).

2. Clarence Day, *Life With Father* (1920; reprint, New York: Washington Square Press, 1963), 101.

3. Braverman, *Labor and Monopoly Capital,* 120–121.

2

William Vickrey

A Modern Theory of Land-Value Taxation

The taxation of land has been approached over the years from a number of widely varied viewpoints. We can start with the Physiocratic view that all taxes ultimately bore on land, so that it would be less disturbing to economic relationships to levy the tax on land in the first place. We can then cross the English Channel to David Ricardo, for whom rent was due to the original and indestructible powers of the soil valued in differential productivity as compared to no-rent land on the margin of cultivation. In his day local transport of people was still largely by foot, while the rural areas were tributary to an urban center, and the marked economies of scale characterizing so much of modern economic activity were still in their infancy, so that it was not all that odd that urban site values were less emphasized. Ecology has shown us that few of the powers of the soil are completely indestructible, and archaeology has sometimes been hard put to determine which were the original powers.

William Vickrey, paper for a session on "New Concepts of Taxation," COPE [Congress of Political Economists] conference (Rio de Janeiro, January 8–12, 1992). Professor Vickrey of Columbia University was the Nobel laureate for economics in 1996, sharing the honors with James Mirrless. Much gratitude is extended to his wife, Cecile, for permission to publish the four essays presented here.

Crossing the Atlantic, we find Henry George watching fortunes being made in California land speculation and coming to advocate what his followers came to call the "single tax." Based on land values, it was intended to capture land rents. These were seen now, in large part, as resulting from the aggregation of human activity and the provision of public services in towns and cities. Many of the newer British colonies did to a degree adopt land-value taxation as a major fiscal resource for localities. But in older countries where property rights in land had deeper roots and had acquired more of a dug-in legitimacy, land-value taxation tended to be regarded as a threat of expropriation by the state of a particular form of private property. Some were willing to support a tax that avoids much of the expropriation taint and is limited to increases in land values, in a *Wertzuwachssteuer* or "capital gains tax." Even this, however, could be regarded as mulcting the landowner of gains that were more or less fully anticipated at the time the property was purchased; also, administrative difficulties and low revenue yields usually led to abandonment after only brief experimentation.

Unlike the governments within the United States, the localities in most areas adopting land-value taxation had relatively light responsibilities, limited to such activities as local administration, street lighting, garbage collection, and the like, with the major items of education and policing handled at a regional or national level. As a result, the importance of the land-value tax was relatively small, far from the near total expropriation of land rents that Georgists advocate.

While many Georgists have argued that the levying of a heavy tax on land values would have as one of its chief merits the forcing of landlords to bring idle land up to its "highest and best use" in order to finance the payment of the tax, mainstream economists have tended to discount this aspect in favor of emphasizing the role of the tax in substituting for various taxes having serious distortionary effects, a tax that comes in a lump sum. It is not, however, all that easy to define land value in a way that will make the tax strictly a lump sum tax. Defining value as what the property would be worth in its original state will not do, as in the case of a suburban lot with redwoods that now would be not an asset but a liability since there is a difficulty in cutting them down without damage to adjacent property. There are also difficulties with valuing land as if it were brought to a standard state: In many cases land would require considerable outlay to bring it to this level, so that a tax amounting to a large fraction of this standard-state value would lead to abandonment.

Such cases could be treated as exceptions, but this would be difficult without spoiling the lump-sum property. One possibility might be to grant a permanent abatement, which could be deducted from the value that is equal to the estimated cost of bringing the property from a fixed base date to the standard state. Even this would involve discrimination between improvements made before and others coming after the fixed date.

The defining quality of a land tax that is to have the effect of a lump-sum tax is that the tax be independent of the use actually made of the property, while never being so heavy as to tempt the owner to abandon the property. On the other hand, the tax should raise as much revenue as possible. It is not necessary, accordingly, that the tax be correlated explicitly with some concept of land value. It could instead be based on a set of indicia that correlate with land value. For example, one could use as a base some figure calculated from the amount of enclosed space existing within various distances of the subject property.

Besides the problem of substandard property is that of dealing with properties under a common ownership. If a set of parcels is under separate ownership by independent owners, improvement on adjacent property will affect the value of a given property. In commercial and business areas, generally in the not too long run, construction of a building would enhance the value of nearby properties, as when the construction of the United Nations building substantially raised the value of adjacent Turtle Bay lots, or construction of a major department store branch at a shopping mall enhances the rental value of the nearby specialty shops. If the properties are brought under a single ownership, directly or through interrelations among owners, these externalities are internalized, and if a tax is levied on land values assessed as though the properties were separately owned, improvement would be discouraged since improvement on one property would increase the tax on the adjacent properties. On the other hand, to assess properties differently according to whether they are in a common ownership relationship with other properties would again violate neutrality.

Actually this distortionary effect of taxing on the basis of an assumed independent ownership is the counterpart of the distortion induced in the absence of the tax when independent owners fail to take account of these externalities in making decisions concerning improvements. Indeed, these externalities could be the basis for subsidizing improvement, as by a credit against the site-value tax, rather than taxing the improvement. Of course, the externalities can be negative as well as positive, as when the erection of one apartment house obscures the view of the sunlight for an adjacent apartment house, in which case a tax rather than a subsidy would be appropriate. While at first glance it might be supposed that a tort payment from the obscurer to the obscuree would be the appropriate remedy, this would not be efficient, however much it might appeal to equity, for it would provide an incentive for structures to be erected in anticipation of such payments.

A related problem arises with respect to the effect of zoning restrictions, which should be taken into account in assessing land value. One advantage of a high land-value tax is that it would mitigate the impact of zoning changes on the wealth of the affected owners, and at the same time change tax revenues in a way that might act to restrain unduly restrictive zoning adopted for fiscal or exclusionary reasons. It would also largely resolve the problem of determining what is a "taking" for purposes of constitutional requirements of due compensation.

It may not be necessary or even appropriate to use total land value as the basis for the tax. It is useful to distinguish value originating from the natural state of the land from that created by the owner's investment in such activities as clearing, grading, fertilizing, irrigating, and the like, and site or location values created by proximity to sources of goods and services provided by the government or by other private parties as a component of urban site value. Where a land tax is used primarily to finance urban services, it would be entirely appropriate to levy the tax only on the excess of site value over the value per unit area of land around the periphery of the area affected, as a proxy for that part of land value created by localized activity. This would also greatly diminish discriminatory discontinuities in the level of taxation at jurisdictional boundaries. Land value not taxed for urban purposes could still be taxed to help defray such services as weather reporting, agricultural research, pest control, and possibly health services, education, law creation and enforcement, and defense. It seems unlikely, however, that a land tax could become a "single tax" financing all services at an efficient level of user charges based on short-run marginal social cost.

3

William Vickrey

Simplification, Progression, and a Level Playing Field

The Property Tax

Localities across the nation, and especially large central cities, are in serious financial difficulties, mainly because of reliance on the property tax as the chief source of revenue, and fear that increased property tax rates will cause a loss of economic activity to competing jurisdictions. The situation is aggravated by competition in "beggar-my-neighbor" attempts to attract business and industry by special tax concessions that often violate principles of uniform application of tax laws and provide occasion for corruption.

The property tax is, economically speaking, a combination of one of the worst taxes—the part that is assessed on real estate improvements and in some cases to a limited extent on personalty—and one of the best taxes—the tax on land or site value. A vast improvement in city finances would result from shifting from a property tax to a land-value tax. A tax on land, properly assessed independently of the use made of the lot, is virtually free of distortionary effects and "excess burden,"

Pages 19–27 of a manuscript dated April 2, 1995, which was slated to be presented by Professor T. Nicolaus Tideman at the conference of the Council of Georgist Organizations in Ottawa (1996).

while the tax on improvements imposes serious burdens on construction, and not only because of the immediate tax. Where a large debt has been accumulated, anyone putting up a costly building is thereby assuming, for the time being, at least, a share in the burden of servicing the debt over an extended period in addition to an increased share in the financing of current outlays.

In some cases municipal debt has reached levels at which the potential burden on new construction has brought it to an almost complete halt. One escape has been to grant special concessions or assessment freezes to those undertaking a suitably specified project. Such concessions have sometimes been subsequently overturned on grounds of unconstitutional nonuniformity. A shift to land-value taxation would offer a nondiscriminatory escape from this predicament. Ultimately, a shift to land-value taxation, by attracting additional activity to the city, is likely to increase the net market value of the land.

With land-value taxation, indeed, the local public debt becomes in effect a collective mortgage on the various lots in the jurisdiction. Reducing current taxes and borrowing a corresponding amount increase the cash balances of taxpayers and reduce the market value of their property by a like amount, leaving their net worth unchanged and their liquidity increased. "Ricardian equivalence" is in full force and the effect of Keynesian fiscal policy is limited to this relatively minor liquidity factor. Transactions in property at the lower market values are easier to finance. There may also be a more substantial advantage to a larger public debt if the interest payable on it is lower than the effective interest rate or rate of potential profit faced by individual taxpayers, so that they would gain by the amount of this interest differential.

Land-value taxation has been successful in New Zealand, parts of Australia, and Johannesburg, South Africa, among other places around the world, and is being used increasingly in Pennsylvania, with notably good results.

Given the high mobility of capital and labor, which tends in the long run to equalize returns to these factors over the region, landlords ultimately reap most if not all of the benefit from an increase in the efficiency of the city, and should, if they fully realized their long-term advantage, enthusiastically support the change to land-value taxation. Even though at first there may be a shift in the tax burden that seems to penalize undeveloped properties, such as parking lots, and benefit highly improved properties, in the long run the relative benefits may actually be the reverse of this, as the relatively bare lots are eventually developed to the higher degree made profitable by the absence of a tax on improvements. Even at lower space rental rates, the profits from the improvement would tend to exceed the profits from the bare lot by more than the increase in tax. On the other hand, the owner of already improved property may see its space rents fall in the face of competition from the new construction, offsetting the reduction in his tax bill.

Congestion Charges

In most large cities, and some smaller ones, traffic densities in the central areas during much of the day are such that less travel is accomplished during a given period than could be accomplished by having fewer cars attempting to move within the area but moving at faster speeds. The cumulative effect of an additional car's progress across midtown Manhattan at 11 A.M. can be as much as 100 to 300 additional vehicle hours of delay over the remainder of the day, since during subsequent periods fewer cars reach their destinations, which backs up more cars on the street, and further slows the traffic in a cumulative fashion.

A sovereign remedy is to adopt congestion pricing, whereby each car entering the area during the congested times is required to carry an automatic vehicle identifier, costing less than $20.00. The congested area is divided into small zones, and scanner units are installed at each crossing of a zone boundary, so that the entry into each congestion zone and exit from it by each car can be recorded "on the fly," the resulting records being processed by a computer to assess a charge to be collected from registered owners at monthly or other convenient intervals. These charges would represent the congestion cost that the crossing of the zone is estimated to have caused to other traffic, as well as the cost to pedestrians.

Where cars remain within a zone for extended periods, an appropriate charge can be added, representing a basic charge for onstreet parking in unmetered spaces; appropriate rebates can be arranged for use of offstreet parking facilities. Taxicabs can be equipped with a supplemental metering device that will be triggered by a signal from the scanning unit at each zone entry to begin recording a charge for mileage within the zone being entered. The charge would be at a rate appropriate to the conditions expected to prevail over the remainder of the congestion period affected by the trip, to be paid by the rider and remitted to the city. The driver would be responsible for the charge while cruising. The meter would have an externally observable display to permit checking that the appropriate charge is being registered.

Those anxious to preserve their anonymity could equip their cars with similar meters, with prepayment by means of cards or tokens purchased and inserted in the meter to add to the unused balance, then being canceled and retained to permit checking against counterfeiting. To assure compliance, video cameras can be mounted at a number of scanning points to provide pictures of cars and license plates that pass without producing a valid identifying signal, and of a random sample of responding cars to permit checking that the identity signal corresponds to the registration.

When the charges are properly adjusted to reflect the costs inflicted on others, traffic densities would be kept close to an efficient level, generally below the maximum flow point. Some trips whose importance is insufficient for the driver to be willing to pay an amount equivalent to the congestion cost would be abandoned or shifted to other modes or destinations. More important is that many trips would be shifted in time in such a way as to reduce their contribution to congestion. Some trips will be shifted to an earlier time when charges are low and their contribution to congestion is less significant. Many trips now made during and after the build-up of congestion will be started at a later time, which again will reduce their contribution to congestion delays; in many cases they will arrive at their destinations earlier than they would have under present conditions. Some additional traffic that formerly could not afford the time for the trip will be attracted by the higher speeds. Where congestion has been severe, in all likelihood total traffic flow over the day would be *increased,* contrary to the popular assumption that it would be diminished.

In any case, speeds would be substantially increased over nearly all the day, air pollution would be decreased, and the locality would obtain a substantial amount of revenue. Businesses, especially the high-level ones, would be attracted by the improvement in the ability to circulate rapidly, property values would increase, and the yield of the land tax at given rates would increase.

In addition to a charge for effects on congestion, a levy can readily be added to reflect the contribution to the costs of air pollution. Each car can be assigned an air-pollution rating on the basis of its new condition, subject to downgrading over time at a near-worst-case assumption, the rating being eligible for an optional upgrading by submitting to an appropriate emissions test at the cost and convenience of the owner. The pollution charge would be varied according to the time and location of use, to reflect atmospheric conditions at various times and places, and added to the congestion charge.

In the event of an impending inversion or other serious atmospheric condition, notification of an increase in pollution charges could be broadcast, giving those who can do so an appropriate incentive to shift the timing of optional shopping and other trips to times less susceptible to pollution. Cars making only weekend trips to the country would not be unduly penalized, while cars found overly costly to upgrade could be sold to rural users not frequenting areas sensitive to pollution.

Parking

In many areas, parking spaces are preempted for long periods by those able to arrive when spaces are available, to the exclusion of many people with more urgent needs whose arrival times cannot readily be adapted. Where coin-operated parking meters of the usual type are used, places for urgent parking are often unavailable because the rate is too low to keep vacant space available, or the time limit on the parking meter is too short for the errand to be accomplished, such as an hour with the dentist. At other times the more convenient places remain underutilized as parkers are driven to use free space less convenient but less expensive or less rationed by time.

A more flexible and universal system of parking charges is needed whereby charges would be sufficiently high at times of greatest demand that a few reasonably convenient spaces would nearly always be available to those prepared to pay a market-clearing price, while charges would be reduced for times when demand is lower, being reduced to zero whenever there would be more empty spaces than are needed for convenience. Many technologies for doing this are available. One of the simpler ones is the use of parking cards purchased in advance in various denominations, to be scratched or mutilated to indicate the time parking begins, with one or more cards displayed in the car to a total value equal to the charge for the intended parking period as indicated by a posted schedule. The rates of charge may be made to vary by time of day. They can also be readily changed to adjust to changing levels and patterns of demand.

More sophisticated and feasible systems would permit the charge to be determined at the end of the parking occupancy at rates that could be varied according to how many nearby spaces have been vacant during the time of parking. If properly calibrated, this would automatically keep the charges at close to the market-clearing level, enhance efficiency, and raise land values.

Subsidies Promoting Efficiency

Land taxes, congestion charges, and parking charges designed to promote the efficient use of the city's space should in most cases be capable of producing sufficient revenue to permit the elimination of most levies that impair its economic efficiency, such as occupancy taxes. It should even be possible to improve efficiency by subsidizing activities with positive externalities or strong economies of scale or density so as to permit their prices to be brought closer to the efficiency-promoting level of short-run marginal social cost.

Transit Fares

With congestion charges on auto use and land taxation in effect, it will be possible to adjust transit fares to reflect the marginal social cost of each type of trip, largely in the impact on other passengers from longer travel times resulting from the time taken in stopping to board and discharge passengers, the increased probability that one will deprive someone else of a seat, or crowding. This will require an additional subsidy to be financed out of land-value taxes in the areas served, but in the long run will result in the enhancement of pretax land rents by more than the required subsidy.

This can be implemented by using magnetic cards and charging a maximum fare on entry depending on time of day and location, and allowing passengers making shorter trips or otherwise qualifying for a lower fare to obtain the appropriate rebate by registering with their card upon exit. This permits most passengers to enjoy the convenience of exiting freely, and eliminates much of the congestion, delay, and equipment cost that would result if all passengers had to register at exit.

Strict application of the marginal-cost pricing principle may result in what appears to be an anomaly. On a lightly loaded bus going from *A* to *B* to *C* to *D*, the marginal cost for a passenger from *B* to *C* is likely to be higher than for a trip from *A* to *D,* if, as will often be the case, the number of passengers delayed by the boarding and alighting will be greater. This cost structure, indeed, is what justifies the running of express buses. The difficulty of explaining such anomalies to the public may be considered justification for tolerating the sacrifice in efficiency resulting from a failure to adjust the fare structure to eliminate them.

Actually, even greater anomalies that lack any efficiency justification occur in practice: In Washington, D.C., a passenger may be able to save money by a free transfer to a bus for the latter portion of a trip that could have been made entirely by Metro. A passenger boarding a train just before the rush hour may pay a lower fare than a passenger boarding the same train a little later after the beginning of the rush hour going to the same destination.

Other Network Utilities

In the case of local network utilities such as water, gas, sewer, electric, telephone, and cable services, land rents in the area served are enhanced by the availability of these services, and the lower their prices the greater the enhancement. Equity and efficiency are both served by having landlords contribute to the network costs of these services so as to enable their prices to be brought closer to marginal cost. In the long run the increased efficiency of the local economy would tend to redound to the benefit of the landlords by raising their market rents by more than the amount of the subsidy. Universal service would be achieved in accordance with the underlying principles by which a free market is justified.

Even those owning land for tennis courts or parking lots and making no direct use of the services will be able to charge higher prices to customers because of the greater convenience of the location. They should be no more excused from contributing to the cost of the service accessibility that is inescapably attached to their lots than one could expect to be able to get a rebate off the rental of a car because one intends to drive only by daylight in fair weather and will make no use of the headlights and windshield wipers with which all cars are equipped.

4

William Vickrey

Henry George, Economies of Scale, and Land Taxation

Principles

Henry George and most of his followers thought of a land tax as being the source from which to finance all of the traditional government functions, and on that basis it would have probably been possible, in George's day, to make the tax a "single tax." Under present-day conditions, with enormous sums being spent for defense and welfare programs, it has become doubtful whether a land tax could indeed raise the revenue required to finance government outlays. In addition, if we consider other localized services with marked economies of scale for which partial financing from land taxes would be appropriate, the likelihood that land taxation could become a single tax becomes vanishingly small. This does not mean, however, that the virtues of a land tax should not be exploited to the fullest extent possible.

An efficient organization of an economy requires that all outputs be priced at their short-run marginal social cost. Otherwise customers will not balance the value of an item to them against the cost to others

---

William Vickrey delivered this paper at a COPE meeting in Rio de Janeiro on January 9, 1992.

occasioned by their use or consumption. For activities without economies of scale, or where these economies are exhausted at a scale that permits vigorous competitive markets to exist, the main virtue of the free competitive market is that it produces approximately this result. For activities with economies of scale, or positive externalities, prices at short-run marginal social cost will in general not cover total costs, so that a subsidy is required if output is to be pushed to the point of taking full advantage of these economies. With some stretching, government itself can be considered an extreme case of economies of scale where marginal cost is zero.

Most taxes that might be levied to provide the required subsidies have distorting effects and excess burdens of their own, and where costs can be covered by prices only slightly above the short-run marginal social cost, operation on a self-financing basis may be appropriate.

Localized Services and Site-Value Taxes

In the case of localized public services, including public utilities such as water, electric power, gas, and telephones, taxes on the site rents generated by the availability of these outputs at efficient marginal cost prices are an efficient, equitable, and adequate source for these subsidies.

Under suitable assumptions it can be shown that these site rents (over and above the rent on peripheral rural land) will be just sufficient, no more and no less, to provide the needed subsidies. Properly assessed in a manner that looks beyond the actual current use of the property, such taxes have no distortionary impact. If landlords in a community could be made aware of their long-run interests, they would voluntarily agree to tax themselves on a site-value basis to subsidize utility rates so as to permit them to be set at close to the efficient level, and find that the rental value of their land had risen by more than the amount of the tax subsidy.

In principle, returns to mobile capital invested in structures will in the medium long run remain at a level governed by rates of return available in regional or even global capital markets, and returns to labor will tend to gravitate to a level also determined regionally or nationally. This leaves landowners, as the owners of the principal nonmovable asset, to reap any gain from the improvement in the operation of the city or locality engendered by bringing utility prices closer to the efficient marginal cost level.

Fire Protection

The principle of financing a large proportion of utility service costs out of taxes based on site values generated by the availability of these services applies even in the case of fire protection. Superficially, the beneficiaries of fire protection would seem to be the owners of combustible property. But the cost of providing fire protection of a given grade to a given area is at least 80 percent independent of the number of combustible structures in the area, aside from pathological cases like the South Bronx. Direct costs of responding to alarms amount to a relatively small part of the total cost, as does the value of the impairment in the service quality resulting from the possibility that the unit may be out on another call when a new call comes in. Costs are chargeable 80 percent or more to land occupancy, and only 20 percent or less to possession of combustible property. The value of a vacant lot will be enhanced if it is within the area served by a fire brigade, but if an appropriate house is erected on the lot, the value will go up by roughly the cost of construction, whether or not there is fire protection, though of course the type of structure selected will differ. The value of fire protection inheres in the lot, not the building.

Utility Services

Many utilities such as water mains, sewers, telephone lines, cables, and power lines must all be carried past property whether the occupant uses them or not, and a large part of the cost is independent of the quantity of the service used. Mail delivery also falls in this category. A driver cannot expect to avoid paying for the headlights or windshield wipers on a rental car merely because one is not going to drive at night or in rainy weather. Tennis players will pay more to play on a court next to the firehouse, because it is located in a neighborhood where these various services are available, and where people live who want to play on nearby courts. They will indeed pay more to play on conveniently located courts, but in the absence of adequate land taxation the landlords will get away with the higher rents without contributing adequately to the higher playing fees. Rents in wealthy suburbs are what they are because bus service is provided to other areas, even though all the residents drive their cars to work and never use buses. People whose homes sit on spacious acreage will not pay adequately for the cost of carrying the mains and cables past their property.

The subsidy necessary to permit prices to be set at levels promoting efficient patterns of use can in principle be provided under any of a number of forms of operation, whether as a public department, a quasi-independent agency, or a private arrangement for profit, though it may be a little more awkward under private than under public operation. Care is needed in setting up the way the subsidy is computed, which should be fixed for reasonably long terms, lest the attention of the management be diverted from operating efficiently to try to extract a larger subsidy.

Efficient Responsive Pricing: Telephone Service

Whatever the form of organization and degree of subsidy adopted, bureaucratic inertia and historical precedent should not be allowed to prevent the adoption of the kind of responsive pricing that tracks short-run marginal social cost as closely as financial constraints permit, in the manner made possible by modern electronic technology. For telephone service, short-run marginal social cost is almost entirely a matter of the expected increased delay to other calls resulting from tying up equipment by a given call. Charges should vary almost instantaneously according to the level of busyness of the exchanges and trunk bundles involved. The current rate can be reported to the user by a voice announcement in place of the dial tone, or, in the case of long-distance calls, by a message given after the destination exchange has been dialed, if the caller wishes to wait for it. If the rate is higher than he is willing to pay, he can then hang up without having occupied any equipment beyond the call register. Not only does this encourage shifting of calls to slack hours, but in the case of emergencies generating a spate of calling, such pricing can ensure that vital calls will get through promptly, instead of being deferred or frustrated by a system overload, often with fatal results. Expensive expansion of the system may become less necessary. Some of these results can be achieved without subsidy from land-value taxation, but subsidy will greatly enhance the achievement.

Transit Service

That transit service stands to gain heavily from an adequate subsidy is evidenced by its being one of the most frequently subsidized of utility services. Even if costs per bus-mile are constant, bus service still presents economies of scale or density in that increased service in response to increased usage will provide more frequent or more varied service, and the value of this improved quality must be credited against the cost of the increased service to get the true marginal social cost of added bus trips. For trolleybuses, trams, or subways, there is obviously the fixed cost of the right-of-way that is not part of marginal cost, and there are also the economies resulting from the use of larger vehicles or longer trains.

In off-peak local bus service, where there may often be plenty of vacant seats, the short-run marginal social cost of added passenger trips consists almost entirely of the delay to the bus, its driver, and the remaining passengers involved in picking up and discharging passengers. This may have the paradoxical result of making the cost of carrying passengers between *B* and *C* greater than the cost of the longer trip from *A* to *D*. In rapid transit service with fixed stops, this cost is negligible, and fares for the shorter trips should be made to vary in proportion to distance at a level sufficiently low to avoid deterring any significant number of trips.

For peak-hour trips, the cost is in depriving others of a seat, where standees are permitted, and possibly also in jostling when vehicles are crowded. For short trips this may be roughly proportional to the distance traveled, but varied according to typical loading conditions. There may be little justification for differentiating between medium-length and longer-haul trips, however, since in most cases the vehicle and its seats must be carried to the end of the line whether occupied or not. Differentiation at this end may be counterproductive if it induces passengers to drive or walk a longer distance to an intermediate station for the sake of a lower fare.

Fares should be varied gradually up to a sharp peak at each rush hour in the main direction of travel, giving all passengers an incentive to move their trips away from this spike even by a small amount. Fares that vary by a single step from a peak to an off-peak level tend not only to generate minipeaks at the time of change, but also to produce little effect on the height of the peak itself since the shift in time of trip required to obtain the lower fare will usually be too great to represent a feasible alternative for a significant number of passengers.

Fares varied by time of day can make successful a campaign for work staggering. Without time-of-day fares, success of a work-staggering campaign may lead to its failure, as firms, observing that peak congestion is no longer a serious problem, begin to drift back to the preferred times and recreate the congestion. Fare variation can provide the incentive that would prevent this relapse.

Stored-value magnetic cards provide a means of collecting fares varied according to origin, destination, and time. Preprinted cards worth convenient round sums can be sold at various outlets, with a small premium value added to the higher valued cards to encourage a reduction in the number of transactions. A maximum fare can be deducted from the value on the card on entry, and for trips with a lower fare, the passenger would register on exit to cause the rebate to be added back. Registers can be programmed to add old card balances that were too small for entry to the value of a new card.

Through fares for trips involving two or more vehicles may be charged at less than the sum of the fares for the component legs, to allow for the less satisfactory nature of such service as compared to single-vehicle trips of comparable length, and the corresponding greater elasticity of demand. But transfers to or from buses especially should bear some charge, to discourage the use of connecting buses for trivial distances, often over the heavily loaded part of the trip.

While passes of various kinds have some advantage in bus and trolley service in speeding the loading of passengers, and appear to have considerable appeal to the riding public, they have no place in a closed transit system, where passing the barrier with a stored-value card is not significantly more time-consuming than the use of a pass. Passes generally fail to provide adequate incentives for passengers to shift travel away from the rush hour, especially where financial constraints are binding, for a given level of net revenue of passes inevitably produces a less efficient pattern of utilization than is obtainable from a properly graduated pay-by-the-ride system.

Pricing of Street Use

On Georgist principles, automobile traffic involves the use of scarce land for the occupancy of which land rents should be collected and used to finance government. Present practices with respect to urban traffic are analogous to Soviet practices in which commodities are underpriced and shelves are empty and there is much wasteful queuing to be on hand when supplies arrive, which is much like driving around looking for a space about to be vacated.

Facilities can be worthless precisely because they are free. Some years ago I observed a ferry crossing the Thames that during peak periods regularly accumulated a queue just long enough so that the total time required to cross the river was the same as that needed to go around through the Blackwall tunnel. No one would get across the Thames any faster if the ferry service were increased or slower if it were curtailed. Overgrazing on public commons is also a classical case in point.

Parking

In street parking, charges should be based on the added difficulty that occupancy of a space imposes on others seeking to park. In practice this can be approximated by a rule that, in a given neighborhood, whenever during a given time slot fewer than 2 to 5 percent vacancies are observed over a suitable period, charges should be increased, and whenever vacancies average 10 to 20 percent or more, charges should be reduced, ultimately to zero.

Parking meters are an inflexible and inefficient instrument, allowing only one rate to be charged. They are often misused in a rationing rather than a pricing mode, moreover, so that those with an urgent need to park for somewhat longer than the specified time limit must risk being assessed a fine or resort to a far less satisfactory alternative. Parking cards purchased in convenient outlets or by mail in suitable denominations can be used. They can be mutilated by the parker to show the time at which parking begins and displayed in the windshield, the time paid for being determined according to posted schedules. Another alternative is to provide ticket-issuing machines, as in Stockholm, where money can be inserted, the time to which parking is paid displayed, and, when a button is pushed, a time-stamped ticket is issued.

Queuing at Bottlenecks

In queuing situations, as at bridges during peak hours, the marginal external social cost of a trip is measured by the time from the passage of the bottleneck to the next gap in the flow of traffic. Rather than charging on the basis of the actual duration ex post facto, one can properly charge on the expected duration estimated from comparable recent periods.

If charges are increased over a preceding period whenever substantial persistent queuing exists at comparable times, and lowered whenever frequent gaps occur in the traffic, likewise at comparable times, eventually each user will be able to reach his destination without any more delay than under the present regime by starting his trip as much later as the queuing delay is reduced, and paying a premium toll above the previous flat toll typically equal to the value of the additional time spent at the starting point. If part or all of the revenue from the premium peak-hour toll is used to reduce the base toll, nearly everyone will be better off. One can guarantee that absolutely no one is made worse off by providing a lay-by in which those who so desire can wait for a period equal to the reduction in the queuing time resulting from the change in regime and obtain a voucher entitling them to pay only the old toll. There is a free lunch!

It is important that the toll rise and fall gradually. Otherwise half or more of the benefit will be lost, and difficulties may be encountered with racing or lagging when tolls change. Implementation can be with magnetic cards or AVI [automobile vehicle identification] units, or for casual users by charging a fixed maximum toll against which rebate vouchers would be issued, realizable as lottery tickets by scratching off a spot, or redeemable at service stations.

Hypercongested Networks and Incipient Gridlock

The most dramatic results can be obtained by applying short-run marginal social-cost pricing to congested street networks. Frequently, for much of the day traffic densities exceed a maximum flow. By pricing street use in such a way as to keep accumulation of traffic in the congested area below the maximum flow point, flows at the height of the peak, and possibly even aggregate flows for the day as a whole, can be significantly increased. Speeds will be increased generally, except possibly for brief shoulder periods where traffic is being shifted out of the peak. The substantial revenues obtained can be used to subsidize transit or reduce other taxes, and noise and air pollution will be reduced.

The simplest implementation consists of AVI units carried by all vehicles moving in the congested area, operating on power beamed from roadside scanners and responding with a signal identifying the vehicle. If the area is divided into zones with scanners at all thoroughfares crossing zone boundaries, charges can be computed on the trip segment at a given time from the entry point to the exit point of each controlled zone traversed. Systems have been available at least since 1959, and have been upgraded and thoroughly tested.

Taxicabs present a special problem: They might pass the charge through to the passenger. This can be handled by charging on the basis of going past a scanning point, the scanner beam being modulated according to the charge and added to the fee on the meter. Or the scanner signal could be made to cause a surcharge per unit distance traveled until the taxi leaves the zone. The taxi operator would be required to absorb any charges accumulated during cruising. Such methods would be less accurate than charging on the zone entry and exit basis, but should be acceptable.

More sophisticated methods being studied involve the use of "smart cards" and moderately elaborate apparatus on the car permitting the driver to be given an immediate indication of charges as they accumulate, as well as providing a privacy "red herring" that preserves anonymity for those concerned. In some versions the charge would be related to the speed or delay experienced by the vehicle itself, but this seems undesirable both because of the incentive it would provide for aggressive driving and because the relation between delay experienced and delay caused by a particular vehicle is at best loose, and indeed often inverse.

Conditions created by adventitious events such as parades, traffic-attracting events, and construction obstructions can be alleviated by suitable surcharges announced in advance.

Air Pollution

Air pollution surcharges can be added, graduated by the emission rating of the car, the locality traversed, and weather conditions. During inversions incentives would be provided to minimize car use. Oil guzzlers used primarily for weekend excursions out of the basin susceptible to pollution would be only lightly penalized. Trading high-pollution cars to rural areas would be encouraged. Results would be much more rapid than from applying standards to new cars. Cars can be given a pollution rating according to model year, and this rating degraded automatically over time, subject to upgrading on the basis of actual testing. Testing could then be voluntary and more stringent and costly, as it would usually be undertaken only when likely to prove worthwhile.

Heavy Trucks

It is increasingly being recognized that heavy trucks account for a very large proportion of the costs of wear and tear on highways. Indeed, it has been estimated that damage to the pavement varies roughly with the third or fourth power of the axle load. While this implies that a truck with axle loads substantially less than the design limit of a highway will do relatively little damage, heavy trucks in the course of a trip will almost inevitably traverse segments of highway for which they press on the design limits or even exceed them. On two-lane roads, moreover, slower-moving heavy trucks often impose significant delays on other traffic, even when traffic is well below capacity; this is especially true on upgrades. In addition, it is apparent that heavy trucks maneuvering through city streets to reach their pick-up and drop-off points often very seriously obstruct traffic.

As weigh-in-motion (WIM) technology is rapidly developing, it appears that combining its use with the requirement that all heavy trucks be equipped with AVI units, and placing scanning units to control alternate routes, would provide a capability for assessing charges in trucks that would reasonably track their marginal social costs closely. This is especially important in promoting an efficient division of traffic between highway trucks and railroads. Other possible effects would be to induce truckers to avoid using roads susceptible to wear and tear from excessive axle loads, and to minimize obstruction to traffic during pick-ups and deliveries by employing additional personnel at these points.

Airport Congestion Charges

Airspace is a resource in fixed supply comparable to land and in principle commanding a socially generated scarcity rent. Airport landing fees should also reflect marginal social cost. Auctioning of landing and take-off slots differentiated by time of day and week is one possibility, though some modifications may be desirable to take into account the differences in strength between the vortexes produced by different-sized planes. Under some conditions the airspace requirements of a small plane may actually be greater than for larger planes because of differences in speeds. Some concessions may also be in order for scheduled flights to or from points with relatively infrequent service, or in smaller planes, in consideration of the stronger economies of scale prevailing under such circumstances.

Aircraft Noise

In addition to fees determined by auction, it may be appropriate to assess additional charges for operations of noisier aircraft. Like pollution charges for automobiles, these are likely to produce a more efficient adjustment of operations. They should make for assignment of the noisier aircraft to trips involving airports less susceptible to noise (possibly through exchange of planes between airlines), the retrofitting of planes, and the like, rather than flat administrative requirements applied across the board to airlines of widely differing characteristics. It might be desirable to vary the charges by time of day, with higher charges at night, but probably not according to the runway used, which might produce undesirable pressure on traffic controllers, who in assigning runways in any case are able to take noise factors into consideration.

Adequacy of Land Rents to Provide Subsidy for Short-Run Marginal Social Cost [SRMSC] Pricing

In a world where prices of goods and services imported to cities and exported from them are established by competition among cities, there is no shortage of sites suitable for the monopolistic position. It can be shown that these site rents generated by the availability of goods and services at prices reflecting marginal social cost (over and above the rent on peripheral rural land) will be just sufficient, no more and no less, to provide the needed subsidies.

The Linear City Model

1. Imagine a city laid out on a strip of ocean front of uniform width. Imports can be landed and exports dispatched indifferently from any point on the frontage, but local (coastwise) transportation has a line-haul cost proportional to distance.

2. Activities with economies of scale can be represented as having a fixed cost consisting of imports, and variable input costs consisting of land, imports, and local outputs of other activities, all varying in proportion to output.

3. If an activity wishes to increase the frontage it occupies, it will thereby increase the distance freight, for it must be carried past this frontage and require encroachment on the rural land at the edge of the city. The marginal social cost of its land occupancy is thus equal to the rural rental of the land plus the line-haul cost of the transportation along its frontage. Total land rents equal line-haul transportation costs added to rural rents for equivalent space.

4. This marginal social cost of land is also a competitive equilibrium rent. If land rent for each front foot is established at a level equal to the peripheral rent in addition to the cost of coastwise traffic in front of it, each activity manager will use land up to the point where its marginal productivity equals this rent, and will shift his location until the freight savings from further shifting would balance the differential in land rents. The freight savings from a leftward shift is equal to the excess of the tonnage of his shipments to and from points on his right, times the cost per ton-mile, times the distance shifted. The density of traffic at his leftward boundary will similarly exceed, by this same differential in the cost of his shipments, the density of traffic at his rightward boundary, so that if the freight savings equal the rent increase, rent differentials will equal freight cost differential; and total rents at any point will equal total freight cost at that point plus a constant of integration equal to the rental value of peripheral land.

5. If the city is in competition with similar cities, and there is no scarcity of land strips on which cities can be established, competition will drive world prices of its inputs and outputs to the point where the city is operating at the minimum point on its average total cost curve, and the city as a whole would just break even, after including in its costs the rental value of the land taken from the peripheral activity. Less favorable prices would cause the city to go out of business, and more favorable prices would stimulate the establishment of new cities.

6. Line-haul distances will vary in proportion to the output and size of the city, as will also freight volumes, so that transportation costs vary as the square of the output of the city. Marginal transportation costs will be twice the average cost.

7. Where average total cost is a minimum, marginal cost equals average cost, so that the total fixed cost equals total transportation cost, which equals the excess of land rents over peripheral rents. Q.E.D.

More Realistic Models

A similar but somewhat more complicated analysis can show the same result for two- and three-dimensional models, except that for the two-dimensional models excess land rent and fixed costs are equal to one-half of the local transportation costs. Also, if we have such elements as locally produced components of fixed costs, land used in transportation, and line-haul transportation costs not proportional to distance, precise modeling becomes dauntingly complex—but the main result is that site rents in excess of rural values will remain just sufficient to provide the subsidies needed to implement marginal cost pricing. This seems reasonably robust. But if city sites with special characteristics such as harbors are limited in supply, the tendency would be to produce rents exceeding the subsidy requirements. There would remain, for the financing of other government outlays, the tax on rural land and the comparable portion of the value of urban land.

5

William Vickrey

Propositions Relating to Site-Value Taxation

The Efficient Competitive State

Site-value taxation for the collecting of rents and attributable to the availability in a city of goods and services produced under conditions of economies of scale, priced at marginal cost for efficient allocation, under competitive conditions would be just sufficient to provide the necessary subsidies.[1]

Urban Versus Rural Site Value

To separate the site value due to urban attractions from that not due to the presence of the city, it would be appropriate to use as the base for a site-value tax for municipal or metropolitan purposes the appraised market value of the site in excess of a flat amount per square foot representing the value of surrounding land for agricultural or other purposes. This would also ease the difficulties of differential rates across jurisdictional boundaries. Value up to this flat amount could for state purposes be the base for a land tax.

William Vickrey wrote this paper in August 1995. It was delivered at the Levy Institute at Bard College, November 2–4, 1995.

Landlords as Beneficiaries

In starting from an inefficient situation, if labor and capital are fully mobile in the long run so that returns to labor and to capital are determined by nationwide or regionwide conditions, any gains from an improvement in efficiency would redound to the owners of the fixed factor, land.

Example: If the landlords of New York City knew what was good for them, they would vote enthusiastically for an added tax on site values to be devoted to lowering subway fares, especially for off-peak and shorter trips, and improving the frequency and quality of the service. Assuming that the subsidy would be used efficiently and not frittered away on administrative overheads, aborted, or put to grandiose construction projects[2] or overgenerous fringe benefits,[3] this would increase the value New Yorkers get for their outlays on subway service, increasing the attractiveness of the city, and in the long run raising site rents by more than the tax.

Short- and Long-Run Impacts of Tax Changing

The differential impact of a shift from property tax to site-value tax on properties on similar sites but differing degrees of current development may be the reverse in the long run of what it may appear to be in the short run. Although the owner of a vacant lot finds his taxes increased while a neighboring owner of a developed property may find his taxes decreased, in the longer run, the removal of the tax on improvements may make it profitable for the vacant lot owner to put up a structure appropriate to the new conditions, recovering much or even all of his tax increase in the process, even in the face of a deduction in the prevailing market-space rental rates; while this reduction in space rents may reduce the rents of the already developed property by much or all of the tax decrease.

Sprawl

Site-value taxation in the long run tends to diminish urban sprawl, increasing densities and site values at the center, and usually diminishing them at the periphery. This tendency will be opposed by zoning practices and established transportation facilities.

Ricardian Equivalence

For a community relying exclusively on site-value taxation, Ricardian equivalence is in full sway and Keynesian fiscal policy is impotent. For a situation in which various site values increase proportionally at the same rate over time, any debt is in effect a joint mortgage on the site value, and any deficit financing will reduce the market value of sites by the same amount as the reduction in current taxes, leaving the taxpayer in effectively the same position.

Where site values increase at different rates, there may be some shifting of net worth among property owners, but the overall macroeconomic effect is likely to be much the same. In any case, there may still be some advantage to deficit financing, if the interest rate on the public bonds is lower than the rate on private mortgages or the return in private investment adjusted to risk. This may be due to scale of economies or lowering of transaction cost for the larger transaction, better credit rating of the public agency than of private parties, or, in the United States, the exemption from the federal income tax of interest on state and local public bonds. There is also a facilitating of the market in real estate as less private funding is needed for transactions where the property has in effect a built-in assumable mortgage.

Where the only tax involved in debt service is on all real estate inclusive of improvements, the presence of a debt can have serious consequences. An investor putting up a building is thereby assuming, for the time being at least, an increased share in the burden of servicing the debt, subject to being partially relieved later on by subsequent builders. This is already a substantial burden over and above the tax levied to finance current outlays, but if a point is reached where doubt is cast on the likelihood of such relief, the doubt may become self-realizing and construction come to a complete halt. Attempts to use deficit financing to take advantage of differential in rate of interest become unwise.

To the extent that a jurisdiction relies on sales, income, or other consumption taxes, debt does not affect property values in this way, Ricardian equivalence does not hold, and Keynesian fiscal policy remains effective.

Rents for Roadway Use

An important type of site for which payments should be made to the public fisc consists of congested streets and highways. Ideally, charges for space use should correspond to the marginal social cost of each such use, regardless of what notional capital value might be assigned to the land involved. The very high cost of street widening or otherwise varying the capacity of facilities gives street space a scarcity value bearing little relation to the value of nearby lots in private ownership.

Parking

In the case of onstreet parking, charges should be adjusted by time and place so that there are nearly always empty spaces available within a convenient distance of any given destination, where parking is permitted at all, but charges should be reduced to zero when empty spaces are plentiful. The usual form of parking meter is incapable of accomplishing this. Alternative methods of collecting charges are available, one requiring very little capital investment: The use of simple parking cards purchased in advance in convenient denominations, to be punched or mutilated to indicate the time of use to be covered, according to posted fee schedules, and displayed on the vehicle. Other methods involving more investment in curbside equipment may enable the charge to be determined at the time the parker leaves, making it unnecessary to guess at the charge in advance, and permitting the charge to be determined in actual vacancy rates. This would track marginal social cost more closely than is possible with a preset calendar.

Commercial and official vehicles should not be exempt. For trucks in the New York garment district, for example, adequate parking charges would encourage more rapid loading and unloading and discourage the use of parked trucks as warehouses, vastly improving the efficiency of the operation as a whole. Delivery trucks making a habit of double-parking should be required to carry a meter to be set to accumulate a charge at an appropriate rate while the truck is double-parked, evidenced by a flag or other visible display. This should end the ridiculous practice of double-parking delivery trucks just ahead of a bus stop, which causes more interference with bus service, to say nothing of traffic generally, than if they had parked at the stop.

Queuing

For bridges, tunnels, and other bottlenecks where queuing regularly occurs, tolls should be varied by time of day, adjusted until the toll at any moment corresponds to the product of the expected time span to the next gap in the flow times on an average value of delay per vehicle hour. For a typical morning rush-hour congestion period, the result that can be expected is that each regular user could leave home later by as many minutes as he now expects to waste in the queue and arrive at the destination at the same time as now, paying a toll in excess of the off-peak rate, if any, by a differential equal to the value of the time saved as evaluated for those with a value of time somewhat lower-than-average.

Where a flat toll is already in effect, the differential peak toll can be used to lower all tolls by a flat amount, leaving nearly everyone substantially better off. If, nevertheless, there are those who regard their time as having so little worth and must travel so close to the peak period that they would be less well off on balance, they can be allowed to wait in a space out of the main flow of traffic for an amount of time equal to the expected queuing delay under the former conditions, and then obtain a voucher allowing them to use the facility at the former toll rate, if any. Everyone would thus have available an alternative substantially equivalent to present conditions or slightly better, if it is preferable, which would guarantee that no one would lose by the change. (The evening rush-hour situation, being predominantly at origin rather than at destination, is not symmetrical and somewhat less clear-cut.)

It is essential that the charge vary gradually rather than simply in a one-step basis setting a peak against an off-peak period. This is not only to avoid inducing aggressive driving or lagging around times of substantial toll change, but, even more importantly, to provide incentives to all rush-hour users to adjust their timing even by a small amount. Otherwise very few users at the middle of the rush hour will shift, and little improvement in conditions at the height of the peak will be realized.

For regular users the mechanics can be handled by electronic or bar-code identifier units. Casual users can pay a flat maximum rate and receive in return a rebate voucher with scratch-off spots, redeemable as lottery tickets, or otherwise. This should enable the toll collection to be handled without increase in toll-plaza facilities. Where tolls are collected in one direction only, they can be charged in the tolled direction on the assumption of a peak return trip, a rebate being credited on the return trip—automatically in the case of regular users having vehicle identifier units, or on the stamping of receipts in registers that need not be at the toll plaza. Those facing tolls in the return trip can be allowed to pick up timed and dated vouchers along the nontolled direction and get them stamped for a potential refund at the tolls on the return trip.

Network Congestion

For congestion on a network of city streets or highways, charges can be assessed by requiring cars entering the congested area to be equipped, permanently or temporarily, with identifier units (scanned electronically, or by bar code, or radar) which can be scanned by wayside equipment suitably scattered around the area so that each vehicle can be checked into and out of arranged zones. The resulting records can be assembled, and appropriate charges calculated by computer and billed to registered owners or charged to credit or debit card accounts at suitable intervals.

Generally, the effect would be to increase traffic speeds and reduce pollution and carbon dioxide emissions, in addition to providing badly needed revenues. In seriously congested conditions amounting to incipient gridlock, such as are prevalent in midtown Manhattan over most of the day from 11 A.M. to 7 P.M., the results are likely to be an increase, rather than a decrease, in the total volume of movement accomplished over the day as a whole: The reduction in the density of traffic during peak hours will allow the fewer cars to move sufficiently faster that the flow in vehicle-mile per hour is increased. More movement, faster movement, more revenue, less pollution!

Casual users can be dealt with in a number of ways. The strictest would be to require everyone not equipped with identifier units to pick one up for a deposit related to the period of validity, subject to a refund on surrendering the unit at departure. Or licenses for a brief period could be sold for a flat fee, or free subject to a restriction on repetition. Some routes for through traffic could be designated as free routes.

Taxicabs and the Like

For taxicabs, to permit the charge to be passed on to the customer, and for people wishing to preserve their anonymity, an on-vehicle apparatus can be provided which, on entering a zone, will begin charging at a rate per mile indicated by a modulated signal emitted from the scanning equipment, the charge being debited against a stored amount periodically augmented by inserting a suitable card or token purchased anonymously.

Fire Protection

Superficially, it might seem that the cost of fire protection is to be charged to the combustible structures that benefit directly from the protection. From the standpoint of marginal social cost, however, nearly all of the cost of fire protection is properly charged against site value. The cost of providing a given grade of protection to a given area is only slightly affected by the number of structures. There is the wear and tear on equipment used and the risk of injury to personnel during the actual fighting of fires, added to the possibility that response time to a second fire may be longer if the local unit is out fighting a first fire and a unit must be brought from farther away. Dense development is associated with traffic congestion that may lengthen response time of fire companies. This cost is to be charged directly to the traffic and not to the property improvements.

These changes are small compared with the wages of the crew on standby and the capital cost of the firehouse and equipment. They amount probably to less than 20 percent of the total. This minor part of the cost of fire protection can appropriately be assessed on the improvements, including tangible personalty, possibly according to what an insurance premium would be for a standard degree of coverage. The owner of tennis courts next door to a firehouse who does not directly use the service can nevertheless afford to devote the land to this use if the convenience of the location for his customers enables him to charge fees yielding a return to the land comparable to what it could get in other uses. He thus benefits indirectly from the presence of the firehouse, without which his customers would be scarcer.

Other Utilities

For other utilities such as water, sewage, gas, electricity, telephone, cable, mail delivery, and the like that are available at that location, the case is the same. That one or more of these facilities do not receive use by the occupant should not excuse the owner from contributing to the cost of carrying these services past his property, any more than a driver can expect to get a reduction in a car rental charge because one will not be using the headlights, the windshield wipers, or the backseat. As matters now stand, electric and gas bills include the cost of carrying the services past the tennis courts and the disproportionate shares of the cost of carrying the services past row houses and two-acre lots. The results are thus not only inefficient but regressive. In addition, land rents and land prices are higher by reason of the availability of these services, but not by so much as if they were available at marginal cost.

Postal Service

In the case of the postal service, an appropriate arrangement would be for the local pick-up and delivery service—where most of the cost varies relatively little with the volume of mail and possibly some window services, especially in smaller communities—to be subsidized out of local urban site-value taxes (with the character of the service in frequency of pick-up and delivery, mailbox locations, and the like) by local governments with reference to local conditions and desires, rather than in accordance with bureaucratic rules and budgets devised in Washington. Bulk sorting and transportation of mail would still be a national responsibility, much as the Tennessee Valley Authority generates and distributes power on a wholesale basis, leaving distribution in local hands.

Competition Among Cities

As long as efficient marginal cost pricing financed by site-value taxes is rare, and labor and capital are mobile, landlords can gain by the adoption of the more efficient modality and thereby secure net rents reflecting the degree to which their efficiency is greater than that of their competitors. As the practice becomes widespread, however, for those cities that are in competition with other cities of a similar character, net urban site value after taxes will be competed away through lower relative prices for their products, to the benefit of the population in general. Net nonurban rents, such as those reflecting agricultural productivity, may remain, as well as urban rents in cities having some degree of uniqueness, such as a harbor, an attractive environment, or a salient position in some special activity such as entertainment, fashion, or finance.

Notes

1. See William Vickrey, "The City as a Firm," in *Economics of Public Services*, Martin Feldstein and Robert Inman, eds. (London: Macmillan, 1997), 334–343.

2. The llustration used is 63rd Street.

3. As an example we can mention the Lindsay settlement allowing for retirement after twenty years' service on a pension equal to half of the final year's total wages and inclusive of overtime and holiday premiums. After a year, it brought these results: The juiciest schedules were picked by workers with seniority and there was a spate of retirements by skilled workers, as well as a serious deterioration in the system's performance.

6

Harry Gunnison Brown

Land Speculation and Land-Value Taxation

Is There Speculation in Land?

The advocates of greater taxation of bare-land values have often contended that speculation in land is a serious injury to the community. It causes economic waste, they say, by compelling the walking and riding of longer distances past vacant lots, and by requiring a greater extent of water mains, gas and sewer pipes, telephone wires, and the like than would otherwise be necessary. It decreases productive efficiency, they contend, and so lowers wages by forcing the use of inferior land when better land would otherwise be available and, through restricting the amount of land in use, by compelling a more intensive utilization of land than would otherwise be economical. Increased taxation of bare-land values, by this argument, would discourage speculative holding of land and would do so in rough proportion to the increase in the tax rate.

That there is some land held out of use by persons speculatively inclined everyone knows. Many of the speculators probably do not consider themselves in this way. They are willing to sell for a "reason-

From Harry Gunnison Brown, "Land Speculation and Land-Value Taxation," *Journal of Political Economy* 35, no. 3 (June 1927): 390–402. Reprinted with permission.

able" price. Some of them want only what the lots they own have "cost" them, including in cost the accumulated taxes and interest on the original price paid. (Since, at 5 percent interest, compounded, a sum doubles in value approximately every fourteen years, a lot purchased for $1,000 and held out of use for ninety-eight years should sell for approximately $128,000, not allowing taxes, in order to repay to the owning family what the land has "cost" it. This might seem a bit hard on the person wanting to buy the land, and the income to the owning family might not seem to have been paid for by any equivalent service rendered. But all that is aside from our present point.)

There appears, however, to be some dissent, among professional economists, from the view that any considerable amount of land is held out of use for speculative gains. This dissent seems to be based on the two assumptions that speculative holding of land is relatively unprofitable and that people will not do what does not pay. Professor Thomas Carver, although favoring land-value taxation, expresses his dissent on this particular point:

> If an individual, Jones by name, has a tract of land which is not being used, there is no reason for believing that he would be averse to getting some income year by year while the land itself is rising in value on his hands. Thus he would get the rise of the value of the land just the same as though it were idle, and he would get, at the same time, whatever income it would bring him. There are not many men who deliberately prefer a smaller to a larger income.[1]

Carver, indeed, goes on to say that after land has been divided into building lots it cannot be cultivated economically; that "the public may be slow in buying the lots for building"; and that "for a number of years this land practically goes to waste." But in view of considerations to be advanced in this paper, I am inclined to believe that Carver underemphasizes both the amount of land speculation and the significance of the human traits that produce it.

As a matter of fact, is a situation anything like this so simple? Not all persons are alike and not all equally find opportunity of gain in the same activity. Even if there are certain persons who would find it profitable to put houses or other buildings on certain lots—in case they owned the lots—it does not follow that those who do own the lots would find it profitable to do so. Still less does it follow that these actual owners would *know* such construction to be profitable. And their speculative anticipations and hopes may cause them to put a price on the lots too high to justify purchase of these lots by others who might see gain from improving them. Nor will it always be feasible for improvements to be made by tenants. Indeed, there must be a good deal of land that is worth using if improved, but not usable to advantage without the construction of buildings or the making of other improvements which tenants will not care to construct or to make, unless they can arrange for long leases or other guaranties on terms not likely to be satisfactory to speculating owners desiring the privilege of sale without notice and free of encumbrances.

Let it not be supposed that we are assuming, for the discussion of land speculation and land improvement, any theories of human action essentially different from what are properly to be assumed in the discussion of other economic problems. Thus, if a rise in the price of shoes makes the production of shoes in general more profitable than the production of steel rails, it will not, on that account, be more profitable for *all* steel-rail producers to begin making shoes instead of steel rails. Most of the steel-rail producers, employers and employees, are so relatively well adapted to steel-rail production and so relatively ill adapted to shoe production that for *them* shoe production would remain the less profitable business. So it is with land speculation as against building. Not all speculators would find building more profitable when and because some speculators would find it more profitable. It does not get us very far to say that if, *in general,* land improvement allows the improver to get both the "unearned increment" and something besides for the *use* of the land and the improvement, therefore *every* owner of land will improve his land as soon as advancing population brings a reasonable demand for the use of such land.

Many and large plots of land *are* held unimproved in the typical city for many years, while streets are built past them, while telephone and electric light wires are stretched over them, while gas and water and sewer pipes are laid beneath them, and while the expanding population builds homes for itself beyond them from the city's center. That the homes are built so far out would seem to be evidence that there is a reasonable demand for these homes. The homes *are* built, indeed, but they are built where their building involves the comparative waste of greater distances for streets, electric wires, water pipes, and travel.

Nor is the evidence convincing that the holding of the intervening lots, *even apart from this incident economic waste,* usually serves the purpose of avoiding the tearing down of houses for the erection of office buildings and the like, saving the vacant land for the latter purpose. Generally, when the intervening areas are first built up, they are built up in substantially the same way as the more outlying districts. Holding the land out of use serves, ordinarily, despite possible exceptional cases, no good social purpose. It merely forces the earlier use of the more distant sites and compels the economic waste associated with such use.[2]

The prospect of a rise in land values stimulates speculation in land by persons who become hopeful of gaining thereby. It causes the holding of land for prices higher than the current market conditions warrant, and so fairly good land may be held out of use while land of inferior location is substituted by those who wish to build. Of course, as a city grows, one after another of the owners of vacant lots decides to build or to sell. The process of building, in any area of a growing town, despite the retarding influence of land speculation, does usually proceed at a more rapid rate than the process of depreciation. For this reason—if for no other—the more centrally located areas of a town are usually built up (sometimes with buildings inadequate to the sites, but at least not absolutely vacant) by the time the town has grown to any considerable size.

Some of the owners who hold land speculatively, even if competent to direct construction and to make money from the improvements, prefer to use elsewhere their surplus funds, if they have any. Of course, this may cause capital construction somewhere, but not on the speculatively held land. Others hold land idle for long periods from mere inertia or indecision. Still others, "land poor," have not the means—and perhaps not the credit—to improve, but keep all their holdings, hoping for a rise. And there are some owners of vacant land who prefer to invest any surplus funds they may have in purchasing more such land, hoping to gain a larger percentage on investment in this fashion, through an anticipated rapid rise, than they could gain by investing such surplus funds in land improvement.

It may be said—it often is said—that, on the average, such large returns are not realized; that, indeed, land speculation usually does not pay. Perhaps, on the average, it does not. Neither, on the average, do lotteries pay. Nor does wagering money on a roulette wheel pay. All such gambling devices are purposely arranged so that the gamblers, on the average, pay in more than they take out. Else how could the proprietors reap any gain? But this does not prevent thousands—should we say millions?—of persons from participating in such gambling. Those economic theorists who picture the "economic man" as a person always choosing the most profitable line of action, and then assume every man to be such an "economic man," are singularly blind to the teachings of experience.

May not the case of land speculation be in some degree analogous? Even if only a minority of the population have the gambling instinct and would participate in land speculation (or in lotteries), that minority may be sufficient to lower somewhat the margin of production by holding good land out of use. It is not so much, perhaps, that speculation in land causes any great decrease in the total amount of land used, although the expectation, a priori, would be of somewhat greater congestion because of such speculation. The more obvious effect, at any rate, would seem to be the forcing into use of poorer and more remote land instead of better and more accessible land.

If There Is Land Speculation, Does Land-Value Taxation Discourage It?

Some of the economists who contend that land-value taxation would not appreciably diminish land speculation perhaps so contend because they think there is practically no speculation to discourage. It is this opinion that we have been critically examining in the preceding pages. Others, admitting the speculation, may believe that increased taxation of bare-land values, and therefore, of vacant land, would do nothing to diminish it. Indeed, it is sometimes impossible to tell, from a writer's comments, which of these views he adheres to. Thus, Professor Frank H. Knight, in a recent book review, refers disapprovingly to "the familiar single-tax heresy that taxes on land value would have any appreciable effect in the way of bringing additional land into use."[3] No criticism is intended here of Professor Knight for failure to make these opinions perfectly clear, in a brief book review, where complete elucidation of his own opinions could not be expected. What is desired is to make the reader see with entire clearness that there are these two possible explanations of the dissent of various economists from what Professor Knight calls "the familiar single-tax heresy," and that the two views must, for the purpose of critical analysis, be sharply distinguished.

Professor H.J. Davenport seems to have taken the position that there is speculation in land, and that land-value taxation, unless all of the rent were to be taken, could not be expected to decrease it.[4] Indeed, he even goes so far as to argue that such taxation (less than 100 percent) would actually increase speculation in land. After intimating that relatively little agricultural land of high grade is kept entirely uncultivated because of speculation, Professor Davenport goes on to say:[5]

> More serious are the speculative aspects of land-holding and land-improving in urban centers. So far, clearly, as the outlook for increased earning power and higher prices tempts a particular class of operators to invest, a class of men with neither the disposition nor the resources for improvement, some land must be retarded in its improvement—those operators who intend a mere gain in price as a return upon investment outbidding the competing offers of the long-run investor. To remove the inducements to speculative purchase by canceling all prospect of the private enjoyment of whatever rent or increases of rent shall attach to the land is obviously to exclude this speculative demand.
>
> But even the more clear is it that to fix a tax, whether present or prospective, at anything short of the entire earning power—to leave a shell of individual property and income—is merely to make the gains still greater in proportion to the investment necessary to control them and is to foster the greater speculative activity that goes with operations on margins.[6]

No criticism is here advanced against the first of the preceding two paragraphs or against the larger part of Professor Davenport's paper. In the view of the present writer, Professor Davenport has carefully analyzed and brilliantly refuted a number of arguments currently directed against greater land-value taxation. And the case for such increased taxation of land values is, indeed, sufficiently strong even if no decrease of speculation could be hoped for because of it. But he is mistaken, I am convinced, if he does not admit the discouraging effect of any considerable increase of land-value taxation, applying equally to used and to vacant land, on land speculation—granting that there is any such thing as speculation in land, and Professor Davenport is not among those who deny its existence. In other words, my criticism—so far as there may be criticism—is leveled against the second of the two paragraphs quoted. It would seem, however, that Professor Davenport must have had in mind, not a general tax on all land value, but only a tax on the rent of used land, vacant and unused land being left untaxed. In such a case, while the tax would hardly encourage speculation, it clearly would not discourage it, unless, as Professor Davenport says, 100 percent were to be taken, and unless possible speculators expected this. But if the tax is applied as well to vacant land, then, as Professor Davenport would probably agree, it could not but be a discouragement to land speculation.

Let us attend, carefully, to the arithmetic of the problem. Suppose a piece of land having an estimated net rental value of $50 a year and a salable value, on a 5 percent basis, of $1,000. A speculator anticipates a rise in its value and buys it to hold for such a rise. He has no training for utilizing the land and intends only to sell again when the time seems ripe. There is no tax on the land. It happens to rise in value at about the rate of 5 percent a year, compound interest, so that at the end of fourteen years it is worth about $2,000.[7] At that time the speculator sells. He hoped for an earlier rise, perhaps, and did not intend to hold on so long, but he congratulates himself that he has secured at least 5 percent on his investment. Perhaps he is lucky. If a value of about $2,000 for this land at the end of fourteen years had been generally foreseen, persons who could use the land profitably during the interim would have been able to offer more than $1,000 at the beginning and would so have been in a position to outbid the speculators. On the other hand, if the speculator wrongly anticipates a rise to $2,000 in a year or two, and users do not share his anticipations, he will outbid them. At any rate, in our example, he has made about 5 percent, compounded, on his original investment. But, it may be said, he would have made more than that had he used the land, since he would have received the income from its use as well as the rise in its value. Such use, however, would have required further investment. In the first place, he may lack the necessary experience and ability to follow such a course. In the second place, he may be unduly optimistic regarding the prospect of a rise in the value of the land, and may so anticipate a larger percentage of return from using all his funds in speculation than from using a part of them in construction.

But our concern here is with the question whether taxation of land would make any difference. Granting that land speculators are, on the average, of the unduly optimistic, gambling, lottery-loving type, does taxation of land values put on them any penalty of such a sort that they are less likely to speculate with such taxation than without it?

In the case we have assumed, there being no tax, the speculator gains about 5 percent, compounded. He might, to be sure, have gained more by improving the land, but we have seen why an optimistic person with a lottery-loving type of mind—as well as some speculative holders of a different type—might be unlikely to invest in improvements. How would the case stand now if the tax rate were high enough to take half of the potential rent, or $25 a year, going up to $50 a year at the end of the fourteen-year period when the land had doubled in value?[8] In that case, the value of the land would be presumably only half as great at every point of time. It would be $500 at the beginning of the fourteen-year period, instead of $1,000. It would be $1,000 at the end of the fourteen years, instead of $2,000. Does the speculator gain a larger percentage than before, or even as large a percentage? His land rises from a value of $500 to a value of $1,000 instead of from $1,000 to $2,000. But he now has to pay an annual tax of $25 a year, coming up to $50 at the end of the period. His net percentage gain is certainly smaller.

If the speculator wants to invest as great a sum at the beginning as if there were no tax, that is, $1,000, he will have to buy twice as much land. If this land rises in value from $1,000 to $2,000 during fourteen years,[9] he will have gained 5 percent, compounded, minus the annual tax which begins (on this larger piece of land having a rental yield of $100) at $50 and works up to $100 at the end of the fourteen years. Is it not clear that the gains from land speculation are seriously reduced by such a tax? The speculating owner certainly doesn't come anywhere near making 5 percent!

But there may have to be faced, in the minds of some economists, another objection. Granting that the returns from land speculation are reduced by such a tax, they may say, "will not the returns from land utilization be reduced in equal degree?" Most assuredly not. The returns from such utilization are as large a percentage as before. The land yields as large a net percentage of rent on its value for the tax being capitalized, so the land can be purchased for a correspondingly lower price. (Indeed, since the price of the land may have depended not solely upon the bidding of would-be users, but partly upon the bidding of speculators, and since this bidding tends to be discouraged by the tax in question, the price of the land may conceivably fall by a greater percentage than the net potential rent.)[10] And the yield of the improvements is certainly no less.

Let us suppose now a higher tax, taking nine-tenths of the potential rent. This will leave $5 net potential rent on the lot, instead of $50, and should make its salable value one-tenth as large, or $100.[11] If the speculator now buys it, and if it doubles in value in fourteen years, as before, it will then be worth $200 (the capitalized value of $10 a year net rent, that is, of $100 minus a tax of $90). The speculator can be said to gain $100, or 5 percent compounded, only if no consideration is given to his outgo of $45 a year, gradually increasing toward $90. Even if the rise of rental value takes place suddenly at the end of the last year, so that the tax is a flat $45 a year for the entire fourteen years, still the speculator has had to suffer an outgo of $630 ($45 × 15) during fourteen years in order that he may sell for $200 at the end of that time the lot he bought for $100 at the beginning.

Or suppose he wants to invest as much in land as the given lot would sell for if untaxed, that is, $1,000. Then he would buy ten such lots. If, at the end of fourteen years,[12] the ten lots have doubled in value and can be sold for $2,000, the speculator cannot consider that he has made $1,000, or 5 percent compounded, *unless he refuses to reckon, as offsetting this gain, the annual tax.* This annual tax on the ten lots, assuming no rise in value until the end of the period, is $450, amounting, during the fourteen years, to $6,300. Clearly, such a speculator not only would fail to gain, but would suffer, relatively to his original investment, a tremendous loss.

Yet a person who wished to buy the $1,000 worth of land at the beginning of the period for improvement and use would be able to make just as large a return upon the land, as such, as if there were no tax. For the diminished rental yield would be as large a percentage of the lower capitalized price as before. And the return on the improvements put upon the land would not be reduced. Indeed, if the heavier tax on land values should make possible a reduction of the tax on capital, the net percentage of return on the improvements might be greater.[13]

If, then, $1,000 invested in land will yield as large a return in future rents when land values are heavily taxed as when they are not taxed at all, provided the land is improved and used, and if $1,000 invested in land held vacant and unused, which happens to double in value in fourteen years, will yield some 5 percent compounded, if there is no tax, but will cause a net loss of $5,300 ($6,300–$1,000) if there is a tax of 90 percent, shall we say that the advantages of use and speculative holding are in the same relation to each other whether there is a tax of zero or of 90 percent? Yes, if the tax is only on rent actually received. No, if it is on potential rent and applies equally to unused, partially used, and fully used land.

But perhaps someone will still say that, even if the land is not taxed, the speculator will really suffer as great a loss through speculating as if it is heavily taxed, the difference being merely that, in the former case, he fails to secure a gain that he might get by using the land, while in the latter case he suffers an outgo in the form of an annual tax.

Let us compare the two cases and see whether there is really no difference. With no tax, assuming the land to double in value in fourteen years, an investment of $1,000 in land not used nets 5 percent. But it might, if the land were used, net in addition $50 a year. (We shall here assume, for simplicity of exposition, that the rent does not rise above this annual sum for fourteen years, when it suddenly becomes $100; but our proposition would be equally demonstrable in any case.) There is, then, a loss of $700 rent in the sense that the speculator might have had this rent in addition to his increment. With a tax of 90 percent, his loss in net rent (what he might then have by using the land) is $5 a year, or $70, and his outgo for taxes is $45 a year, or $630, making $700, as before; but his gain from rising value is only $100 ($100 to $200). Or if he buys a piece of land ten times as large, so investing an equal sum, $1,000 at the start, then his loss of net rent from holding the land idle is $50 a year, or $700, and his outgo in taxes, $450 a year, or $6,300, making a total of $7,000 as against a rise in value of $1,000.

Summary and Conclusion

The percentage of increase in the originally invested sums may be as great—if the land rises in value as the speculator hopes—whether there is a tax or not; but the annual penalty is much greater in proportion as there is a heavy tax. It is as if a person who risked $1,000 in a lottery, on the roulette wheel, or in some other gambling venture had to pay a tremendous sum in taxes for the privilege of engaging in the lottery or other venture, a sum which would probably more than equal his gains even if there should be gains. Would not such a tax diminish land speculation? Shall we say that it does not diminish land speculation because there isn't much of it, on the theory that it doesn't pay on the average and that people won't do what doesn't offer probabilities of paying? Shall we say that a tremendously heavy tax on persons participating in lotteries and other gambling in proportion to the amount of their participation, so that they could hardly gain under any circumstances, would not diminish gambling because there wouldn't be much anyhow, since on the average, gambling does not pay, and since people don't do things that do not pay? In truth, gamblers differ. A low tax would discourage some of them. But a sufficiently high tax, if it could not be evaded, would discourage nearly all of them.

There is nothing in the nature of men as we know them to justify an a priori conclusion that no appreciable speculation in land ever takes place. On the contrary there is, a priori, every reason for expecting a considerable amount of such speculation. For we know that many persons will "take a chance" at ventures when the average result to participants must be a loss.

Will those who are trying to show that there is no such speculation of importance fare better by examining the "actual facts"? It would be necessary to show that practically no land, except marginal land, is so held out of use; that land appreciably more isolated, or requiring more travel back and forth, or otherwise poorer, is not resorted to because of such speculation, and that rent is not increased because of it.

At any rate, if there is any such speculation at all worth mentioning, it must be admitted that heavy land-value taxation, resting equally on land whether used or unused, must discourage it. Should it be established that there is not enough speculative holding of land to do any significant amount of harm—and it seems unlikely that such a conclusion can be established—then those who believe that heavier land-value taxation is desirable must thereafter confine their attention to the other advantages of such taxation. I have been in the habit of putting emphasis rather upon such other possible advantages; but I am nevertheless strongly inclined to suspect, despite the deprecating comments of Professor Knight and others, that the discouragement of holding land idle and of thereby lowering the margin of production might be a real, even though a relatively minor, advantage of such taxation. As long as the unused land is better than the marginal land, its use by the owners, or by persons to whom they may lease it, or by persons to whom they may sell it, tends to increase production. And this is not only true when the owner is compelled to sell without securing an increment in price over what he paid. It is equally true if he must sell for a price less than he paid. Holding land out of use to avoid selling for a low price has the same kind of effect on production as holding it out of use in the hope of selling for a high price.

Notes

1. Thomas Carver, *Principles of National Economy* (Boston: Ginn, 1921), 737.
2. See further the author's critical comments in *The Taxation of Unearned Incomes,* 3d ed. (Columbia, MO: Lucas Brothers, 1926), 126–128.
3. Frank Knight, "Theoretical Issues in the Single Tax," *National Municipal Review* (June 1925).
4. See the later suggested interpretation of his statement.
5. That it is improved and cultivated as it might be does not follow.
6. H.J. Davenport, *American Economic Review* (March 1917): 16.
7. For simplicity of exposition by the avoidance of fractions, it will be assumed throughout the rest of the article that 5 percent compound interest means doubling in value in fourteen years. This is not exactly true; a little longer is required.
8. As was pointed out, it is not quite true that 5 percent compound interest means doubling in fourteen years. The period required is a little longer.
9. A little over fourteen years, but nearer fourteen than fifteen.
10. Insofar as the value of land is determined by users rather than speculators, a tax that reduces the net rent of land tends to reduce its salable value in the same, but in no greater, proportion.
11. See, however, foregoing remarks regarding possible effects of discouraging speculation.
12. Fourteen years, plus.
13. The larger net return on capital, unless and until increased savings reduced the rate of return at the margin, would involve capitalizing *land* at a higher interest rate, so that the net rent of *land* would be a *higher* percentage of its salable value than if there were no tax on the land.

7

Mason Gaffney

Tax Reform to Release Land

Introduction

Taxes on land and buildings are important influences on land use, and are within the control of government. Real estate taxes are a major source of revenue to local governments (LGs) in the United States, as well as being a major cost of owning property. Currently under legal attack in the United States is the local real estate tax as the backbone of public school finance. The premise is that children should not be deprived of reasonable education because their school district lacks an adequate tax base. Regardless of any reforms in this system of local taxing for local services, it seems probable that real estate taxes will persist at some level of government—they are too important a source of revenue to be abandoned. They might or might not be reduced.

Real estate taxes do more than raise revenue; they influence land use, often strongly. Their influence arises not merely from their level, but from the relative tax on land versus that on buildings, from the relative tax on unimproved land versus that on improved land, from the frequency and reasons for reassessment of property, and from other

---

Mason Gaffney, "Tax Reform to Release Land," in *Modernizing Urban Land Policy,* Marion C. Clawson, ed. (Baltimore: Johns Hopkins University Press, 1973), 115–151. Gratitude is extended to the Johns Hopkins University Press for permission to reprint this essay.

aspects of the imposition of such taxes. Some of the land use effects may be unintended by the legislators and administrators responsible for the taxes, but many of the effects seem clearly to be desired and sought. Real estate taxes cannot absolutely compel some land uses or absolutely forbid others, as can zoning or building codes; but they provide powerful economic incentives, which are operative constantly over long periods of time and in the long run may be as effective as absolute prohibitions or mandates.

Local real estate taxes affect the landholder directly, and also indirectly by affecting the way local governments use other land use controls. Most local zoning today has become fiscal zoning, calculated to fortify the local per capita tax base. That is not news, but it is only the most familiar example of the role of the real estate tax in the pattern of local particularism.

The purpose of this paper is to describe the many ways in which real estate taxes influence urban and suburban land use. Some of these effects are rather obvious and expected; but others, on analysis, turn out to be different than a quick and intuitive judgment would predict. In general and in total, real estate taxes as administered in the United States tend to favor the land speculator over the builder, the larger owner over the smaller, and the suburbs over central cities. De facto, real estate taxes as ordinarily administered are an instrument of economic discrimination. They might, if properly restructured, become instruments for socially more constructive land use.

Motives of Local Governments

The art of central government is that of motivating local governments to act in the wider public interest—to serve the nation by serving themselves. Local governments have objectives and operate under constraints and incentives just like persons and firms. Economists have analyzed persons and firms since at least Adam Smith and examined how public policy can work with the market to harness private motives to public ends. But they have neglected the analogous question about LGs, and so have political scientists.

Local governments borrow the sovereignty and police power of the state, and are assumed in law to represent a public interest. But what public? Each represents a small and particular public. There are even cases—in California, of course—of special service districts that are armed with sovereignty and its trappings, immunities, privileges, and exemptions representing as few as one landowner.

Since local governments borrow the sovereignty of the state, the states have the power and duty to structure local incentives to constrain LGs to serve all by serving themselves. And so the states do, in many ways, but they have fallen behind the problem. Today the tension between parochial LG interests and broader public interests approaches the flash point. It is past time to be defining the tensions and aiming to resolve them. This is the point of this paper.

That the local turf is more completely open to the movement of labor and capital differentiates the local viewpoint from the national. The LG is defined as an area of land. Men and wealth come and go, and the level of their returns is set by national market forces, much as the waters of the sea find a common level by interflowing. So the benefits of local spending lodge mainly in higher local land values, because land alone is stationary for long. By the same token, the cost of taxes lodges in lower land values. Land is the equity interest in the municipal corporation. Land income is the bottom line of its income statement. Many municipal motives may best be understood, therefore, as efforts to get the most they can of land income and values.

There is a harmony here between local and national interest. The private owner maximizes net income from a given land area by carving it up and improving and using it so as to bring to the highest level its net service flow. The private owner's greed, harnessed by the market, makes him allocate his land for housing and complementary life-support facilities in a surprisingly socially oriented way. "Highest and best use" is sometimes belittled as though it were a public nuisance, but basically it means the use serving the most human needs. That basic rule must be qualified to account for external effects, but the qualifications are not the rule.

The same rule holds for the LG, which is a group of landowners in league to preside over the collective capital that they use jointly. The LG is a halfway house between the individual landowner and the state. Landowner control is modified by democracy, which gives the whole system some of its characteristic tensions and compromises. But landowners, as the permanent party of every LG, take a strong and steady interest in local government out of proportion to their numbers. It is reasonably accurate for many purposes to think of the LG as a collective landowner, seeking the highest land income. In so doing it serves the national good.

While there is that basic harmony of local and national good, LGs feel at least four pecuniary incentives that make their goals clash with the larger metropolitan and national welfare. LGs want to avoid dilution of the tax base. They want to keep down tax export. They want to fence off local public goods from aliens. And they want to avoid pure competition among their members. No doubt there are more, but these are prominent, and a sufficient basis for the problems of local exclusivism that vex us today. The factor of ethnic bias is treated elsewhere.

Avoiding Dilution of Tax Base

The states delegate to LGs certain service duties and certain tax powers to finance them. Many duties, such as drainage, vary as functions of area rather than of people; but others, notably education, vary with population. The property tax is redistributive. So old settlers in each LG are sedulous to see that immigrants contribute as much in taxes as they require in added spending. Indeed, they go further. They try to limit new entry to people who will enrich the tax base by the maximum possible amount. Added to this is often a crabbed and misanthropic outlook on strangers, and a lack of urgency to develop annexed vacant land, which has led to extremes of exclusivism.

Whoever said Americans idolize motherhood never looked into suburban zoning. Whoever said the property tax is regressive is not listening when the rich grumble about taxing property to finance services to people. For the state to require LGs to "tax the rich man's property to educate the poor man's child" is to invite them to fence out poor families. What partly resolves the tension is that good schools are, like other local services, capitalized into higher real estate values. The bromide that property benefits only from services to property and not from services to people is false. But it is true that school benefits are in proportion to children and not to taxable real estate. The municipal manager finds it his duty to keep out children without a large complement of taxable real estate, and wears a black armband on Mother's Day.[1]

This attitude is not limited to suburbs. Milwaukee's Mayor Henry Maier, president of the U.S. Conference of Mayors, advocates removing "whole square miles of people" from central cities.[2] Big city mayors have been doing that for several years, with federally subsidized programs for highways, urban renewal, land clearance, slum clearance, code enforcement, airport expansion, purchase of open space, attraction of industry, campus expansion, harbor expansion, street widening, and so on. It is not just the lure of the suburbs that has lowered the density of central cities so far below what it was thirty years ago.

This exclusionary attitude is not an urban monopoly by any means. Cities have at least some tradition of welcoming immigrants—that is how they became cities. Some rural and sylvan areas never have wanted growth, which is often one reason they remained rural or sylvan. Northern Maine is a celebrated case, owned by a handful of timber companies that have opposed the incorporation of any towns that might tax them to finance schools and attract immigrants. In the settlement of the West the very formation of counties was fought by large ranchers whom the counties might tax. Planting smaller farmers everywhere, the Homestead Act overcame the resistance in most counties, and the need for farm labor softened the exclusionary attitude. Today, as the average native student demands longer and costlier schooling, and as migrant labor competes, every rural county feels a new impulse to exclude the poorer people. Migrant labor does the job without requiring schools and without voting.

Minimizing Tax Export

LGs like to help their constituents avoid paying taxes to higher levels of government. This takes several forms.

Within counties using the property tax, smaller LGs try to underassess real estate. Boards of equalization fight this competitive underassessment with overt success but sometimes fail to redress covert underassessment. Low-use zoning is underhanded underassessment, because it depresses resale values during the period before the zoning is breached or lifted. The LG in effect sets its county assessment low by its own motion. This ploy is invidiously reserved for LGs whose citizens can collectively afford to forgo resale value during a prolonged holding period before the zoning is changed.

A complement of low-use zoning is tax assessment based on present use rather than market value. Local assessors often find this acceptable to boards of equalization that would reject more overt forms of competitive underassessment.

Any local tendency to encourage commerce is discouraged in states that levy heavy sales taxes and, unlike Illinois and California, do not return a share to the LG where collected. With no return, any local sacrifice of environment to build up commerce would only pour more taxes into the state treasury.

Property assessment also plays a central role in avoidance of state and federal income taxes. Income property is tax depreciable. Law and Internal Revenue Service (IRS) practice allow repeated depreciation by successive owners, ridiculous as that may be. The law recognizes that land does not depreciate, so each successive owner can depreciate only the building, not the land. When he buys he must allocate the cost between depreciable building and nondepreciable land.

Enter the local tax assessor. It is IRS practice to accept the local assessor's allocation of value between land and buildings. Local assessors, by undervaluing land relative to buildings, thus help their constituents depreciate land and so avoid a large share of the income tax due on real estate, and help convert it from a tax payer to a tax shelter. This is the modern version of competitive underassessment, costing the federal treasury billions annually and going virtually unchecked. This practice creates a strong local bias to underassess land, which in turn tends, through its direct effect on landowner incentives, to keep land from serving the needs of the median consumer.

The income tax hits ordinary income much harder than capital gains—more than twice as hard, when an investor knows the angles on capital gains—and the tax-avoidance game works by converting income into capital gain. The LG helps. Rather than use public money to help established industry and commerce earn ordinary income, the LG extends its capital infrastructure into new land to create capital gains, selling tax-exempt municipal bonds to raise the capital. The "unearned increment" on the land is the untaxed increment as well.

The LG also devotes extra effort to securing state and federal spending and public works that will raise local land values. To this end, it reserves sites, holding them ready for a new branch of the state university, a military base, a highway interchange, a defense plant, or whatever. To this end it also seeks to attract citizens with influence at court, which adds to its bias for the wealthy.

Blending into the minimizing of tax export is the maximizing of outside aid. An entire culture of local politics has grown up around the art of pleading poverty. Cities are always "strapped," in "crisis," requiring "relief," and so on, in spite of the rise of their real estate tax base. This is silly, but a game people play in dead earnest as they compete for federal dollars. Underassessment is a central part of the game, sequestering latent fiscal assets. So is regressive assessment, assuring that local taxes hurt and arouse sympathy, and an image of desperation.

Fencing Off Local Public Amenities from Aliens

LGs provide many public services, such as schools, parks, police and fire protection, libraries, and others. These municipal amenities yield a flow of services to their users, a form of income to these persons that is tax free. Local taxes used to finance the production of these local amenities are deductible from the individual's taxable income, unlike cash payments for items of individual consumption. The availability and quality of these local services raise local land values, as anyone who seeks to buy a house in a neighborhood with good schools quickly learns; and the capital gains provisions of income tax law keep largely free of taxes the increases in land values. At a time when a penny saved is two pennies earned before taxes and tax-free income is almost the only kind worth having, these are weighty values.

The problem here is restricting the use of these local amenities to local residents. The goal is a tenure or right of use that is common but not too common—common within the small group of local residents, but private against outsiders. This source of pressure is often very strong. All residents of the local area have much to gain from exclusive use of local amenities but only the large landowner has something to sell if aliens invade the local area by purchase of property. The tenant and small owner have little or no salable tenure in local amenities—only a shadow equity in the old swimming hole based on use and custom, familiarity, and their scantiness in numbers. They can suffer real losses from the invasion and crowding of their old haunts.

To maintain the unstable balance between common amenities and limited access, suburbanites have developed the cult of open space, a philosophy that transmutes the exclusionary particularism of the golf course into the nobility of naturalism. The apotheosis of open space is to suburban particularism what "national defense" is to the federal budget. The anomaly of open space behind cyclone fences is a contradiction only to whoever doesn't get the subliminal part of the message.

Every movement requires a philosophy and naturalism has been recruited to serve the local treasury.

Avoiding Pure Competition

The historical mercantilistic city was a monopoly, using municipal policy to exploit its trade territory by restricting competition. Today the increase in mobility somewhat lessens motive, but it is by no means dead. Owners of old buildings are sensitive to competition from new ones, which pull away tenants. They know that renewal at higher density adds to supply and helps lower rents, while renewal at lower density is removal, which delivers tenants into the hands of landlords. They mask this with talk of "good planning," "human scale of density and size," psychoses of crowded laboratory rats, birth control, saving historical shrines, aesthetic absolutes, and other diversions and digressions. So far they have gotten away with it.

Local Mercantilist Policies

Local governments have other, more basic incentives on which the four discussed here are superimposed. They want to serve their constituents well at low cost (subject to Parkinsonian tendencies among bureaucrats, of course). They seek efficiency, internal equity among voters (even including tenants), renewal, ordinary (that is, productive) income, growth of the local market, and succession of land to higher uses serving more human needs. There is a continual tension between the goals, to understand which is to understand much of municipal behavior.

LG response to these combined incentives is municipal mercantilism or particularism, interchangeable terms emphasizing the pursuit of parochial self-interest at the expense of outsiders. LGs pursue mercantilism by bending all their powers to the goal. These include establishing boundaries, taxing, zoning, allocating capital budgets, planning public works, policing buildings, pricing municipal services, influencing utility rates, negotiating for new industries, and a few others.

Balkanization

The basis of local particularism is segregating the tax base by creating and defending tax enclaves. Industrial tax enclaves are one type, but they get more than their share of the spotlight. Resources are a larger member of the family. "Trees don't go to school," says the timber owner, "why should I pay taxes?" Mineral owners don't say anything. They just lie low with nearly total success. Farm landowners, whose real estate weighs in at over $200 billion, have sold themselves as a collective welfare case. (Their national average property tax rate is about 1 percent of market value.) Factory owners, on the other hand, are blamed for schoolchildren, as though hiring were siring.

It is a double standard to ponder, as national unemployment rises to crisis levels while the birthrate drops toward zero population growth. Creating jobs is not really antisocial; it just seems that way to the local school board. Those who deploy their capital to employ men are doing a favor to the nation, and are not adding a bit to national school costs. So the establishment of industrial enclaves, which exclude residences, should not be singled out for avoiding school taxes, any more than farmland, timber, minerals, and utilities. Employers should pay taxes because they own property, not because they hire fathers.

Enclaves established to provide tax havens resist "growth" not of everything, but only of population. They love to annex land and attract taxable capital. From the parochial viewpoint of modern municipal mercantilism, the best industry is the industry most intensive in capital that hires the fewest fathers per dollar of tax base. Such industries are hypersensitive to property taxes, and so tend to attract one another and cluster in low-tax enclaves. This is splendid for them, but hard on everyone else.

Some suburban residential enclaves, often mixed with rural ones, have effectively excluded racial and ethnic minorities and low-income people of every race. Such enclaves have recently been the center of legal and political efforts to desegregate races and classes and to tap segregated tax bases by invasion. The enclaves may deserve the invasion, but let us not forget the larger tax bases not touchable in this way: forests, farms, minerals, vacation resorts, factories, utilities, stores, and warehouses. A move to statewide property taxation for schools will do more to equalize school resources than anti-zoning cases. And let us not forget that invading a segregated tax base will almost surely result in relocation of people and businesses in areas they might not have chosen but for the lure of the richer tax base they could share there. Again, statewide school finance has the advantage of equalizing fiscal resources without requiring or inducing people or businesses to move in quest of more favorable tax treatment. Some of the longest leaps in the annals of suburban sprawl have resulted from developers' pioneering in peripheral rural counties to enjoy their low tax rates.

Administrative Modification of the Property Tax

Assessors have much latitude, de facto. Most assessors are, for better or worse, chameleons of municipal policy, and use their latitude to help effect predominant local goals as seen by the local powers.

Regressive assessment has been found in many LGs, although never in pure form. It is mixed with other biases. Some, like the bias against newer buildings, tend to countervail regressivity. But most biases probably reinforce it—for example, the bias for land, the lag in revaluing declining areas downward and new areas upward, the bias against subdivision, the bias against the unorganized and possibly against blacks, the wholesale rate given to large speculative acreage and larger lots, and basing assessment on present use rather than value.

Some recent studies showing or suggesting regressive assessment are by Oliver Oldman and Henry Aaron in Boston; Theodore Smith in Hartford; the Urban League in Atlanta; and Mason Gaffney in Milwaukee.[3]

It may be hard to prove regressive or racist motives. They may not even prevail, although I believe they are an influence. The point of consistency is fiscal particularism, the desire to protect and enrich the local tax base.

"Hearth-tax" assessment is a strong tendency. A site is assessed in part by value, but adjusted for the number of families there. The result, and I surmise the idea behind it, is to remake the property tax into something more like school tuition.

Sites without buildings are assessed most lightly of all. No hearth, no tax. We shall see that taxing buildings reduces population while taxing land increases it. The LG fighting immigration will naturally hit buildings harder.

Land assessment based on present use is part of the pattern. It is not true that taxing ripening land ad valorem forces premature use, but it is true that raising land assessments at the time of subdivision or other conversion to higher use is a powerful force postponing such conversion. It creates a locked-in effect, like the capital gains tax that waits on sale. The assessor's propensity to assess land use rather than value is reinforced and abetted by low-use zoning, discussed later.

There is tension here, and ambivalence. LG taxpayers would like the undeveloped acreage to share the load. But they hold back, in an uneasy truce: We don't tax you; you don't crowd our schools.

The property tax is also modified by exemptions provided by state law. LGs are not omnipotent over this, but they have a choice of what exemptions to fight. The Milwaukee tax commissioner, for example, fights to disexempt dormitories, hospital annexes, and nursing homes—capital that serves people's needs. On the other hand, he does not fight to tax cemeteries that preempt as much land as industry and hold most of it in reserve for future burials while life-support systems are taxed instead. Nor does he fight to tax the vast grounds surrounding many institutions, or to assess golf courses at market value. Cities blame the states and plead impotence, yet much of the exempt land is owned by institutions of the city itself: industrial land banks, harbor commissions, redevelopment authorities, and many agencies with advance sites. Thus cities evince a preference for the kinds of tax exemption that reduce the supply of buildings (other than private schools, which help hold down school taxes).

Forcing Property Consumption by Direct Control

One way to enrich the property tax base is to require every resident to use no less than a standard complement of land and capital, and exclude those who will not. This is forced consumption.

It is a pretty expensive indirect way to collect taxes, something like Charles Lamb's description of a mythical Chinese practice of burning down a house to roast a pig. It could raise a family's yearly debt service or other yearly capital costs by $10 in order to increase tax returns by $1. The lower the tax rate, the greater the forced consumption of real estate required per dollar of tax revenue. And low tax rates do not weaken the motive, which is to avoid *increasing* rates, from whatever level.

LGs force land consumption by using zoning, subdivision control, building codes, and condemnation power.

Zoning

Low-density zoning is the focus of today's perception of this set of devices. It is simply forced land consumption. Indirectly it also forces the individual to consume more capital, because large homes go with large lots. It greatly and directly forces LGs to sink more capital in all public works, the costs of which vary as functions of area, not population.

It is ironic that low-density zoning is viewed by some as a defense against urban expansion. It forces urbanites to consume more land, and cities to spread out, even if working ideally. The way it normally works, it thwarts demand for better land and sends developers probing outward seeking weak spots in the zoning umbrella. High-density land use thus erupts capriciously here and there, and threatens everywhere, rather than clustering where it belongs. The protection of nature and open space against man, purportedly a reason for low-density zoning, is not achieved. Man is frustrated in his quest for land, and more of nature is displaced than if he were satisfied. Zoning to protect nature is a boomerang policy. Touted as a solution, it has become a large part of the problem.

It is ironic that zoning is used as a defense against higher school enrollments and hence against higher taxes, for low density inflates most other public costs. Jumpy, uneven, unpredictable sprawl inflates them even more. The added costs are net social costs to the nation; the school savings are just transfers, local gains achieved by imposing the cost on others, or depriving children altogether. The national result is a tragic waste of resources to no purpose.

Agricultural zoning is the most extreme kind of exclusionary zoning, followed by large-lot zoning in horsey exurbs. But zoning is universal. Zoning extends clear to the center of the city, where it takes the form of floor-area ratios, height limits, and setbacks. At every stage it interdicts market choice for more intensive use. Usually this is a direct bias against the poor. Luxury high-rise apartments and some office buildings cater to the affluent, but the indirect effect of suppressing them also hits the poor, as the rich are forced to bid for more land.

As you might expect, LGs overzone for uses regarded as fiscal surplus generators, and underzone for deficit-makers. There is often a lack of careful counting of supply and demand, and a tendency to reserve most of the land for a small share of the regionwide market. The fiscal motive is mixed with a variety of subjective value judgments and weakly based, strongly held opinions about high-rise apartment living, ethnic outgroups, and aesthetics. Some results of exclusionary zoning are capricious and hard to explain rationally with any human endeavor: What is regarded as a local liability often reflects more prejudice than analysis. But even perfect knowledge would not eliminate a zoning bias.

In most cities, too much land is zoned for commerce and industry. Some rich suburbs zone them out as nuisances, but that is the exception: Few can afford the luxury. The classic rationale for zoning is to protect ivy-covered cottages from gas stations and rendering plants, but in most LGs the zoning gives these nuisance uses a wide choice of sites among dwellings. The ivy-covered cottages are the nuisance: They produce the fiscal pollutant, schoolkids. Many have to invade industrially and commercially zoned land, because so little is zoned residential.

The main limit on commercial zoning is imposed by influential merchants to stifle competition. Zoning boards entertain as quite legitimate, legal, and respectable the plea that commercial zoning be denied a newcomer because it would hurt someone else's business. The common-law rule against monopolies is easily forgotten. This is in keeping with the historical municipal mercantilism of monopolistic city-states.

Zoning often determines property tax assessments. From the land speculator's viewpoint, the ideal is farm zoning and a low-assessed value during the ripening period, with the option to secure high-density zoning at the time of his choosing. Many have succeeded in achieving this. The rest of the community appreciates the speculator's not diluting the local tax base by developing, but would also appreciate his enriching it by paying taxes. There are other pros and cons in each case, too, and great variety in the compromises struck. But there is a common theme: Zoning is used to hold down property tax assessments on ripening land. Zoning helped to change the property tax from a tax on present and potential land value to a tax on land use, activity, and human occupancy. It reinforces and legitimizes the assessment discrimination that occurs even without zoning. The assessment discrimination, in turn, helps keep land in low-density use or cold storage, withheld in either case from the poor.

Subdivision Control

LGs have power to refuse subdivisions, and can make them meet standards. It is an obvious occasion for upgrading, and goldplating street improvements has become the rule. An aerial photograph shows vast areas in subdivision paving, planned to repel through traffic, used entirely for local access. The result: expensive lots, as intended.

Some LGs impose what are in effect special taxes on new building tracts by requiring donations of land for school sites. These add to the price of new houses, limiting supply and excluding poorer buyers.

A pernicious byproduct of imposing extra costs on subdividing is an exaggerated propensity to build without subdividing, where possible. This means stringing buildings out along trunk roads financed by city, state, or the United States. Interior land is sterile, or worse, divided into bowling alley lots. Settlement is linear, which guarantees the least linkage, and the most interference and congestion. The resultant low density makes public transport uneconomic, leading to total dependence on private autos—another exclusionary device.

Building Codes

The worthy purposes of codes, like other devices, are easily subverted to exclusionary ends, and probably have been. "Every building a Cadillac" is hard on Datsun budgets. Occupancy limits further require that the Cadillac have empty seats.

Grandfather clauses let standards be focused on new buildings, the cutting edge of supply, without threatening old ones. This, too, acts against renewal.

It is grotesque to watch the Department of Housing and Urban Development (HUD) struggling with its Operation Breakthrough, as though cheap housing waited on engineering advances. The theory of "cultural lag" has been a commonplace for decades, yet technocratic minds keep seeking physical solutions to institutional problems. For as long as the life of the theory of "cultural lag," American industry has offered us a good cheap dwelling unit called a trailer. The reason it does not solve our housing shortage is to be found not on the assembly line, but in the assembly chamber. Largely because they dilute the tax base, LGs will not let them in.

Condemnation

Many cities condemn old buildings for reasons of safety and health. This does, where applied, bring euthanasia to structures forced into the geriatric stage by policy. But the emphasis is on clearance, riddance, and removal, not on rebuilding. Like federal urban renewal, condemnation lends itself to policies of exclusion.

If welfare were all locally financed, LG authorities would condemn old buildings more vigorously. Large federal sharing in welfare makes old slums much less a local liability than otherwise. The schoolchild remains the main local liability.

When a forsaken gargoyle, cornice, aesthetic or "historical" antiquity is threatened by market forces, condemnation operates in reverse. People who look the other way when poor families are driven from their condemned homes may often be found rallying to save a shrine that symbolizes what they define as history or tradition. If it stands in the way of a housing project, so much the better.

Taste Conformity

Some LGs have architectural review or fine arts commissions and the like, with certain powers to save antiquities, prohibit nonconforming styles, and so on. Ostensibly they are concerned with aesthetics, and no doubt they are, but taste standards are subjective and often absolutist. An objective factor in taste is waste, as Thorstein Veblen taught, preferably dignified by age and obsolescence, tempered by modesty in display. But modesty in display entails setbacks that lead to immodest land requirements, the ultimate symbol of financial respectability, reserve power under leash, and priority of status. Class bias may masquerade as anger at the greed of developers, and fear of children as love of beauty. The result is another fence against the poor.

Regressive Regulatory Bias

Utility rate regulation nearly everywhere fails to consider the fact that distribution cost gets lower as density rises and gets higher with distance from the load center. Yet at today's low densities, distribution (or collection) has become far and away the major cost in almost all utilities, so total costs are dominated by density of settlement. The cost varies as a function of area primarily, and only incidentally with volume per meter. Rates do not reflect these differential costs. Discounts, indeed, go to the large individual buyer irrespective of density. Many large individual buyers are at low density and far out, and should pay higher rates.

Thus "rich territory" subsidizes the lean, and small lots subsidize the large. Utility rates are a regressive tax. Owners of large lots and of undivided vacant land are spared part of the costs of services available to them and hence are under less pressure to subdivide their land.

If the surpluses wrung from small users of land in this fashion went to local school boards, LGs might welcome the poor. But the surpluses are pooled, instead, over utility networks covering many LGs. The local school district is hit with the cost of the children living at high density, while the benefit of low utility costs per capita is diffused over a wide system. As a result many LGs use their power over certain mass systems, mainly sewer and water, to control immigration. They can block subdivision with "sewer power" by refusing sewers, pleading undercapacity—and then fail to increase capacity.

Meanwhile, building continues at the low densities appropriate to private individual water wells and septic tanks. Capital costs are high, and screen out the poor. Large-tract platting preempts land and precludes subdivision. For sewer and water service this pattern of land settlement makes no sense at all. It is a device of local fiscal particularism, calculated to fortify the tax base per capita. And it is growing. Those who put much hope in cracking snob zoning as the route to reform, take note. LGs have several lines of defense.

Allocation of Municipal Funds

The tendency of cities to tilt capital and operating budgets toward the upper classes is widely observed. In recent years, Milwaukee cleared a large urban renewal project area, evicting scores of families stacked up in the ghetto—but scheduled all its capital budget for city utilities into expansion onto raw land, zoned for large lots. The specifics are available but the point is not Milwaukee. If it were just one city, we could laugh at the human circus. But this is a national epidemic, and where are these "whole square miles" of poor people to find a resting place short of the whole square miles of tax-exempt land reserved for cemeteries?

Industrial Promotion, Federal Programs, and Other Policies

Seeking industry involves a hierarchy of desirables. It is based largely on capital intensity. Capital means taxes; labor means schoolchildren. Cities seeking industry use all their selling wiles to favor capital over labor.

Cities have primary control over sales of cleared land under federally subsidized urban renewal programs. In keeping with other policies, sales and conditions are dominated by fiscal bookkeeping.

There are dozens of ways that city policy affects land use—too many to catalog here. Step by step, a city's motives determine the result. Today, the motive is to repel poor people, and many programs develop that thrust.

Without itemizing every policy, note the very fact of their numerousness. If local government is to function meaningfully it must have powers and areas of discretion. Anti-mercantilist policies of central government should aim at restructuring incentives, therefore, rather than at imposing federal control on every specific power, as by categorical grants. The virtues of local autonomy are its independence, human scale of organization, contact with local needs, and quick responses. These are to be preserved and cherished. To overcome LG mercantilism by direct controls is to destroy local autonomy, a price too high to pay, especially since we don't have to. The alternative is to make it fiscally advantageous for LGs to attract people so that they will compete for families instead of for capital and land. This brings us to the subject of taxes.

The Property Tax, Land Use, and Municipal Mercantilism

The property tax is at the heart of fiscal mercantilism in today's American cities. It is a control over land use—the most powerful and pervasive of all, and the most flexible. It has been used as an exclusionary device, but it can be, and to some extent has been used as a promotional device, depending on how the assessor allocates real estate value between land and buildings. The property tax can be a lever for the reform of LG mercantilism.

Property taxes affect several aspects of land use: intensity, frequency of demolition and renewal, size of parcel, choice of location of improvements, and the time when land is ripe for higher use. In the aggregate, property taxes affect the supply of buildings and floor space in each LG jurisdiction. The property tax not only raises money, it controls land use, redistributes wealth, and dominates LG mercantilism. It wants a close analytical look. Analysis may entail some pain. But, as your dentist says, it only hurts a little, and it should improve your bite.

The property tax is at least three taxes: one on land, one on buildings, and one on personal property (in practice, business inventories).

Each has its distinctive effects. I treat the first two separately, and in the interest of brevity omit the last, which is the smallest.

The effect of property taxes depends, among other things, on how high the real rate is. A rough national mean today might be about 1.5 to 2 percent with a wide dispersion about the mean. At these levels the tax rate is still not very high next to interest rates at 8 percent or so, and annual inflation at 4 percent or thereabouts. But because the tax is a cash outgo, the effect of the tax rate may outweigh the effect of interest at an equal rate if the interest is only forgone interest on equity. In many LGs, too, real rates are above 3 percent, or are threatening to be. There are a few up around 7 percent with Newark and Boston. Here the property tax is a major control.

Intensity of Use

Taxes on Buildings

The property tax on buildings is a percentage of their value and is therefore something like an increase in the mortgage interest rate. Interest is the largest cost by far in building, as it is with all very durable goods; over the life of a building, interest on investment is greater than the principal, the latter representing payments to construct the building. The property tax added onto this cost and recurring annually for fifty to a hundred years is the second largest cost, unless rates are uncommonly low.

The effect of raising building costs is to reduce building or to make submarginal everything about a building that is marginal. Every individual site, considered in isolation, is less intensively improved. Chopped off are marginal increments to quality, beauty, safety, pollution control, convenience, fireproofing, quakeproofing, insulation, durability, height, and all aspects of intensity (excepting lot coverage, discussed separately). In essence, less capital is applied per unit of land. It is a matter of diminishing returns of capital applied to land.

Egoism precedes altruism, and much of what is marginal to an owner is that which is there to please and avoid offending or endangering his neighbors. What is marginal to the owner is of more than marginal value to the health of neighborhoods, so the loss of marginal increments to one owner's capital is a collective loss of consequence. In some jurisdictions it has been found that building owners neglect exterior appearance specifically and selectively because they believe it influences assessors. The celebrated case of the Seagrams Building assessment in Manhattan, although extreme, lends credence to this notion. The Seagrams Building assessment was raised 50 percent because of its good looks.[4]

Taxing buildings makes capital dearer, motivates people to substitute land for capital, and encourages horizontal spread. Vertical rise meets increasing capital costs, whereas horizontal spread enjoys decreasing capital costs, up to a point, and saves on capital by consuming more land.

This produces the anomaly that taxing buildings, although it lowers intensity, acts to increase lot coverage. By putting a premium on horizontal spread, it encourages the building to invade the yard. This might be overcome by enlarging the lot, but here the owner runs directly into his neighbor trying to do the same thing. A corollary is artificially forced demand for land, and higher land prices. In time this also leads to urban expansion and larger lots.

High rise is sometimes painted as a desperate expedient of poverty, but it is more accurately seen as a luxury that lets us enjoy the benefits of closer living without walling off all open space. The luxury is available when capital is cheap. Taxing buildings makes capital artificially dear and prices this luxury out of the market.

Where lot coverage is limited by zoning and buildings are taxed, horizontal spread cannot substitute for height. The result is limited height and a reduction in the carrying capacity of the land of the LG. The tax is another form of forced land consumption—less direct than zoning, and with other side effects.

Taxes on Land Value

Under the simplifying but unreal assumption that there is a perfect market for capital, these would be neutral in their effect on land use. The tax cost does not add to the interest cost of holding land, but displaces it. Forgone interest on equity falls as the tax lowers the price of land. Simple algebra shows that the decline of interest cost exactly equals the increase of tax levy—that is the classic theory of tax capitalization.[5]

But in fact, interest rates vary among people. They are regressive—the poor pay more. Land taxes, assuming true assessment, are not regressive. Substituting taxes for interest therefore undoes the effect of regressive interest rates. It hits the rich owner harder than the poor. This is the theory of *differential* capitalization of land taxes. It gives the land tax a progressive quality.[6]

Differential capitalization increases the bidding power of the poor for land, causing them to encroach on lands held by the rich. This occurs through subdivision of large holdings, accelerated release of ripening land to higher uses, consolidation of very small holdings, and sales of land from the rich to the poor.

The effect of land taxes on intensity of land use is therefore not a simple plus or minus. The effect is equalizing as among classes. Land taxes let the poor, who live crowded on poor land, live less crowded and move to better land. They lower density for the poor by raising it for the rich, who own most of the land.

That is not widely understood. It is often advanced that land taxes "force land into use," and result in higher density. This simplicity is catchy and will not easily give way. But it is misleading. Land taxes crowd the rich, but open up more land for the poor. Only from the standpoint of the wealthy are land taxes simply intensifying. The land tax is rather redistributive.

In finding land to house and serve the mass market and the poor, this kind of redistribution is a virtue. But at the local level, it runs counter to mercantilist needs by increasing population, attracting immigrants of only average wealth, and whetting competition. This is why the exclusive taxation of site values has not been more widely supported by LGs. The state and national incentive structures are not gauged to make its results unambiguously attractive to them.

Land taxes focused on central land also tend to lower intensity of land use in fringe areas by forcing the use of central land. Those who choose to go exurban thus also achieve lower density.

Timing of Demolition and Renewal

Short-Run Effects

When a building is old, the effect of building taxes is probably to lengthen its life, and certainly to defer the renewal of its site.

It is not the taxes on the old building itself that lengthen its tenure. On the contrary, they may cause premature demolition and replacement by a parking lot or even nothing if the owner can count on the assessor's then lowering the valuation, a point on which local practice varies.

What does defer renewal is the threat of taxes on the successor building. Building on a parcel of real estate is the occasion for a large increase in the tax bill. This throws a weight into the scales of decision between old and new. The year that would be optimal for renewal in the absence of taxes now looks premature to the owner.

So long as taxes depend on the use to which land is put, they intercede in the competition of the market in favor of the lower taxed use and alter decisions at the margin. Here it is a matter of one particular application of that general principle: the margin of decision between old and new. Building taxes are heavier on the new and weigh the decision against it. They may defer renewal for any number of years and decades, depending on particulars. In its mutually reinforcing effects throughout the neighborhood, what defers renewal of the individual site for twenty-five years may defer renewal of neighborhoods and cities for fifty years or in some cases forever. The city may die. Some cities are dying in this way. Perfectly good land is abandoned, rendered unrenewable by the cumulative neighborhood effects of counterproductive tax policy.

Land taxes are more neutral than building taxes in the renewal decision, and in perfect capital markets they might do so completely. In practice they accelerate renewal because they drain cash from holdouts waiting for high bids from builders. According to the portion of tax theory that looks at marginal incentives and ignores the wealth and liquidity effects of taxes, land taxes are simply neutral, and in an important sense that is true. But taxes affect behavior in more than marginal ways. They affect it through changing relative wealth and holdout power and credit ratings. The effect of a cash drain on a holdout far outweighs the effect of an equal value of forgone interest on equity because the cash drain lowers his wealth and liquidity. The cash drain of land taxes also conveys information to many owners who are only vaguely aware that they are holding a resource of high salvage value to society. Land taxes build a fire under sleeping owners. Anyone who talks with owners of ripening land soon learns that many who are not in debt perceive as their holding costs taxes more than their forgone interest, though the latter be five to ten times as high; and in any legislature assembled they put their faith in preferential low assessment of ripening land when they want to forestall its urbanization. If money talks, the tax dollar outtalks the interest dollar, at least the dollar of forgone interest on equity, which speaks in a whisper.

Long-Run Effects

Taxes also affect the planned life of buildings. In acting like higher interest rates, they discourage durability, which may be perceived as substituting capital for labor. From this, it is easy to infer that building taxes act to shorten planned life. Easy, but wrong, for the taxes also force substituting land for capital. In the discussion of intensity of use, that meant spreading out in space. Here it means spreading out in time, letting structures stand a long time before demolition.

So we seem to have two contrary forces at work. Building taxes cause us to build less durable structures, but then to defer demolition. These two forces are consistent in helping save on capital. They are at odds only insofar as the first appears to shorten life, the second to lengthen it.

The matter is resolved by distinguishing service life from carcass life of buildings. Taxing buildings makes us shorten service life, but lengthen carcass life. Houses are built for faster recovery of capital but slower recovery of site, so that the shells of old structures, the ghosts of departed values, stand to haunt us after they have been drained of most of their serviceability.

This reinforces the short-run effect. Old buildings stay with us a long time, thanks to taxes on buildings, and they stay with us yielding less service.

There are those who oppose demolitions on the ground that they destroy housing for the poor. Federal Urban Renewal Programs and other removal programs have been frightful in this respect, and wanton demolition for slum clearance is surely to be condemned. The proposal made by John and Ursula Hicks to exempt new buildings while taxing old is to be faulted for forcing premature demolition.[7] But taxing buildings as generally practiced in the United States today is not defensible on the grounds that it defers demolition, for it does so only by weakening the profit motive to rebuild and increase supply. Indeed, taxing old buildings, taken by itself, often causes premature demolition, long before land is ripe for renewal. In tandem with the tax threat against new buildings, it lengthens the dead period between buildings when land is held out of service.

As to land taxes, they are again more neutral, subject to the qualification that the market for capital be perfect. But taxes affect behavior in at least two ways. There is the effect on marginal incentives, already discussed; then there is the effect on wealth. Land taxes are neutral in respect to marginal incentives, but they have a definite wealth effect, especially in contrast to the taxation of buildings. Taxing buildings drains wealth from builders and creates liquidity crises for them; taxing land serves the same discipline to nonbuilders and to the holders of obsolete and inadequate improvements. By this mechanism land taxes affect the market sharply.

Size of Parcel

We have seen that taxing buildings causes the substitution of land for capital. The immediate impact is increased lot coverage. The secondary impact is bigger lots. If there is just so much land in a city, lots cannot get bigger, and the result is simply higher land values. But if a city can spread out, under this influence it does.

Similarly, taxing buildings discourages subdivision where that means more capital per acre. It discourages converting old estates to middle-class housing, for example, because the tax bill would rise.

Apartments might seem to be an exception because they involve assembly, but the exception is only specious. The ownership of apartments is unified, as a rule, but the *use* is subdivided. So subdivision, broadly construed, includes the building of apartments. A tax on buildings is quite consistent in its bias against this kind of land use.

For a reason already cited, land taxes are not neutral in their effect on the size of parcels. Interest paid or forgone is the main cost of holding land. Interest rates are regressive, and as a result, the use of land is regressive. This means that those who enjoy low interest rates spread out over land which at the margin yields them less service than it would yield their credit-pinched rivals. Land taxes displace by a tax cost the interest cost of holding land. They fall harder on those who enjoy lower interest rates and larger land holdings. They tend, therefore—assuming true assessment—to equalize land holdings.

Choice of Location

The effect of taxing buildings is not merely incremental in the manner treated so far. It changes the relative bidding power of different uses, and changes the structure of cities.

In a perfect market, uses needing high accessibility cluster around a center of maximum access. Access is mutual, so the presence of those seeking access is a net benefit to others seeking access, and clustering is self-reinforcing, up to a point. Likewise, uses needing specific mutual access, or access to the same people or things, cluster in specialized neighborhoods and districts. For any level of linkage, aggregate transportation needs are lowered. There is a logic to market decisions—the "highest and best" use in the market sense also has a good claim to approximating "highest and best use" in an ultimate sense of social good.[8] So it is a social cost of moment to deny the market allocation of land without some good reason like a playground, minipark, or street.

Two rival uses having the same imputed site value, *S,* compete on equal terms for land, and represent equally high and good use.

$$S = PVR - C \tag{1}$$

where *PVR* is the present value of revenues (net, discounted), and *C* is cost of construction. It is the *difference* between *PVR* and *C* that makes site value, not the absolute size of either. Thus a gas station can sometimes compete with an apartment; though present value of revenues is less, so is construction cost. But the effect of building taxes varies with *C,* the tax base. As between two uses equally high and good, that is, with an equal *difference* of *PVR* and *C,* the building tax intercedes in favor of that bringing a lower construction cost *(C)*. Although its revenue is less, the gas station outbids the apartment because the apartment would have paid more building taxes.

This is a matter of leverage. A given percentage increase in cost cuts deeper into the residual land value afforded by the more intensive use, because its cost is higher relative to the land value. Let us give that some precision and generality.

We begin by converting to a lump sum, their present value (*PV*), the stream of future building taxes. "Present value" of the stream means if you borrowed *PV* and paid it off on the installment plan over the life of the building, your annual payment would be the amount of your building tax. The *PV* of an annual payment of $1 over sixty years is a lump sum of around $13 (discounting future dollars at 7 percent per year compounded). So a property tax rate of 1 percent of building cost is equivalent to a present value of 13 percent of building cost.

This comes out of what a builder can bid for land. He reduces his bid by 13 percent of the cost of the planned building (*C*). The higher *C* is, the more the disadvantage.

Let us couch this in the percentage drop in what competing uses can bid for a site. The absolute drop, for each 1 percent of tax rate, is:

$$-\Delta S = 0.13C. \tag{2}$$

That drop as a percentage of site value is:

$$-\Delta S/S = 0.13C/S. \tag{3}$$

C/S for a high-rise structure might run 8/1. Since 8 × 0.13 = 104 percent, the tax reduces the bid by more than 100 percent and so wipes out the site value.

For a $70,000 gas station on a $140,000 hot corner, *C/S* is 0.5. Since 0.5 × 0.13 = 6.5 percent, the oil company can bid only 6.5 percent less than if there were no taxes. The effect of building taxes is to give the less intensive use a comparative advantage over the more intensive.

That does not mean the total abolition of high-rise buildings everywhere. This is not the way the world works. It means gas stations get more land, and better land. (They also spread out.) Apartments get less land, and worse. (They also are built shorter.) Gas stations move into the center; apartments move outward. This helps account for the anomaly that intensive uses pop up on poor land and mix in with much lower uses, while low uses preempt much of the central land. In general there is a poorer matching of buildings and uses with sites.

That is a picture of urban disintegration. Our ways of imposing taxes play a role in making cities sprawl. Sprawl, in turn, with attendant suburban enclavization, weakening of metropolitan community ties and facilities, and automobile dependency, spawns many of the problems of class conflict that concern us now.

More directly, the bias against uses with a high ratio of building-cost to site-value (*C/S*) is a bias against the poor, who as a rule live crowded at much higher density than the rich and on land of lower unit value.

I have noted earlier that the tax on buildings affected incentives somewhat as would a rise of interest rates. Here we reach the limits of that parallel. The building tax is more specifically targeted against intensive use than is the interest rate. In the extreme, on an unpaved parking lot yielding income with no building, the building tax does not lower its value a bit, while a higher interest rate would lower the value. More generally, in (1), building taxes are proportional to *C*, while higher interest rates have an effect that is proportional to *PVR*. Thus the artificial scarcity of capital caused by the building tax is more disruptive to the integrity of urban linkages than is a natural scarcity of capital reflected in high interest rates. Indeed, high interest rates would also make roads and allied infrastructure costlier, raising horizontal transportation costs and raising the premium on central location.

Ripening of Land for Higher Use

Criteria of Ripeness

Under dynamic conditions, land is often in transit from one use to another and usually toward higher use. In anticipation of a move, it develops an "expectation value," or speculative value, that is higher than income from the current best use will support. When should the owner take the quantum jump and initiate the higher use? When is the land ripe for the change?

The choice of ripeness date (*D*) is difficult because a durable building, indivisible in construction, must be placed on the land to shift its use. As demand for the site grows with each succeeding year, the hypothetical optimal improvement that the owner would put up if he were going to build in that year changes. Each succeeding year's optimal building yields more net present value to the land.

To avoid premature, preclusive underimprovement or other irreversible errors, the owner postpones building—but not forever. Richard T. Ely, in arguing the case for deferral, identified himself with the doctrine of "ripening costs," but he failed to supply a criterion for ripeness. *D*-date (ripeness) arrives when the value imputed to the site by each succeeding year's hypothetical optimal building stops rising faster than the interest rate.[9] (This is the same as selecting the date that maximizes present value of the land as of any fixed calendar year.) By not building in Year 1, you forgo—and thus in effect invest—the present value of site (S_1) realizable by building in Year 1 to gain S_2 in Year 2, or S_3, S_4, . . . , S_n. If any

$$S_n > S_1(1 + i)^{n-1} \qquad (4)$$

then the value of holding the uncommitted site grows faster than money in the bank and is a good investment.

In addition, there is current site income ($a1$) from the tag end of the prior use, or from some interim use. A site, then, is not ripe so long as

$$(a_1 + \Delta S)/S_1 > i. \tag{5}$$

Note that ΔS is not just the yearly rise of land value in the market, but is $S_2 - S_1$ as defined in the previous paragraph. S is "use value." It is below market value until the optimal year of building, at which time use value has risen to equal market value. Market value is use value at D-date (ripeness) discounted, so market value grows at the investor's rate of interest. Use value *(S)* grows faster than that until ripeness, by definition of ripeness.

Taxing Buildings Affects Ripeness

We have seen that taxing buildings reduces site values derived from buildings and applies leverage against intensive building. It follows that taxing buildings affects the growth rate of site values, assuming that the optimal ratio building-cost to site-value (C/S) changes with ripening. Thus taxing buildings affects the date of ripeness.

As land ripens, the effect of taxes on the ripeness date depends on whether further waiting would lead to a higher or lower C/S ratio. Normally it leads to a lower ratio; C rises, but S rises by a higher rate. The effect of taxes is then to retard ripeness. They encourage the owner to sacrifice an earlier for a later use.

This is the kind of elusive relationship that algebra was invented to nail down. To simplify, assume no current income from a prior or interim use. To simplify the notation, the present value of the stream of future net revenues, PVR in equation (1), is denoted simply as R. The growth rate of use value (S) is:

$$\frac{\Delta S}{S} = \frac{\Delta R - \Delta C}{R - C}. \tag{6}$$

Let T be the present value of future building taxes, expressed as a percentage of C. (We previously illustrated T as 13 percent for a 1 percent tax rate; about 15 to 40 percent is normal, depending on the tax rate and the discount rate.) After taxes, assumed to lodge in lower site values:

$$\frac{\Delta S}{S} = \frac{\Delta R - \Delta C\,(1+T)}{R - C(1+T)}. \tag{7}$$

Taxes proportional to ΔC reduce ΔS, because ΔC comes out of ΔS. But taxes also reduce S, the denominator of the rate. Which factor prevails? The rules of algebra provide an answer.

The effect of taxes is to raise the growth rate of S if:

$$\frac{\Delta R - \Delta C\,(1+T)}{R - C(1+T)} > \frac{\Delta R - \Delta C}{R - C}. \tag{8}$$

By cancellation (or inspection), (8) implies

$$\frac{\Delta C}{C} < \frac{\Delta R}{R}. \tag{9}$$

By inspection, (9) is true if C/R is falling. I shall call C/R the cost/benefit ratio. From (1), R is $(C + S)$, the sum of building and land value, so:

$$\frac{C}{R} = \frac{C}{C+S}. \tag{10}$$

Thus C/R is simply the share of building cost in real estate value. Falling C/R implies falling C/S as well.

Intuitively we think that land ripens into higher intensity, but intuition is a blind guide here because it compares incommensurables: building *value* per unit of land *area*. Economic intensity compares commensurables: building value and land *value*. Our C/S and C/R are proper indices to economic intensity.

For several reasons, I believe ripening usually entails a drop in C/R. C rises, but R rises at a higher rate, so C/R falls. These reasons are developed in section II of the Appendix. So the usual effect of taxing buildings is to retard ripeness by raising the percentage growth rate of the use value of the site. I conclude that the paramount effect of building taxes on ripeness is to defer it.

The demonstration must be tempered to allow for the evasive action of the taxpayer faced with the threat of a tax on buildings. This modification is in section III of the Appendix.

Occasionally, ripening would lead to a higher *C/R*. Then the effect of building taxes is to advance ripeness by making the later use relatively less attractive. The point of consistency is that intensity loses either way. Taxing buildings makes landholders more patient to wait for lower uses, but less patient to wait for higher uses. But section II of the Appendix shows that excessive patience is the rule.

Neighborhood effects add to the retarding influence of building taxation. Part of ripening is waiting not so much for greater demand but for greater certainty. Certainty means waiting for neighbors to commit themselves. But Alphonse waiting for Gaston simply perpetuates uncertainty when Gaston is waiting for Alphonse. Much of the rationale for ripening is hyperindividualistic and does not bear examination from a social viewpoint and can only be painted a social good by committing the fallacy of composition. "We have no plans," said a San Francisco land speculator, "we're waiting for other people's plans." In such a context, whoever leads off ripens his neighbor's land and shortens the sterile downtime of land between major improvements. Building taxes that retard the improvement of one site thus retard the ripeness of neighboring complementary sites by generating uncertainty. Uncertainty of this kind in a highly complementary urban neighborhood is an external nuisance every bit as noxious as odors, fumes, noises, and shadows.

I remarked earlier that the property tax on buildings affects the behavior of the investor somewhat as a rise of the interest rate. In respect to ripening, that is not true. A higher interest rate would also require the use value of sites (*S*) to grow faster to remain unripe; but a higher building tax rate has no such effect. Indeed, the macro-nationwide effect of having buildings taxed in all jurisdictions is to lower the level of interest rates that investors require land to earn.

Land taxes would be largely neutral if credit markets were costless. It is widely believed that they speed up ripening, but the belief has been wrongly rationalized. It rests mostly on assuming that land taxes are piled on top of interest costs of holding land. But land taxes are capitalized into lower values, and thereby supplant interest costs rather than supplement them, as already noted. The reason that land taxes hasten ripening is that ripening land is mostly held by strong hands whose comparative advantage lies in holding assets where the main cost is paying interest on loans and forgoing interest on equity. Hastening the ripening of such land is simply an aspect of the transfer from rich to poor that land taxation effects via differential capitalization.[10]

Frequently the date of ripeness is outside the owner's direct control and depends on when public works are extended. Today, in many suburban areas, sewers are a controlling factor. Here, land taxes cannot speed ripening until sewers are built. But they can then speed private building to match public building and effect great savings on public capital of all kinds.

Land taxes also have important distributive effects. Future sewers have a present value to landowners. Values rise above farm levels—not once and for all, but incrementally along a line wiggling around a basic compound interest growth curve. This annual accrual of value is a current income, in the true economic sense, just as depreciation is a current cost. Land taxes levied ad valorem on the base of this selling value are a way of tapping this accruing income for the public. Appreciation is proportional to value; the tax is proportional to value; therefore the tax is proportional to the appreciation.

Arguments against taxing appreciating land do not therefore hold water on the grounds on which they are usually presented—that is, that ripening land yields no income. They do, however, make sense to the local interests whose welfare is the ultimate aim of the municipal enterprise. Land taxes redistribute income from landowners to other voters and immigrants. From the parochial mercantilist view, this is bad. From the national view, for which the welfare of migrants and labor is a greater concern, it might be valued more positively.

It is traditional to blame premature building and sprawl on ad valorem assessment of ripening land. Premature extension of public works is more guilty, coupled with postmature conversion of ripe land close in, made unripe or submarginal by taxes on building.

Aside from effects on wealth, land taxes are neutral in their effect on date of conversion, so long as they are not contingent on the date selected. Noncontingency is the same principle that makes land taxes neutral toward other land use choices. Suppose someone were panicked by rising land taxes into premature urbanization of farmland, as is sometimes feared. What would he gain? Either he would over-improve and lose money the first few years; or he would gauge his building to the slim early market, and in a few years be locked into an underimprovement while his land assessment and taxes kept on rising.

If he behaves rationally he will not in reaction to tax-carrying costs convert land sooner. The time permanently to convert land use, with or without taxes, is when the rapid rise of value begins to taper off. Then the land is ripe. This happens when the city has grown out to abut the land in question. Land taxes should tend to help conversion be less disorderly than now by equalizing carrying costs among owners of different credit ratings. Land assessments should also be given a quantum jump when public works are supplied, triggering action, prompting owners to fill in compactly and developers to sell quickly, lest the public investment in the works be sterile.

Land taxes would encourage premature conversion if the assessor maladministered them, that is, if he raised them until the owner improved the land, then locked the assessment at that level. Under that system, the owner could buy himself a low assessment by early underdevelopment. Some assessors do maladminister like that. The solution is the building-residual method of assessment: Assess the land at what it would bring if vacant, then assign the building the residual value.

Aggregate Local Effect of Property Taxes on Supply of Buildings

Building Taxes

The overall effect of taxing buildings is to reduce the service flow from a municipality of a given area. We have seen this to happen in several ways.

Intensity falls in quality, durability, and especially height. There is some compensatory tendency toward increasing lot coverage, the strength of it depending on whether people have somewhere else to go. If they do, lots get larger as buildings ramble.

Site renewal slows down greatly. This slowdown, coupled with a lesser durability of buildings, creates slums and out-of-service land. Each old building robs neighboring sites of their renewability, and the extreme result is nonrenewable abandoned neighborhoods.

Building taxes magnify the motive to withhold land for ripening. The virtue of avoiding premature commitment is distorted into the vice of postmature commitment. Within a neighborhood the delay can be indefinite as each separate owner, waiting for certainty, imposes uncertainty on others. In the entire metropolis, postmature building in truly ripe areas disperses demand outwards. Development takes place in outer areas that are made to look ripe from a local viewpoint, even after taxes, but are grossly premature in the regional plan. This is the more likely when central city tax rates become substantially higher than suburban.

Taxing buildings tends to favor larger parcels and discourage subdivision and apartments. Taxing buildings weakens the relative bidding power of more intensive uses in competing for land, and changes the structure of cities. Gas stations and parking lots push high buildings out of the center. Out-of-service lands break up complementary clusters, and cause urban sprawl.

The combined effect is to reduce the service from any given amount of land and to diffuse demand over a wider area than is necessary, economical, or socially desirable. This result is a kind of forced consumption of land, in addition to forced consumption of capital, as sprawl inflates the infrastructure costs of urbanization. This heavy capital cost dashes the hope that moving out to cheap land in the old frontier tradition may open up land for housing the mass market.

Land Taxes

The overall effect of taxing land is toward equalizing the intensity of use between rich and poor by displacing regressive interest costs with the tax. That means intensifying the use of land, because most land is held by the rich; but it means more land per family for most families, because the median family is far below the mean in income and even lower in wealth.

Taxing land is redistributive, the more so when the proceeds go to finance schools and welfare. So long as localities were infected with a wish to grow, and an egalitarian philosophy, land taxes found strong support. In today's flood of local mercantilism, which questions growth and leans to elitism while still seeking local efficiency and community, tension and ambivalence surround the local taxation of land.

Efficiency, Equity, and Policy

Policies of forced consumption of land and capital achieve their ends at high cost in social efficiency. They reduce density below what sovereign consumers evidently desire, running up heavy public costs in the process. They retard renewal and create slums. They frustrate the mass market desire for cheap land and cheap housing.

In several ways they make cities disintegrate. Building taxes weaken the relative power of intensive uses to compete for the most accessible land. Underemphasis on land taxes, as by underassessment and zoning dodges, causes the most rentable land to go to the strongest hands with superior financial power, rather than to the most productive use. A weak seller far out often looks better to a builder than to a strong holdout close in. Zoning as we practice it is self-defeating, because a builder's biggest profit comes from breaking the zoning rather than following the rules and paying a high price for land already zoned to his needs. Long extension of the ripening period creates too many niches for shoddy interim uses that disfigure the American city.

The policies force consumption of more land and capital than consumers want. And they inhibit adequate development of mass systems like transit and sewerage that depend on high density.

The set of policies also militates against social equity and sense of community. Consistently biased against the poor and school-age children and their parents, they contribute to class division and the generation gap. They are biased against people, contributing to the unemployment problem that federal policy alone has now proven powerless to abate. If Richard H. Tawney was right that a society is rich when material goods are cheap and human beings dear, then these policies work to impoverish society. They treat people as pollutants.

Remedial policy can be at once radical and conservative. It needs to be radical in the sense of being pervasive and transcendent. That is, we need policies that will change local incentives and nudge local decisions in the humanist direction, as opposed to a series of running battles forcing local officials to go against what they perceive to be their interest.

Policy can be conservative in the sense that small changes can tip the balance between exclusionary and philanthropic policies. Cities have powerful incentives to attract people, as well as to resist them. The two large forces are about evenly balanced. It was not long ago, after all, that the growth booster was an American stereotype. Heaven protect us from his most barbaric manifestations, but he does display a set of motives for welcoming immigrants. What is needed now is to tip the scales of local incentive in favor of receiving human immigrants, as opposed to exclusive emphasis on capturing capital, public works, and territory.

Policy can also be conservative in retaining local control over local matters. There is great administrative efficiency in having each local government handle as much as possible, motivated toward efficiency by having its own interests to maximize. It is not important that the profit or equity be large. It is important that profit vary with local efficiency, reward it, and motivate it.

It would not work to withdraw local zoning power. Zoning and other exclusionary devices are means to ration access to local public schools, and in lesser measure to parks, streets, and other common properties. To take away the LGs' exclusionary powers would cause them to starve the teachers and sell the parks for commerce. They would not pay for good schools if these simply attracted more large, poor families to share the schools and dilute the tax base. Fighting the good fight against snob zoning will boomerang on the warriors if it results in lowering school support. The object, after all, is access not just to land for housing, but also to good schools. The object is not only to equalize school access, but to improve schools.

The most important feasible policy change, both radical and conservative, to achieve these goals today is to shift "foundation" school financing to the state level, and the property tax along with it. A year ago that was considered far out.[11] Suddenly it is imminent and probable.

Schoolchildren entering a community complete with a generous voucher or tuition, social dividend, or other device for allocating state funds by school population would be a local fiscal asset. LGs would compete to attract them. It would become financially respectable to be a human being.

Much else would then fall into place as a result of voluntary local action. And the property tax itself, as a state institution, could be remodified: All the exclusionary features that characterize local assessment practice could be changed. The site-value tax with exemption of buildings would make more sense than it does now from the local viewpoint. And rates could be much higher than now, with less fear of repelling fiscal surplus generators. Property could carry more of the tax burden, lightening the load on regressive sales and payroll taxes.

A concurrent change should be a higher emphasis on user charges gauged to social cost. Exclusionary policies now are an indirect device to ration use of local commons. They are very inefficient devices with more side effects than favorable effects, and readily perverted to anti-social goals, as we have seen. If we don't like autos, we should tax autos, not houses.

User charges today are perverse. We tax water supply and exempt private wells, tax sewer use and exempt septic tanks, tax mass transit and exempt autos and streets, and so on. Within mass systems, rate regulation makes rich territory (which houses poor people) subsidize lean territory and rich people. All this needs to be worked over, on marginal cost principles. The effect on land use would be a conservative, economical, humanitarian revolution directed by accountancy.

Changes in federal tax policy are also needed. Congress needs to take the fun out of land speculation by hitting capital gains in a dozen ways, thus encouraging cities to use their capital budgets to serve their median citizens rather than the strong hands who hold speculative land and inveigle councilmen. Washington might also share the social dividend of school finance, raising the revenue by kinds of tax reform that encourage better land use.

Cities could expand with sharp edges, coordinating zoning and tax assessment with extension of municipal services, developing close-in land compactly for median citizens, letting the wealthy average-raisers outside pay their own way.

Congress needs to stop the competitive underassessment of land by local assessors, which makes a mockery of the federal income tax by letting people avoid taxes by depreciating land not just once, which amounts to complete exemption of land income, but several times, which amounts to a large subsidy for holding title to land. There is no substitute for federal review of assessments—a federal board of equalization, in effect. Otherwise, local assessors will continue overvaluing buildings relative to land to inflate the depreciable share of real estate owned by their local constituents.

These economic policy suggestions do not displace the legal steps discussed by others here, but supplement them in our mutual quest for the lost sense of American community and purpose. These are exciting times, and there will be much excitement in implementing and detailing the policy shifts sketched above. Nobody said it was going to be easy.

APPENDIX

I. Differential Capitalization of Taxes on Land Value

Let a = annual net income of land before land tax (but after other taxes)
i = rate of interest
t = rate of yearly property tax on land value
V = market value of land = assessed value of land.

With $t = 0$

$$V = \frac{a}{i}. \tag{1}$$

This is simple "capitalization" of income into value.

With $t > 0$

$$V = \frac{a - tV}{i},$$

$$V(i + t) = a, \tag{2}$$

$$V = \frac{a}{i + t}.$$

Equation (2) is the classic algebra of tax capitalization: The tax is capitalized into a lower value.

Now assume that credit rationing divides the capital market into two groups, Poor and Rich, who pay (or forgo) two different interest rates, p and r.

$$p > r. \tag{3}$$

Equation (2) now tells us what each group can bid for land, using p or r in place of i. This is *differential* capitalization. Rich outbids Poor for land yielding each the same net income *(a)*, and even for land yielding Poor more income, up to:

$$\frac{a_p}{a_r} \geq \frac{p+t}{r+t}. \tag{4}$$

But taxes (t) lower the bids of Rich more than bids of Poor. Bids of the Poor are cut in half when $t = p$, but bids of the Rich are cut in half at the lower $t = r$. More generally, equation (4) says that raising t dilutes the effect of p's being higher than r, tending to equalize the bidding power of Rich and Poor.

I have simplified by omitting that the lower bidder must figure on taxes on a value established by the higher bidder, but the simplification merely understates without changing the conclusion.

To restate by reference to yearly carrying costs, c,

$$c = V(i + t). \tag{5}$$

The Poor pay more to carry a given piece of land, because the cost is mostly interest. Again I understate by simplifying. The Poor not only pay higher rates, but borrow on shorter terms, so their carrying costs include a heavier amortization factor as well. The self-financed landowner has no debt to amortize, and no cash drain but taxes.

But as t is made larger, V falls, so Vi falls, and the impartial tax cost displaces the regressive interest cost.

The effect of the tax is greater when land is appreciating. Let V rise yearly by g, a percentage. Deduct this from c (we could instead have added it to income). Now

$$c = V(i - g + t). \tag{6}$$

(6) shows that g leverages or fortifies the effect of p's being greater than r, in contrast to t, which dilutes the effect.

Thus, appreciating land gravitates to "strong hands," that is, those who borrow at the prime rate, or don't have to borrow at all. And by the same token the equalizing effect of land taxes is most pronounced when applied to appreciating land. A numerical example based on (6), when $p = 0.08$ and $r = 0.05$, follows.

Ratio of Carrying Costs $\frac{c_p}{c_r} = \frac{0.08 - g + t}{0.05 - g + t}$

$t \backslash g$	0	0.02	0.04
0	8/5	6/3	4/1
0.02	10/7	8/5	6/3
0.04	12/9	10/7	8/5
0.06	14/11	12/9	10/7
0.08	16/13	14/11	12/9
0.10	18/5	16/13	14/11

II. Why Land Generally Ripens into a Lower Intensity

Let C = capital cost of building
R = present value of future net revenues or cash flow from building
S = use value of site = $R - C$.

$$\frac{C}{R} = \frac{C}{C+S} = \textit{cost/benefit ratio (C/R).}$$

1. There is a hierarchy of land uses, qualitatively different. While each is of variable intensity, they are discrete, with a quantum jump from one step to the next, as from grazing to row crops, row crops to orchards, acreage to lots, singles to walk-ups, walk-ups to high-rise, and so on.

Demand is generally rising, and land succeeds from one generation of use to another. Each use has an inner margin where it is the lower use, less intensive than its inner rival; and an outer margin where demand is weaker, or land is less suited, and it is the higher use, more intensive than its outer rival.

"Marginal" land connotes low intensity, but the connotation is misleading. It is based on a physical concept or acreage, while economics is concerned with values. The essence of economic marginality is that $C/R = 1$, the cost/benefit ratio approaches unity. In these terms, marginal land is the *most* intensively used. As demand rises and costs fall, land yields a surplus. As the rings in the hierarchy of land uses expand, and a site shifts from the outer to the inner margin of its ring, it becomes less marginal and more rentable, and C/R falls.

2. Land ripens because of falling building costs as well as increasing demand. Obsolescence is a continuing expectation, an ineluctable factor in all decisions (independent of inflation and overstated fatalism about union wage rates, not at issue here). Of course, falling *C* means lower *C/R*.

Another general reason to expect falling *C* is economy of scale. As demand grows, a larger building is appropriate. There are great economies of scale in building.

Land can also ripen into a new generation of use at lower density. A quarter or more of many central business districts has ripened into parking lots, for example, and many a house has been knocked down to expand a gas station apron.

Another kind of falling cost generally to be expected is lower borrowing rates of interest. This results from increase in creditworthiness of land as the proposed use becomes less marginal, innovative, or experimental in an area. As the land ripens into a better credit rating, *R* rises because it is the discounted value of future revenues, and a lower discount rate is relevant.

This last factor is partly circular, but that is the nature of credit ratings. It depends on the cumulative process of forming conventional opinion among lenders, few of whom supply much venture capital.

3. Empirical studies generally show that *C/R* is lower on better lands. It is very low in Champaign County, Illinois, or Benton County, Indiana, the best grain land. It is very low in Kuwait, the best oil land. It is quite low in Manhattan, the best urban land; generally lower on retail land than on residential; lower in central cities than on fringes; lower in rich than in poor suburbs. It is lower for Site I timberlands on the western slope of the Coast Range in Oregon than for Site VI lands in the high Cascades. To some extent that may reflect underutilization of better land due to cartel behavior, the soporific effect of surplus income on owners, and other institutional factors, but it probably is more basic than that—basic as that is!

4. Time generally brings public works, paid by others, to lower costs. This is one factor in increasing demand, already postulated, but it is also a factor in lower costs. Thus extension of city sewer and water precludes septic tank and well.

Figure 7.1 is a schematic representation of these relationships.

Figure 7.1 **Costs, revenues, use values of sites, and intensities (or cost-benefit ratios), comparing succeeding discrete generations of uses as land ripens into higher uses.**

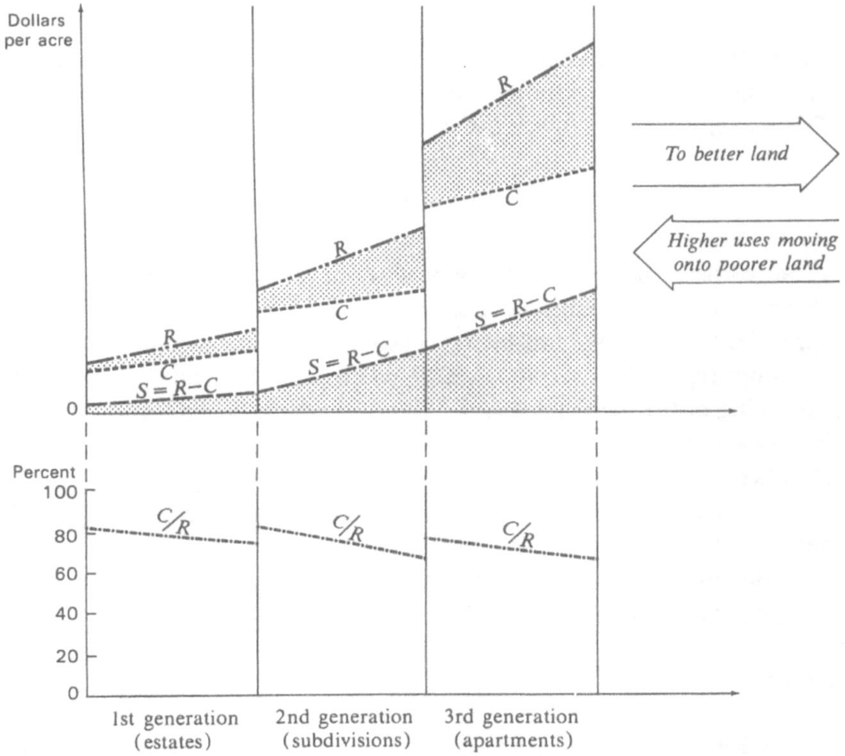

III. Effects of Building Tax on Intensity and Ripeness Combined

In equations (7) and (8) in the text, I proceeded for simplicity as though C and R in each year would be the same despite the threat of building taxes. Actually, the landowner would turn to less intensive alternatives, so C/R would fall. This would almost certainly entail an absolute decline in both, as well.

Thus, consider all cases where

$$C(1 + T)/R > 1. \qquad (1)$$

That means

$$R - C(1 + T) < 0, \tag{2}$$

that is, the use value is negative: Taxes have made the particular use of land submarginal. But they have not made the land itself submarginal. The owner can find a lower use whose

$$C(1 + T)/R < 1. \tag{3}$$

Now posit a base intensity-path, without taxes, following the course charted in the preceding section of this Appendix, with C/R falling; apply building taxes, and let the taxpayer change his path, to avoid taxes optimally. He will lower C/R where it is highest, that is, at the beginning of the path. Thus C/R will be lower at the start and will drop less along the path. This, in turn, reduces the high growth rate of S after taxes, and reduces the retarding effect on ripening.

The net effect of all this is a combination of two evasive wiggles. In general, the owner builds less, later. The emphasis depends on particulars. He may build much less and a little later; or a little less much later; or any combination.

Notes

1. Indeed, our current Malthusian agitation may derive its plausibility and social status by committing the fallacy of composition on the problems of school finance in suburbs where many social leaders live and form their views of the world, seeing it as a spaceship suburb threatened by school taxes. It is an unfair extension: Children do not dilute world wealth in the same way they dilute suburban tax bases.

2. "Presidential Address, U.S. Conference of Mayors, New Orleans," *Washington Post*, June 18, 1972, C12.

3. Oliver Oldman and Henry Aaron, "Assessment-Sales Ratios Under the Boston Property Tax," *National Tax Journal* 18, no. 1 (March 1965): 36–49; Theodore Smith, "Real Property Taxation in the Urban Center" (Hartford: J.C. Lincoln Institute, January 1972); "Report of the Atlanta Urban League on the Fulton County Property Tax," mimeographed, (September 1971); Mason Gaffney, "What Is Property Tax Reform?," *American Journal of Economics and Sociology* 31, no. 2 (April 1972): 149; and "The Property Tax Is a Progressive Tax," S.J. Bowers, ed., *1971 Proceedings of 64th Annual Conference of National Tax Association* (Columbus: National Tax Association, 1972), 415.

4. *Life,* August 16, 1963, 4.

5. See Appendix, section I.

6. See Appendix.

7. J. and U. Hicks, *Report on Finance and Taxation in Jamaica* (Kingston: Government Printer, 1955), chapter 10.

8. For further discussion and sources, see Mason Gaffney, "Land Rent, Taxation, and Public Policy," *Papers of the Regional Science Association* 23 (1970), 141–153 and "The Sources, Nature and Functions of Urban Land Rent," *American Journal of Economics and Sociology* (July 1972): 241–257.

9. Mason Gaffney, "Replacement of Individual by Mass System," *Proceedings of American Real Estate and Urban Economics Association* 4 (1969), 21–68. This piece also treats the effect on ripeness of later generations of use, a point omitted here.

10. See Appendix, section I.

11. This essay was written in 1971.

8

C. Lowell Harriss

Fundamental and Feasible Improvements of Property Taxation

Introduction

Property taxation in the United States can be substantially improved. The structure can be changed so that the adverse nonrevenue effects will be lessened without reducing revenue. The method? Reducing rates on buildings and other man-made capital and getting more revenue from land.

Such change is feasible. It can be small or large at any one time. It can be effected in steps over several years. Each community can act for itself as permitted by the state. The necessary changes in administration would be quite modest.

Economically, Two Levies, Not Just One

In an economic sense, the tax base consists of two quite different elements:

1. Land and other products of nature and

Views expressed are the author's and not necessarily those of any organization with which he is associated.

2. Buildings and other things people have produced.

To a business or an individual, an investment in land may seem much the same as that in buildings or machinery. But for anyone concerned about the economy of a community or a state, the difference is profound. The quantity of land has been fixed by nature (with minor exceptions). In contrast, the quantity of man-made capital depends upon human actions. The amount of housing, machinery, and so on that will become available in an area as time passes can vary greatly. New funds for such capital will go where prospects seem best, after consideration of the property tax and the services from government spending.

The amount of housing and other man-made capital in a community in the near future will not be materially depleted if the tax rate rises next year. But over time, the capital that means so much in life must be adversely affected by heavier against less burdensome taxation of such man-made property.

Not so with land. The quantity of land will not be reduced by an increase in tax. Land will not move or take a vacation. In fact, the quantity of land actually made available for more, or most, productive use may be enlarged by tax pressure on owners to pay more tax in cash as against holding land essentially idle or below its potential.

"The Best of Taxes, the Worst of Taxes"

Every community in the United States relies to some extent, and often to a large extent, on property taxation. From one place to another there are large differences but also many similarities. Until well into the twentieth century, this was *the* American tax. It paid for schools, police, and streets and most of the government services, except mail delivery, that touched family life. It still finances much of those local services, but rarely on the state level. The differences among communities and states require caution in making generalizations. It is certain, however, that this revenue source will continue to be important.

Some criticism of this tax is justified, but not all; some reasons for its condemnation have been mitigated significantly in some localities. Remedies already used successfully in some places could be extended. Inequality and inaccuracy of assessments, for example, can be greatly reduced by methods already used more and more widely. Circuit breakers can moderate burdens on low-income owners or occupants. Taxes from large installations, such as utilities, can be distributed beyond the immediate locality to more of the consuming areas served.

Is this tax really "the best of taxes"? Yes, to the extent that it falls on pure land rent (or its capitalization into land values): rent in the sense of payment above what is necessary to call the resource into existence. And the tax is "good," certainly, to the extent that the present burden had been capitalized in the purchase price paid by current owners: They bear no real burden compared with what they would be sacrificing (in tax, plus interest and income loss) if the tax had not existed when they bought the property. "An old tax is a good tax." In contrast to national and state taxes, moreover, property tax payments generally finance benefits for the well-being of people in the community who bear the cost.

"The worst of taxes"? Let us not explore our system searching for the worst (per dollar of revenue). Property taxation does have some bad nonrevenue results, but they can be reduced. The undesirable but largely unrecognized results occur most notably by discouraging new building and upgrading machinery and equipment.

Taxes Do More than Collect Revenue

If we do not pay for gasoline, we will not be able to obtain it. But when individuals or businesses do not pay taxes, we shall probably receive just about the same in government services because others continue to pay. Incentives to escape some or all of a tax are real and often powerful. A family or a business may find it worthwhile to take what in real productivity is a second- or third-best alternative. For instance, the investor decides on a project that yields $80 instead of one producing $100 because the latter would involve $30 more in tax. He "sacrifices" $20 to save $30 in tax. Good for him. But the economy loses $20 of potential output.

The taxpayer—"tax-escaper"—loses something and the government does not get what is lost. There is "deadweight loss": Society suffers. The economy operates less productively than it could. People have less real income than they could have. To rephrase for emphasis: In voluntary exchange in markets there is a quid pro quo. Where taxes are involved, in contrast, the individual gets neither more nor less service by paying more or less tax. Sometimes it is better for the taxpayer to arrange affairs accordingly and to accept results that in a fundamental sense are a second or third choice to save on taxes. There is real loss since the resources could have been used to better advantage. The government treasury does not get the revenue. There is excess burden, real but largely hidden. The government loses, and so does the taxpayer. But the taxpayer would be worse off if he had chosen the inherently most productive alternative and paid the higher tax.

Burdening Man-Made Capital

An annual tax of 1.5 to 2 percent or more on full capital value must equal a significant fraction of market value. Convert to income tax terms. Or convert this tax on capital to an equivalent sales tax on purchases from its yield; or a substantial multiple of any existing one-year state sales tax.

New, well-constructed, excellent buildings are taxed more heavily per unit of space than are slums and junk. In many areas new machines are taxed more heavily than old ones. Is it not foolish for society to decree that if a family or a company supplies more and better capital facilities, it must also pay more toward the costs of government? Can such discrimination be justified by the difference between the two types of property in cost imposed on local government (per unit of occupied space or machine used)? Probably not. Badly run-down buildings may in fact be associated with the greater costs per unit of usable interior space and yet be taxed less heavily.

The tax on buildings discourages maintenance and modernization. That is due in part to the realities of assessments as made, and also to what people believe that the assessor will do, so that maintenance and improvement of existing structures must lag. Cities that need to replace obsolete and decayed buildings nevertheless place tax impediments in the way of progress. No one deliberately attempts to base local finance on a tax that would to some extent favor holding on to decrepit structures and penalizing new ones. The person who wishes to shift from poorer to better housing, or business structures, cannot do so without also paying more toward the costs of government. Is this perversity not both irrational and self-defeating? The tax on buildings penalizes the kind of human actions that benefit society.

The property tax on buildings produces a rarely recognized effect that imposes excess burdens. Taxes on structures as a cost of occupancy will tend to induce, among other things, smaller rooms. We lose potential benefits. The expense per cubic foot of construction declines as the size of the house, office, display area, apartment, or other unit increases (within varying limits). Unit cost drops as room size increases, one of the major things generally desired. Content grows more than proportionally to floor, wall, and ceiling area. Much the same plumbing, wiring, kitchen, heating, and other facilities, moreover, can serve larger as well as smaller rooms and buildings through a range of sizes. Human well-being can be served better (within eventual limits) by the construction of larger rather than smaller rooms. Resource allocation in the economic sense will be more efficient when labor and material go into more commodious housing, offices, and other uses.

Per dollar of revenue, the tax on structures and equipment may or may not be our worst one, but there is much in it to condemn, especially if rates are high enough to pay a good portion of local government and school expenses. Communities can reduce the use of the bad element of property taxation and get more revenue from the part that draws upon pure land rents.

More than a century ago Henry George and his followers supported a single tax on land. The singleness in his program was explicitly designed to eliminate taxes on capital and labor (consumption). The vast increase in government spending has eliminated any hope of abolishing all taxation of capital, income, and consumption. But communities can reduce the burdens on buildings and other man-made capital while making up the revenue loss from higher taxes on land—moving toward George's proposal.

Restructuring of Property Taxation

Opportunity does exist for local government to obtain revenue while actually improving the net incentive structure. Let us take some of the burden off man-made capital and get more from the property since its supply is fixed—the land.

The practical opportunity is not the elimination of taxes on structures and placing full reliance on a tax on land. What *can* be done is to shift to a two-rate or split-level tax, perhaps a three-, or four-, or five-to-one ratio of the land-to-building rates. Several Pennsylvania localities do have lower rates on man-made capital than on land. And following adoption of the rate differentials, their permits for new construction have been noticeably larger in the localities that have adopted the reform than in generally comparably sized communities in the area. Caution is necessary in implying causal connection, but clearly the results have been consistent with what logic would predict.

Studies find that many homeowners (voters) would get some tax reduction, though in most cases little change in their tax bills. Some would pay 2 or 3 percent more, some less by a similar percentage. Owners with exceptionally fine improvements, such as an outstanding building or a well-equipped factory, would see their taxes decline, and owners of vacant land or land with improvements decrepit and far below optimal, an increase in the tax bills.

The higher tax on land would incline to reduce the price of the parcel through the process of capitalization. Landowners would not be able to shift the tax-rate increase to consumers by reducing the quantity of land.

The reduction of tax rates on structures and machinery would make them more profitable, sending upward the demand for land in the community as investment in structures rose and actually benefiting some landowners. The duration and the amount of any increase in the value of structures would be restrained by the reproducibility of man-made capital. Over the years, competition would tend to force businesses to pass along to consumers the benefits of tax-rate reductions on buildings.

Unearned Increments as Suitable Sources of Local Government Revenue

Over the years, in many situations, land prices have risen more than the general rate of inflation. That is for reasons quite independent of owners' efforts and investments: general community development, government investment in schools, streets, parks, population growth, and rising incomes. Landowners have received unearned increments, some very large indeed. Community development has brought gains to many landowners. Such gains would be exceptionally suitable sources of revenue for local government, which for some Georgists would epitomize justice in taxation.

While some advocates of land-value taxation would urge efforts to capture past gains, my emphasis is on the future. And what would be the means? Not, I believe, some special levy on gains as such, but an accurate assessment for property tax purposes under a two-rate system on all increases in land prices alone, as distinguished from capital gains on structures.

Special Provisions to Capture Values Created by Government Action and Property Taxation

Government actions, notably the construction of transportation facilities, sometimes bring significant changes in the values of specific parcels of land. Such changes are especially attractive as sources of revenue to pay for the projects themselves and even other government services. "Value capture" might be used more widely. Street and highway development, for example, can make some land much more valuable. The capture of some of these increments can help pay for the project.

This action could be part of a general program tying in nicely with property taxation and become an economist's dream! The principle: Use some (or much) of the community's pure land rents to pay for fixed or overhead costs of facilities that require relatively large amounts of capital. Customer charges could then be nearer incremental costs. Usage would be encouraged. The community could make fuller use of its fixed capital. Real incomes would be higher than if usage had to bear both fixed and variable costs. The community's increase in real incomes would tend to boost land values.

Why Have These Benefits Not Been Adopted?

The case for reducing taxes on structures and getting more revenue from taxes on land was made very clear by some Georgists generations ago. So why have we not utilized these opportunities? Much of the explanation must be in the absence of active, focused support from those who would have benefited, and in the lack of public understanding.

Virtually everyone as a consumer of residential space and other goods and services would benefit. So would persons as homeowners. But the benefits for the typical family would be modest at best. People would not be overtly aware of the difference. But encouragement of building and other investment in capital goods along with pressure for higher and better use of land would profit the economy and bring gains, neither labeled nor identified, and coming more gradually than suddenly.

Additional Reflections

Land taxation is essentially evasion-proof. Land cannot be hidden, moved to foreign tax havens, or placed in a Swiss bank account. If the taxes are not paid, the local government can take the land and sell it for the money due. Buildings are unmovable, but the funds for new construction are very mobile.

American states and localities now actively compete for business firms (and the economic base generally). One element of competition can be offers of property tax holidays or exemptions.

A discussion of these benefits should distinguish between the land and the buildings and machinery elements of property. Any relief for the land portion will not add to the land in the local economic base, but there might be capital gains for someone—most probably the present owner as against a future user. The value of land will reflect the demand, in which capital and the profitability of its use are indeed important.

Concluding Comment

Property taxation can be improved by human actions, including several beyond the discussion of this paper, such as improvements in assessment and other aspects of administration. Much has been done in a number of communities, especially in Pennsylvania. Americans *can* make fuller use of the best revenue source—pure land rents. A shift of taxation off improvements and onto land *can* reduce tax-created obstacles to new and better housing and other facilities.[1]

Note

1. A letter to the editor of this anthology from Mayor Anthony Spossey of Washington, Pennsylvania, reports:

> In 1984 we realized that our tax assessments and methods of taxation were outdated. A report by the Pennsylvania Economy League proved that our ratio of assessed to market value was quite out of balance. This problem could be solved by the adoption of Washington County's more recent assessments. After careful deliberation, we took that step.

In conjunction with the new assessment, the idea of a two-rate tax was explored to see what changes it would have on our homeowners. A sampling of approximately twenty homes in each of the eight wards was examined to determine how a switch to a two-rate system would affect these property owners. The study proved, without a doubt, that those homeowners, usually the elderly in the older more populated wards, would immediately pay less taxes than under a single millage rate. Those people living in the newer neighborhoods and business property owners would pay more. The latter, however, were more likely to make capital improvements and also benefit from a lower millage on buildings.

With the information available that the majority of our residents would save money by a switch to the two-rate system, the city council and myself decided that the responsible thing to do was to adopt it. During this initial phase public meetings were held and with the facts readily available to our residents, very little resistance was encountered.

What followed was not totally unexpected since building millage rates became lower. There was a substantial increase in renovations throughout the city. The renovations and additions to existing structures rose to an all-time high and continue to remain consistent even in 1998. There was also new construction—it was most welcome since Washington does not have many available developable tracts. These positive changes, of course, add to the value of a community both aesthetically and financially.

We have found that one of the benefits of the two-rate system not anticipated was the impact this change would have on assessment appeals. More often than not, with an appeal, the building value is decreased and we have convinced our appeals board that although a building value may have perhaps changed, the land value has remained constant. As a result, negative effects on our revenues have been lessened since our land revenues have not been reduced, where there is, of course, the higher millage.

Washington has benefited greatly by our two-rate system and I must stress again that we still did not get complaints from our property owners since it is more equitable. Renovations and additions continue to flourish and we lose less revenue on appeals due to our higher rate on land.

9

T. Nicolaus Tideman

Taxing Land Is Better than Neutral: Land Taxes, Land Speculation, and the Timing of Development

Abstract

Several writers have claimed that taxes on the value of land distort land development decisions by advancing the time of development inefficiently. This conclusion rests sometimes on logical errors and sometimes on analysis of taxes that are not taxes on the value of land. While some of these errors have been pointed out previously, the false conclusion continues to be widely cited. In fact, properly administered taxes on land are neutral when markets are perfect, and when markets are imperfect, they improve decisions about land development by reducing the socially inefficient return to land speculation and by ameliorating imperfections in lending markets.

Introduction

Donald Shoup, Athanassios Skouras, and Brian Bentick have argued that an ad valorem tax on land can generate economic distortions by altering the time that will bring the greatest profits from land develop-

The research for this paper was supported by the Lincoln Institute of Land Policy in Cambridge, Massachusetts. The Institute is a tax-exempt and nonprofit educational institution established in 1974 to study and teach about land policy, including land economics and land taxation.

ment.[1] But Shoup's conclusion does not follow from his premises. Skouras analyzes a tax that ceases when the land is developed. And Bentick assumes that the value of land varies with the manner in which it is developed. Despite these defects, the arguments have often been cited with approval.[2]

As early as 1910, B.M. Anderson Jr. pointed out that if a tax does not vary with how land is used, then it does not alter the timing of development. The tax subtracts a fixed amount from receipts at each point in time, so that whatever actions maximize the present value of returns before the tax continue to maximize the present value of returns after the tax.[3] But so many mistakes have been made in analyzing taxes on the value of land, and some of these mistakes have been copied so many times by other writers, that it is worth identifying precisely the errors in the most prominent works in this tradition. To provide a foundation for the identification of these errors, this paper begins with a rigorous derivation of the mathematics of land development.

The conclusion that a tax on land is neutral employs the premise, implicitly if not explicitly, that markets are perfect. When markets have customary imperfections, a tax on land is generally better than neutral. In particular, if there are unarbitraged disparate beliefs about the optimal future use of land because of the lack of a futures market in land rent, then a tax on land helps prevent a "winner's curse" from generating an artificial scarcity of land for current use. And if there is dispersion in discount rates because of imperfections in lending markets, a tax on land helps to put land into the hands of persons with high discount rates, whose investments are generally more productive than those of the persons with low discount rates who would otherwise have held the land.

A further insight that emerges from the analysis is that in a dynamic setting, "the rent of land" should not be defined as the net return to land after payments to other factors, because then "the rent of land" would vary arbitrarily with the timing of development. Rather, "the rent of land" should be defined as the opportunity cost of leaving unimproved land unused.

The Mathematics of Rent, Land Development, and Land Taxation

Define these symbols:

i, t = time

H	=	planning horizon
T	=	time of development
T^*	=	profit-maximizing time of development
r	=	interest rate
a	=	ad valorem tax rate
$N(i, t)$	=	net return from a site per year before taxes at time i, if the site is developed in the way that maximizes profit when it is unimproved at the prior time t
$R(t)$	=	rent of a site at time t, that is, the opportunity cost of leaving the site unused at time t
$S(t, a)$	=	selling price of an unimproved site at time t if an ad valorem tax is levied at a rate of a
$V(t, a, T)$	=	present value, discounted to time t, of the net income from a site after ad valorem taxes at a rate of a, if development occurs at time T
$C(T, a)$	=	present value, discounted to time T, of the net income from a site after ad valorem taxes at a rate of a, if development occurs at time T, that is $V(T, a, T)$.

Some of these terms represent distinctions that have not previously been made in the literature. Note in particular the distinction between $N(i,t)$ and $R(i)$. The net return from a site at a particular time, $N(i,t)$, depends on the time when use of the site began. The rent of a site at a particular time, $R(t)$, on the other hand, is defined to be independent of when use of the site happened to start. To achieve this independence, rent is defined not directly by what can be achieved by use of a site, but rather indirectly, by what is lost from lack of use of the site. If rent were defined in the more traditional way, as the net return after payments to other factors, then rent would be negative whenever investments were needed. $R(i)$ can be defined by reference to $N(i,t)$ by

$$R(t) = N(t, t) - \int_t^{\infty} [\frac{d}{dt} N(i, t)] e^{-r(i-t)} \, di . \tag{1}$$

Take an unimproved site at time t. The cost of leaving the site unimproved is the return that can be earned from immediate use at time t minus the present value of change in all future returns that results from postponing the start of use of the site.

The rent of a site can also be specified in relation to the site's changing selling price, as the present value of the cost of postponing the date from which a user has use of a site:

$$R(t) = -\frac{d}{di} S(i, 0)\, e^{-r(i-t)} \Big|_{i=t} = rS(t, 0) - \frac{d}{dt} S(t, 0).^{4} \qquad (2)$$

The first term of the derivative in (2) is the cost of postponing the start of a given flow of income, and the second is the cost of the change in the size of the flow that comes from postponement. It can be seen from (2) that if a site is appreciating at the interest rate, then there is no cost to postponing use, and its rent is zero.

If rent can be defined either by (1) or by (2), then the two should be equal, and they are. This emerges from manipulation of a general expression for the selling price of an untaxed site:

$$S(t, 0) = \int_{t}^{\infty} N(i, t)\, e^{-r(i-t)} di. \qquad (3)$$

Differentiating (3),

$$\begin{aligned} \frac{d}{dt} S(t, 0) &= \int_{t}^{\infty} \left[\frac{d}{dt} N(i, t) + rN(i, t)\right] e^{-r(i-t)}\, di - N(t, t) \\ &= \int_{t}^{\infty} \left[\frac{d}{dt} N(i, t)\right]\, e^{-r(i-t)}\, di + rS(t, 0) - N(t, t). \end{aligned} \qquad (4)$$

Using (4) to substitute for *d/dt S(t,0)* in (2) yields (1), establishing the equivalence of (1) and (2).

When an ad valorem tax on land at a rate of a is introduced, (3) becomes

$$S(t, a) = \int_{t}^{\infty} [N(i, t) - aS(i, a)]\, e^{-r(i-t)} di. \qquad (5)$$

That is, the present value of all future taxes is capitalized into the selling price of land. Note that this analysis takes no account of how the proceeds of the tax are used. In any practical application, it would be important to ask whether the rental value of land was increased by public services financed by the tax.

Equation (5) seems to suggest that the determination of a current selling price of a site would require that the selling price at every future time be determined first. But a simplification is possible. Differentiating (5),

$$\frac{d}{dt} S(t, a) = \int_t^{\infty} [\frac{d}{dt} N(i, t)]\, e^{-r(i-t)} di + rS(t, a) - N(t, t) + aS(t, a). \tag{6}$$

Substituting from (1) and combining terms,

$$\frac{d}{dt} S(t, a) = -R(t) + (r + a)S(t, a). \tag{7}$$

The general solution to differential equation (7) is

$$S(t, a) = \int_t^{H} R(i) e^{-(r+a)(i-t)}\, di + S(H, a) e^{-(r+a)(H-t)}, \tag{8}$$

where H represents the horizon of the time under consideration. This may be verified by differentiating (8) and observing that (7) is obtained. When H is ∞, (8) becomes

$$S(t, a) = \int_t^{\infty} R(i) e^{-(r+a)(i-t)} di. \tag{9}$$

Thus the selling price of land that is subject to an ad valorem tax can be expressed as the present value of future rent, discounted at the sum of the interest rate and the tax rate. Note that the rent employed in (9) is not the income received from use of the site, but rather the opportunity cost of leaving the site unused, as specified in (1).

The fraction of the value of land that is taken by an ad valorem tax at a rate of a can be expressed as:

$$\frac{S(t, 0) - S(t, a)}{S(t, 0)}. \tag{10}$$

If $R(i)$ is constant, then (10) is $a/(r + a)$. If $R(i)$ grows at a rate of g, then (10) is $a/(r + a - g)$. Thus an ad valorem tax falls more heavily on land that is growing in value than on land that has a constant value.

Erroneous Arguments That a Tax on Land Is Non-Neutral

The idea that a tax on land could shift the timing of development that maximizes profits when markets are perfect seems to have originated with Donald Shoup.[5] He analyzed a situation in which there is a site that yields no return prior to development, and the return that can be achieved depends on when the site is developed. Considering first a situation without taxes, Shoup said:

> let $V(T)$ stand for the development value of the land at any future time T *if it is developed in its highest and best use at time T. . . .*
> If there are no operating expenses and no interim rent receivable for the use of the land in the period preceding the time of development, the present value (at time t) of the land, $P(t, T)$, for any future development date, T, is given by the formula:
>
> $$P(t, T) = V(T)e^{-r(T-t)}, \ t < T \tag{1a}$$
>
> where r is the (instantaneous) rate of discount applicable in the real estate market.[6]

There is an ambiguity and a possible mistake in this statement. Two true statements, in the standardized terminology introduced in the previous section, are:

$$V(t, 0, T) = C(T, 0)e^{-r(T-t)}, \ t < T \tag{11}$$

and

$$S(t, 0) = C(T^*, 0)e^{-r(T^*-t)}, \ t < T^*. \tag{12}$$

In other words, the present value of returns associated with future development at any specified time can be computed by discounting the present value of returns from the time of development back to the present. But the sale value of the site is found by discounting returns from the profit-maximizing time of development back to the present. For Shoup's statement to be true, he must mean by *P(t,T)* and "the present value (at time *t*) of the land," the present value of returns associated with a particular plan and not the sale value of the land.

Shoup showed that at the profit-maximizing time of development, his *V(T)* will be growing at the interest rate. This is true. Shoup then introduces:

> ad valorem property taxes which are (or ought to be) levied on land as a fixed proportion of its market value. Let us assume that the tax is levied each period as a fixed percentage, *a*, of the market value of the land in the same period, and that the development value of the land, *V(t)* [that is, in standardized notation, *C(T, a)]*, is figured after all taxes. Then equation (1a) is altered to
>
> $$P(t, T) = V(T)e^{-r(T-t)} - \int_t^T aP(i, T)e^{-r(i-t)}di.^7 \qquad (5a)$$

For this to be a true statement about an ad valorem tax, the *P(i,T)* in the integral must be *S(i,a)* in standardized terminology, the sale value of the site at time *i*. But the *P(t,T)* on the left-hand side, as indicated above, must be not sale value but rather *V(t, a, T)* in standardized terminology, the present value of future returns associated with a particular plan. At a minimum, Shoup's terminology does not distinguish properly between these concepts, and he may have made a conceptual error.

Shoup shows that when the tax is levied, his *V(t)* must grow prior to development at a rate equal to the sum of the interest rate and the tax rate, so that the after-tax return will be the interest rate. This is true. Shoup then concludes:

> Thus the effect of the property taxes on vacant land is to bring development when the rate of increase of the development value, *V′(T)/V(T)* [that is, *C′(T, a)/C(T, a)* in standardized notation], of the bare site equals the sum of the interest rate and the tax rate. It is interesting that the difference between this optimal development timing condition and the one found previously in the absence of a land tax is one sense in which even a pure site-value tax may not be perfectly neutral in its effect on resource allocation, as is frequently claimed.[8]

It is true, as Shoup said, that when land is taxed, the rate of growth of the value after taxes at the time of development that will maximize profit is the sum of the interest rate and the tax rate. However, this does not entail a shift in the timing of development, as long as the tax is a true ad valorem tax. Shoup appears to have believed that the rate of growth of value at any point in time is the same with the tax as without it. This is not true. The introduction of an ad valorem tax on land changes the sale value and the rate of growth of sale value at each point in time, but the time when the condition for development that will maximize profit is satisfied remains unchanged.

To see this, note first that the present value of future returns net of taxes can be found by subtracting taxes from the present value of future returns in the absence of taxes. Thus:

$$C(T, a) = C(T, 0) - \int_{T}^{\infty} aS(t, a)e^{-r(t-T)}dt. \tag{13}$$

The rate of growth of C, taking account of taxes, is therefore

$$\frac{\frac{d}{dT}\left[C(T, 0) - \int_{T}^{\infty} aS(t, a)e^{-r(t-T)}dt\right]}{C(T, 0) - \int_{T}^{\infty} aS(t, a)e^{-r(t-T)}dt}. \tag{14}$$

At T^{*}, $C'(T, 0)$ is $rC(T, 0)$, so at T^{*} (14) is

$$\frac{rC(T^{*}, 0) - r\int_{T^{*}}^{\infty} aS(t, a)e^{-r(t-T^{*})}dt + aS(T^{*}, a)}{C(T^{*}, 0) - \int_{T^{*}}^{\infty} aS(t, a)e^{-r(t-T^{*})}dt}. \tag{15}$$

which is

$$r + \frac{aS(T^{*}, a)}{C(T^{*}, a)} = r + a. \tag{16}$$

Thus the rate of growth of net income after taxes and other expenses, at the time of development that maximizes profit in the absence of taxes, is the sum of the interest rate and the tax rate. The shift of the time of development that Shoup discusses to the time "when the rate of increase of the development value . . . of the bare site equals the sum of the interest rate and the tax rate" is no shift at all.

If one interprets *P(i, T)* in Shoup's equation (5a) as *V(i, a, T)* in standardized notation, to be consistent with the terminology on the left side of the equation, then what is described is not an ad valorem tax, but rather a peculiar tax that has been the subject of much inadvertent theorizing, though there is no evidence that any legislature ever sought to implement it. Under this tax, an assessor would be told to assess undeveloped land not according to its sale value, but rather according to the present value of a forecast of its price at the time when its owner plans to develop it. This means that an owner of land could change the tax that was currently owed by changing the date for which development was planned. This makes no sense. But because such a tax comes up so often in discussions of land taxes, it needs a name. Such a tax will be called a tax on the "present value of planned net income," or a tax on PVPNI.

The assessment of already developed sites on the basis of PVPNI would involve a different set of complications. An assessor would need to determine how much of the value of the combination of land and improvements should be attributed to the improvements. The residual would be the value of the site. But any attribution of value to improvements that cannot be economically removed from a site, other than what the improvements add to a previously determined value of the site, would be inappropriate. If, as in the real world, unanticipated changing circumstances generate fluctuations in the value of the combination of land and improvements, any independent attribution of value to improvements would be even more dissociated from economic meaning. Shoup avoids this problem by not explicitly modeling improvements.

Because of the conceptual problems that arise both with undeveloped land and with developed land. . . a tax on PVPNI . . . [is] a theoretical construct that does not correspond to any real or plausibly potentially real tax.

A kernel of truth in Shoup's analysis is that a tax on PVPNI is non-neutral. With such a tax, it is possible to lower tax liability by selecting a plan with a lower present value of planned net income. That a tax whose magnitude can be changed by taxpayer action should be non-neutral is not at all surprising.

Skouras had a different interpretation of Shoup's work.[9] He analyzed a tax on undeveloped land that ceases as soon as land is developed and described such a tax as "the concern of Shoup's analysis." This interpretation of Shoup is hard to justify. It seems clear that Shoup had in mind a tax on land that continued after land was developed, because otherwise it would be pointless for him to mention that development value was figured net of taxes. Skouras showed that the tax he analyzed brings development forward, to the time when the rate of growth of developed value in the absence of a tax is equal to the sum of the interest rate and the tax rate.

Criticizing Shoup, Skouras observed,

> Shoup's conclusion that "the effect of the property tax on vacant land is to *decrease* the value of the land but to *increase* its rate of appreciation" is very misleading. There is no reason why the tax should affect the rate of appreciation which depends on development potential. What the tax does is to increase the rate of appreciation required *if a site is to remain undeveloped*. In other words, the tax accelerates land development.[10]

This criticism would be valid if Shoup had analyzed a tax that ceased when land was developed. The introduction of an ad valorem tax on land, however, does both decrease the value of undeveloped land and, while it is economical to hold it undeveloped, increase its rate of appreciation. But it does not accelerate land development.

Michael Owen and Wayne Thirsk offered a model similar to Shoup's, but without referring to Shoup.[11] They defined $P(0)$ as the present value of land, $V(t)$ as "the net-of-tax expected value of land in period t in its highest and best use" and b as the tax rate. To characterize the profit-maximizing time of development, they differentiated

$$P(0) = \int_0^t -bP(i)e^{-ri}di + V(t)e^{-rt} \tag{17}$$

and showed, as Shoup did, that the rate of growth of the price of land at the time of development that maximizes profit will be $r + a$. And like Shoup, they asserted that this involved a forward shift in the timing of development.[12] But then they criticized the conclusion on the ground that "it suggests that current landowners would be able to shift some of the burden of future property taxes onto future purchasers of land." Making sense of this puzzling comment requires the presumption that Owen and Thirsk had been assuming (strangely) in their earlier analysis that the selling price of land would not be affected by taxes on land. In any case, Owen and Thirsk then developed an equation in which postdevelopment taxes are subtracted from their $V(t)$. Thus it seems that they meant to define $V(t)$ not as the net-of-tax value of land, which they had said, but rather as the *gross*-of-tax value. Thus Owen and Thirsk said that the true expression for the sale value of land is

$$P(0) = \int_0^t -bP(i)e^{-ri}di + V(t)e^{-rt} - \int_t^\infty bV(i)e^{-ri}di. \qquad (18)$$

If $V(t)$ is a gross-of-tax value, the tax described here falls prior to development on sale price and after development on what the sale price would be in the absence of taxes. This makes no sense as a tax, and it also falsifies the subsequent assertion that $P(T) = V(T)$ when T is the development date. On the other hand, if $V(t)$ is a net-of-tax value, then Owen and Thirsk have subtracted taxes twice.

Owen and Thirsk made a further mathematical error when, in differentiating (18) with respect to t, they failed to note the fact that t appears in limits of integration.

The Owen and Thirsk analysis was criticized by Bentick.[13] Bentick argued that:

> the model provides only one use for the land and this use does not commence until some time T. Therefore land *must* remain vacant until this time.[14]

This interpretation of Owen and Thirsk is unjustified. While their definition of $V(t)$ is ambiguous, it is hard to see how anything they said provides a basis for Bentick's inference that they assumed, in standardized notation, that $V(t, a, T) = 0$ for $T < T^*$. In reply, Thirsk said that he and Owen did not intend to assume the condition that Bentick attributed to them.[15] He said that what they meant by $V(t)$ was the sale value of land in the absence of taxes. This is clearly not what they said, although it does justify their assertion that taxes needed to be subtracted from their first result. But this still leaves them with a bizarre tax and errors of logic and mathematics.

Bentick went on to say:

> Now introduce property taxation into the model: [Owen and Thirsk] do this by correctly subtracting from [Bentick's equation] (1) the capitalized value of all the taxes levied between 0 and time *T*, and of all taxes levied from time *T* thereafter. They then go through the above present value maximization exercise which I have argued is inappropriate.[16]

While Bentick's words here are somewhat ambiguous, it appears that he has endorsed the double subtraction of postdevelopment taxes.

Overcoming what he saw as the principal limitation of the analysis by Owen and Thirsk, Bentick developed an example of the effects of taxing land that incorporates a choice between two development possibilities:

> Consider a piece of land which may be used in two alternative projects, 1 and 2. Project 1 offers the land immediate rentals of $1 per year in perpetuity, while project 2 offers higher rentals of $*c* in perpetuity, but only after a gestation period of *T* years. . . . Project 2 will be selected if
>
> $$e^{-rT}c/r > 1/r \ldots . \tag{1b}$$
>
> Now impose . . . an annual wealth tax, . . . at rate *b*, which is based on the current market value of land. Investors will now require a gross rate of return of $r + b$ in order to continue enjoying a net return of *r*, and capitalization of the tax will cause the present values to decline so that project 2 will have to pass the more severe test
>
> $$e^{-(r+b)T}c/(r+b) > 1/(r+b).^{17} \tag{3b}$$

It is not correct for Bentick to equate a wealth tax with a tax on land. And his example of two development possibilities is more limited than the continuum of possibilities that Shoup used and Owen and Thirsk contended that they used. If Bentick's analysis were correct, the two possibilities might show the effect more clearly than a continuum. But the analysis is not correct. Inequality (3b) is inappropriate because it assumes that the tax is not an ad valorem tax, but rather a tax on PVPNI. The tax varies, depending on which development option is chosen. If the tax is an ad valorem tax, inequality (3b) has no bearing on which project is more profitable.

Citing Bentick, Mills says:

> [T]hat part of the property tax which falls on unimproved land is widely thought to be neutral. . . .
>
> This view of the tax on land is badly mistaken. It is true that a (less than 100 percent) tax on land *income* is neutral, but this does not extend necessarily to a tax on capitalized land *value,* or changes therein.[18]

I criticized both Bentick and Mills on the ground that they were implicitly assuming that the value of land could be something other than what it would be worth if it were unimproved.[19] Bentick replied,

> I agree . . . that . . . the current market value of a site is the price at which it would sell if it were not committed to any particular activity, and that this is the highest present value of net income streams that begin with bare land today. . . .
>
> My original article shows that a tax on the market value of land is not neutral between uses of land which are *mutually exclusive.*[20]

The last sentence is not true, for the analysis did not follow the rule that the previous sentence endorses.

Mills replied, accepting the neutrality of a true ad valorem tax, while saying:

> The point of my previous note stands, however: when land value is computed (appraised) to include rent accruing to irrevocable previous commitments, the nature of induced nonneutrality is to favor land-uses with early-payoff income streams.[21]

If this is an assertion that a tax on PVPNI is feasible, it needs to be strengthened with a more complete specification of how assessors are to make their assessments. But the statement could also be interpreted as making the valid point that it is possible that assessors, who are supposed to assess land according to the value it would have if unimproved, are instead influenced by the development decisions that owners of land make, and if such a bias in assessments is predictable, it motivates inefficient development decisions.

It would not be necessary to spend so much time on erroneous theory except that these papers have become widely cited and followed. For example, after citing Bentick and Shoup, Richard W. Douglas said:

> As previously stated, it has been (and still is) commonly believed that the site value tax is neutral. The model presented in the previous section shows this is not true as long as the pattern of development can be

altered to bring rental income nearer to the present. The key to the result is that, because of the lock-in effect produced by a development project, land value in a future period may be determined in part by the existence of capital on the land in that period.[22]

Noguchi, citing Bentick, said, "Foresters have long recognized that the classical proposition that a tax on land value is neutral does not hold in an intertemporal setting."[23] Mathis and Zech said, "Mills . . . identifies two market distortions inherent in the real property tax: the traditional one that penalizes improvements and another which favors properties with early payoff income streams. The implementation of [land-value taxation] eliminates the first distortion but enlarges the second."[24] Fischel, citing Bentick and Mills, observed, "The property tax on undeveloped land raises the holding costs of farmers and other speculators . . . and may tempt them to sell too soon for a low-density use that cannot then easily be reversed."[25] Prest, referring to Bentick, said, "The consensus would now seem to be that [land-value taxation] will not be neutral, at least in certain circumstances, in that it will provide an incentive to convert land to higher uses sooner than in the absence of the tax."[26] Citing Bentick and Shoup, Ellson and Roberts contended, "Value-based taxation favors near-term projects relative to far term."[27] Pillai, citing Bentick, wrote, "It is true that a tax on the value of land . . . may be non-neutral if, for example, (1) the time profiles of future income streams from various parcels of land differ from each other."[28] Turnbull, citing Bentick, remarked, "because land-value tax does not synchronize tax payments with rental receipts over time, it distorts the relative present values of mutually exclusive land uses . . . and alters development decisions."[29] Lim cited Skouras, Mills, and Bentick and said, "the land value tax is non-neutral as this tax changes the optimal timing of land development."[30]

If any of these writers realized that they were discussing the properties of a tax on PVPNI rather than a tax on the value that land would have if it were unimproved, they do not make it clear.

Other writers have understood some or all of the errors in the tradition holding land tax to be non-neutral. David E. Wildasin made clear the source of the non-neutrality conclusion. He said:

[I]f one defines some *use-independent . . . standard value,* a tax on this standard value will be equivalent to a use-independent per unit tax, and

> thus neutral. This does not contradict the Bentick-Mills conclusions because these authors consider taxes on the *current market value* of land and because . . . physically homogeneous units of land will in general have values that differ over time depending on use.[31]

While Wildasin's description of what must be done to achieve neutrality is correct, his description of the tax base projected by Bentick and Mills as "the current market value of land" is not accurate. Their tax base is the present value of planned net income. To describe this as "the current market value of land" is to suppose that there is a market in which it is possible to observe the net returns from the planned use of land. But no such observation is possible. What can be observed is the current market value of the combination of land and improvements. Any attribution of value to land alone, other than what the land would be worth if it were unimproved, is hard to justify.

Wildasin also mentioned that a tax on the current rental income of land is non-neutral if tax rates change from year to year, because investors will tend to choose income streams that are heavy in years when taxes are light.[32] While this is true, a tax on the rental value of land as defined by (1) or (2) is neutral even if rates change from year to year, because this definition is independent of how land is actually used. A tax on the rental *income* from land, even if rates are constant, is likely to be non-neutral in practice, because of the difficulty of separating the realized return to land from the returns to capital and entrepreneurship.

Steven C. Bourassa says:

> Bentick shows mathematically that the effect of a land tax may be to give the stream of land rents from the immediately developable project the higher present value. If it were correct, Bentick's result would be significant because it shows that taxes on land are not neutral in their allocational effects. . . .
>
> Upon examination, however, it becomes clear that Bentick's analysis is incorrect. The fatal problem with his analysis is its confusion regarding the normal base for taxes on land.[33]

This is correct.

The effects of any real tax on land, of course, depend not on theoretical calculations, but on the behavior of tax administrators and on the expectations of citizens about their future behavior. What economic theory shows is that there is a set of instructions for tax administrators that, if anticipated and followed in a world of perfect markets, would motivate owners of land to use it in the same way that they would use it if there were no tax. In particular, if a tax on land is not affected by how the land is used, and if the possessors of land believe that the present value of future tax payments will never exceed the present value of future rent, then the tax will have no distorting effect on the use of land, though it may have income effects. The next section shows that, in a world of imperfect markets, taxing land can offset some of those imperfections and produce more efficient land use than is attained in the absence of the tax.

How Land Taxes Do Affect the Timing of Development

Martin Feldstein showed that, under certain assumptions, a tax on land can lower the interest rate and raise the equilibrium of capital stock. He also described a portfolio-composition effect of land taxes that generates a change in the relative prices of land and capital, which would affect the rate of capital accumulation.[34] Wolfgang Eckart described a similar effect.[35] These effects all represent general equilibrium responses to changes in the sale value of land. While they could affect the timing of development, they do not entail any excess burden of taxation. Furthermore, if the tax receipts were used to provide local public goods of equal value to the same persons, there would be no changes in the value of land and the effects would disappear.

Henry George argued that a tax on land curbs land speculation: That is, a tax on land affects the timing of land development.[36] He regarded as socially beneficial this impact of taxing land on the timing of development. The theory presented in the previous section might conclude that George was mistaken in his economics and needlessly concerned about the possibility that holding land unused would be inefficient. The theory of maximizing behavior would make for the conclusion that the owner of any asset employs it in such a way as to maximize the present discounted value of future returns. That the owner of some parcel of land leaves it unused should be regarded as part of a plan by the owner for use of the land that would maximize profit through time. Efficient use of developed land requires durable immobile structures. It would be wasteful to build these before they can be used, so it should be expected that land will be undeveloped for some span of time before it is used intensively. On this basis, Richard T. Ely argued that the incomes of land speculators come from undertaking successfully the socially valuable activity of determining the best time for land to be developed.[37]

Ely's argument raises the question of whether land speculators are properly compensated for the service they perform, or overcompensated or undercompensated. But before addressing that question, it is useful to understand how a tax on land affects the quantity of land speculation; that is, how a tax on land can affect the timing of development.

The way that a tax on land can reduce the amount of land speculation was explained by Harry Gunnison Brown, who pointed out that the participants in a market can have different beliefs about the future, and that taxation can affect the relative value of land to persons with different beliefs.[38] In particular, land taxation takes some of the gain that would otherwise accrue to those who leave land undeveloped because they foresee rises in rent that others do not foresee. Thus a tax on land generates greater reductions in offer prices for those who foresee rises in rent of land than for those who do not, thereby making some land more valuable to persons who wish to develop it immediately than to the land speculators who would otherwise be the highest bidders for it.

This point can be clarified by using a more modern model than the one Brown used. Suppose there is a site near a mine, which would be a good place to put a restaurant for the miners. But it is not certain how much ore is in the mine, and therefore what the demand for restaurant services will be. Whatever the amount of ore, the mine will be worked for just two periods; the site will have no value after the second period. If the ore that has already been discovered is all that will be discovered, then there will be 100 workers in period one and 100 in period two. The best use of the site then is Plan A, building a small cafe, which will generate a net return to the site of 100 in each period. It is possible that at the end of the first period, a second seam will be discovered, leading to the use of 200 workers in the second period. If it were certain that that would occur, the best use of the site would be Plan B, operating out of trailers for the first period and building a large restaurant for the second period. This would lead to a net return to the site of 50 for the first period and 180 for the second. If Plan A is undertaken and the second seam is discovered, then the return in the second period is 110, because the cafe can adjust by accommodating more customers and raising prices. If Plan B is undertaken and the

Figure 9.1 **Returns in First and Second Periods as Functions of the State of Nature and Action Taken**

	No Discovery	Discovery
Plan A	100, 100	100, 110
Plan B	50, 50	50, 180

second seam is not discovered, then the best use of the site in the second period will be to continue to use the trailers and achieve a return of 50 in the second period. The possibilities can be considered a two-by-two game against nature, as shown in Figure 9.1.

Assume that money in the second period is discounted by 10 percent to convert it to present value. If there is no discovery, Plan A with a present value of 190 will maximize profits, and if the discovery occurs, Plan B with a present value of 212 will maximize profits.

If some people believe that the discovery will occur and others that it will not, then the land will be most valuable to those who believe that the discovery will occur, and Plan B will be implemented.

Now suppose there is an ad valorem tax at a rate of 25 percent. What effect, if any, will this have on how the site is used? The analysis begins with the second period and works back. If there is no discovery, then the value of the site in the second period, if it is unimproved and is subject to a 25 percent ad valorem tax, will be 40, so that the tax of 10 plus the value will be 50. If there is a discovery, then its value in the second period will be 144, so that the tax of 36 plus the value will be 180. Subtracting the present value of the second-period tax from the first-period value of the site in the absence of a tax yields 181 as the value before first-period taxes for a proponent of Plan A who does not expect the discovery, and 179.6 as the value for a proponent of Plan B who does expect a discovery. Since the expected value prior to first-period taxes is higher for the proponent of Plan A, this is the plan that will prevail. An ad valorem tax had changed the use of the land to maximize profit.

This tax-induced change in the use of the land occurs independently of what is actually most efficient; that is, whether the discovery will actually occur. Thus, in a world with nonuniform beliefs, a tax on rent can either improve or worsen the allocation of land.

This rather surprising result is a consequence of a lack of complete markets. The proponents of Plan A and Plan B have different beliefs about the rent of the site in the second period. In a world with complete markets, these disparate beliefs would be arbitraged through the determination of a market-clearing probability of the discovery, and hence a market-clearing expected rent in the second period. If the probability of the discovery is p, then the present value of the expected return from Plan A (in the absence of land taxes) is $100 + 99p + 90(1 - p)$. The present value of the expected return from Plan B is $50 + 162p + 45 (1 - p)$. These two quantities are equal if $p = 95/108$. If p is greater than 95/108, then Plan B has the greater expected return. If p is less than 95/108, then Plan A has the greater expected return.

The present value of the expected rent of the site for the second period is $162p + 45(1 - p) = 45 + 117p$. With complete markets, a person who was considering implementing Plan A could purchase for this price an insurance policy that would pay the rent in the second period. The rent that such a person would be willing to pay for the first period, believing that the probability of discovery is p, would be $100 + 99p + 90 (1 - p) - 45 - 117p + 145 - 108p$. For a person who planned to buy an insurance policy to pay the rent in the second period and implement Plan B, the first period bid would be $50 + 162p + 45(1 - p) - 45 - 117p + 50$. The first-period bids of those who contemplate Plan A and those who contemplate Plan B are equal if and only if $p = 95/108$.

Thus with complete markets, the market for insurance policies to pay the second year's rent yields a price that informs people in the first period whether Plan A or Plan B is better (in the market-clearing probability that the discovery will be made). Without a futures market in land rent, those who place a high probability on a rise in the value of land can trade on that prediction by buying land. Brown's concern was that this concentrates land in the hands of those who have the most extreme beliefs about future rises in land values.

The idea that it is socially costly to concentrate land in the hands of those who believe that future land rents will be highest is a variation on the theme of the winner's curse.[39] This is the phenomenon that, when people have disparate beliefs about the value of a thing, the highest bid is made by the person who makes the most extreme upward error in valuation, and this person loses by succeeding in acquiring the thing.

The less land is taxed, the greater will be the weight of extreme beliefs about high future land rents in determining bids for land, and the greater will be the artificial scarcity of land for current use that will be created by land speculation. The winner's curse will be shifted to society.

Turn now to the question of whether land speculators are properly compensated for the service of identifying the profit-maximizing time of land development. Ely is correct in saying that identifying this time is a socially valuable service.[40] But it does not follow that institutions that award all of the rent of land to private owners provide the proper incentive for the performance of that service. The social value of withholding land that would otherwise be developed is measured by the increase in total return that results from postponing development. In the example above, if the discovery is going to be made, then, from Figure 9.1, the social present value of using Plan B rather than Plan A is 212 – 199 = 13. But the private present value (with respect to this one site) of knowing that the discovery will be made, if everyone else believes that it will not be made, is the return to Plan B under discovery minus the return to Plan A with no discovery, or 212 – 190 = 22. Awarding all of the increase in value to the person who makes the decision to withhold land from development would equate private and social returns only if early development would eliminate *all* of the gains that the currently unforeseen possibility would allow. The excess of the private return over the social return will not only concentrate land in the hands of those who have the most extreme beliefs about future possibilities, but also induce an inefficient flow of resources to the activity of trying to be the first one to perceive future opportunities.

This excessive return to those who discover new opportunities has been discussed previously by Paul A. Samuelson, who said:

> Suppose my reactions are not better than those of other speculators but rather just one second quicker. (This may be because of the flying pigeons I own or quickness of my neurones.) In a world of uncertainty I note the consequences of each changing event one second faster than any one else. I make my fortune—not once, but every day that important events happen. Would anyone be foolish enough to argue that in my absence the equilibrium pattern would fail to be reestablished? By hypothesis, my sole contribution is to have it established one second sooner than otherwise.[41]

Similarly, discussing the returns to invention, Jack Hirshleifer said:

> Do we have reason to believe that the potential speculative profits to the inventor, from the pecuniary effects that will follow release of the information at his unique disposal, will be so great that society need take no care to reserve for him any portion of the technological benefit of his innovation? The answer here is indeterminate. There is no logically necessary tie between the size of the technological benefit on the one hand, and the amplitude of the price shifts that create speculative opportunities on the other.[42]

A tax on rent reduces the gain from being the first one to perceive future opportunities. Therefore such a tax will sometimes make it unprofitable for those who foresee future opportunities to bid land away from premature development. In this or in other situations in the economics of discovery, it is difficult to devise a set of institutions that provides the right incentives. But rewarding speculators with the opportunity to pocket some or all of the increases in the present value of future rents is a relatively unpromising way of motivating them to invest optimally in discovering future opportunities. Rises in future rents are what will occur with or without their activity. What is saved by forestalling premature development is the loss in the value of immobile and durable capital that is inefficiently placed where future opportunities will make it prematurely obsolete. To avoid these losses, it makes more sense to promote markets in which those with a skill for identifying future opportunities can sell insurance to those who want to use land now, against the possibility that future increases in rent will reduce the value of their capital. If the identification of future opportunities can be efficiently rewarded through an insurance market in future land rent, then there will be no efficiency losses to offset the efficiency gains that taxing land provides through reduction in the excessive application of resources to identifying future opportunities, and through reduction in the artificial scarcity of land for current use that arises when the winner's curse is shifted to society.

Another way in which land taxes improve resource allocation has been identified by Mason Gaffney.[43] He pointed out that land taxes improve the efficiency of land development decisions by mitigating the effects of friction in the lending market. Land speculation, he suggested, is an activity that is attractive to investors with low discount rates and high opportunity costs of their time. It requires little attention; unlike investments in ongoing enterprises, land is unlikely to fall greatly in value as a consequence of neglect. Potential users of land, on the other hand, are likely to be people who have above-average discount rates. The combination of differing capacities of borrowers to offer collateral and the difficulties in identifying borrowers who will be good risks allows for an equilibrium in which competing bidders for land have quite divergent discount rates. In such circumstances, the taxation of land ameliorates the variation in discount rates. The taxes are capitalized into lower purchase prices, so the tax has the effect of substituting a recurring annual charge for a one-time charge. This makes land relatively more attractive to people with high discount rates and relatively less attractive to people with low discount rates. When evaluated at a common discount rate, the projects of those who have high discount rates and become the highest bidders when land is taxed have greater present values than the projects of those who have low discount rates and are displaced by land taxes. Thus a tax on land improves economic efficiency, mitigating lending-market imperfections. If Gaffney's characterization of persons with high and others with low discount rates is correct, the mitigation of lending-market imperfections also shifts land out of the hands of people who will leave it idle and into the hands of people who will develop it.

Conclusion

Taxes on land seem almost too good to be true. Not only do they have no excess burden, unlike almost all other sources of public revenue, but they actually improve allocation. The idea that taxes on land could induce inefficient decisions in the timing of development might have made them seem no better than any other tax. But that allegation is unsupportable. It rests on logical errors or on an analysis of something other than a tax on land value.

The mathematics of land taxes is tricky. It is important not to confuse the value of land with the present value of planned net income. To have a definition of the rent of land that does not become negative when investments are needed, rent must be defined as the opportunity cost of leaving unimproved land unused, rather than as the net return after payments to other factors.

The allocative improvements from taxing land arise because land taxes mitigate market imperfections. In a world with incomplete futures markets for land, the distribution of land among persons with different beliefs about whether it is efficient to develop land now or hold it idle varies with the level of taxes on land. Not taxing land creates a "social winner's curse"—an artificial scarcity of land since land will be worth the most to those who have the most extreme beliefs about future speculative gains from land.

In a world with imperfect lending markets, a tax on land makes land relatively less attractive to those with low discount rates and relatively more attractive to those with high discount rates. This improves efficiency and accelerates development.

Notes

1. Donald C. Shoup, "Advance Land Acquisition by Local Governments: A Cost-Benefit Analysis," *Yale Economic Essays* 9 (1969): 147–207; Shoup, "The Optimal Timing of Urban Development," *Papers of the Regional Science Association* 25 (1970): 33–44; Athanassios Skouras, "The Non-Neutrality of Land Taxation," *Public Finance* 33 (1978): 113–134; Brian L. Bentick, "The Impact of Taxation and Valuation Practices on the Timing and Efficiency of Land Use," *Journal of Political Economy* 87 (1979): 859–868; and Bentick "The Capitalization of the Property Tax and Idle Land: Comment," *Land Economics* 55 (1979): 545–548.

2. Richard W. Douglas, "Site Value Taxation and the Timing of Development," *American Journal of Economics and Sociology* 39 (1980): 289–294; Yukio Noguchi, "On the Intertemporal Non-Neutrality of Taxes on Land: A Dynamic Market Clearing Model," *Hitotsubashi Journal of Economics* 22 (1981): 20–31; William A. Fischel, "The Urbanization of Land: A Review of the National Agricultural Lands Study," *Land Economics* 58 (1982): 236–259; Edward J. Mathis and Charles E. Zech, "An Empirical Test: The Economic Effects of Land Value Taxation," *Growth and Change* 13 (1982): 2–5; David E. Mills, "Reply to Tideman," *National Tax Journal* 35 (1982): 115; A.R. Prest, "Some Issues in Australian Land Taxation," *Environment and Planning C: Government and Policy* 3 (1985): 97–110; Vel Pillai, "Property Taxation in Thailand: An Uncommon Combination of a Land Tax and a Rental Tax," *Singapore Economic Review* 32 (1987): 43–53; Geoffrey K. Turnbull, "The Effects of Local Taxes and Public Services on Residential Development," *Journal of Regional Science* 28 (1988): 541–562; and Duck-Ho Lim, "The Nonneutrality of the Land Value Tax: Impacts on Urban Structure," *Journal of Urban Economics* 32 (1992): 186–194.

3. B.M. Anderson, "'Unearned Increments,' Land Taxes and the Building Trade," *Quarterly Journal of Economics* 24 (1910): 811–814.

4. I introduced a discrete version of this definition in a 1990 paper. "Integrating Land-Value Taxation with the Internalization of Spatial Externalities," *Land Economics* 66 (1990): 341–355.

5. Shoup, "Advance Land Acquisition by Local Governments: A Cost-Benefit Analysis" and "The Optimal Timing of Urban Development."
6. Ibid., "The Optimal Timing of Urban Development," 37.
7. Ibid., 38.
8. Ibid., 39.
9. Skouras, "The Non-Neutrality of Land Taxation," 113–134.
10. Ibid., 130.
11. Michael S. Owen and Wayne Thirsk, "Land Taxes and Idle Land: A Case Study of Houston," *Land Economics* 50 (1974): 251–260.
12. Ibid., 252.
13. Bentick, "The Capitalization of the Property Tax and Idle Land: Comment."
14. Ibid., 545–546.
15. Wayne R. Thirsk, "The Capitalization of the Property Tax and Idle Land: Reply," *Land Economics* 55 (1979): 549–552.
16. Bentick, "The Capitalization of the Property Tax and Idle Land: Comment," 546.
17. Bentick, "The Impact of Taxation and Valuation Practices," 861–863.
18. David E. Mills, "The Non-Neutrality of Land Taxation," *National Tax Journal* 34 (1981): 125.
19. Nicolaus Tideman, "A Tax on Land Is Neutral," *National Tax Journal* 35 (1982): 109–111; Bentick, "The Impact of Taxation and Valuation Practices"; and Mills, "The Non-Neutrality of Land Taxation."
20. Brian L. Bentick, "A Tax on Land May Not Be Neutral," *National Tax Journal* 35 (1982): 113.
21. Mills, "Reply to Tideman," *National Tax Journal* 35 (1982): 115.
22. Douglas, "Site Value Taxation and the Timing of Development," 291–292.
23. Noguchi, "On the Intertemporal Non-Neutrality of Taxes on Land," 20.
24. Mathis and Zech, "An Empirical Test," 3.
25. Fischel, "The Urbanization of Land," 253.
26. Prest, "Some Issues in Australian Land Taxation," 102.
27. Ellson and Roberts, "Managed' Urban Land Markets," 477.
28. Pillai, "Property Taxation in Thailand," 45.
29. Turnbull, "The Effects of Local Taxes and Public Services on Residential Development," 557.
30. Lim, "The Nonneutrality of the Land Value Tax: Impacts on Urban Structure," 186–194.
31. David E. Wildasin, "More on the Neutrality of Land Taxes," *National Tax Journal* 35 (1982): 105.
32. Ibid., 107.
33. Steven C. Bourassa, "Economic Effects of Taxes on Land," *American Journal of Economics and Sociology* 51 (1992): 110.
34. Martin Feldstein, "The Surprising Incidence of a Tax on Pure Rent: A New Answer to an Old Question," *Journal of Political Economy* 85 (1977): 349–360.
35. Wolfgang Eckart, "The Neutrality of Land Taxation in an Uncertain World," *National Tax Journal* 36 (1983): 237–241.
36. Henry George, *Progress and Poverty* (1879; reprint, New York: Robert Schalkenbach Foundation), 436.

37. Richard T. Ely, "Land Speculation," *Journal of Farm Economics* 2 (1920): 121–135.

38. Harry G. Brown, "Land Speculation and Land-Value Taxation," *Journal of Political Economy* 35 (1927): 390–402. This article is reprinted here as chapter 6.

39. Paul Milgrom and Robert J. Weber, "A Theory of Auctions and Competitive Bidding," *Econometrica* 50 (1982): 1089–1122.

40. Ely, "Land Speculation," 121.

41. Paul A. Samuelson, "Intertemporal Price Equilibrium: A Prologue to the Theory of Speculation," *Weltwirtschaftliches Archiv* 79 (1957): 209 (reprint; *The Collected Scientific Papers of Paul A. Samuelson,* ed. Joseph E. Stiglitz, vol. 2 [Cambridge: MIT Press, 1966], 946–984).

42. Jack Hirshleifer, "The Private and Social Value of Information and the Reward to Inventive Activity," *American Economic Review* 62 (1972): 572.

43. Mason M. Gaffney, "Ground Rent and the Allocation of Land Among Firms," in *Rent Theory: Problems and Practices,* Frank Miller, ed., North Central Regional Research, Publication No. 139, *University of Missouri Research Bulletin* No. 810 (1961): 30–49 and 74–82 and Gaffney, "Tax Reform to Release Land" in *Modernizing Urban Land Policy,* ed. Marion Clawson (Baltimore: Johns Hopkins University Press, 1973), 115–152. This last cited article is reprinted here as chapter 7.

10

Robert V. Andelson

Interest Originating from Invested Rent: Social or Private?

Henry George contends that *rent,* even when derived from land purchased with the fruits of honest toil, cannot justly be privately appropriated, because *land* (not being a labor product) can have no clear moral title, and because its value is produced not by the owner but by society. Although he does not explicitly address the ethical propriety of interest earned by *capital* originating from invested rent, his writings yield this implicit analysis: Even as rent should be returned to the community, abstract justice also demands that *interest* on capital that stems from rent should be returned to the community. But there is no feasible way in which to implement this demand, since it is scarcely ever possible to separate interest derived indirectly from private rent from interest not so derived. But this poses no real problem if we seek *justice* for the present and the future instead of reparations for *injustice* in the past. For the socialization of rent would render accumulations of

This article is a slightly amended version of a paper presented on June 13, 1991, at the first Lafayette College Conference on Henry George in Easton, Pennsylvania. It was originally published in *The American Journal of Economics and Sociology* 51, no. 3 (July 1992) and is reprinted here with permission.

private capital, regardless of how obtained, impossible to sustain (absent special privileges conferred by government) unless directed toward the satisfaction of public demand as reflected in the marketplace.

Although George considered the taxation of land values a good thing in itself from the standpoint both of equity and of economic efficiency, one of his main reasons for advocating it was that he saw it as a substitute for the taxation of wages and interest, which he regarded as both inequitable and inefficient.[1] But some interest, instead of being the fruit of capital (that is, wages invested in production), stems at least indirectly from the fruit of privilege—private appropriation of the rent of land.

Passages in at least three books by George assert that rent cannot justly be privately appropriated even when it is derived from land purchased in good faith with the fruits of honest toil.[2] This is because land is a good to which, by its very nature, there can be no clear title, and because its value is produced, not by the owner as such, but by the community.

Moreover, says George, the assertion applies much more strongly to rent than it does to stolen labor products:

> For this robbery is not like the robbery of a horse or a sum of money, that ceases with the act. It is a fresh and continuous robbery, that goes on every day and every hour. It is not from the produce of the past that rent is drawn; it is from the produce of the present. It is a toll levied upon labor constantly and continuously.[3]

To produced commodities, the principle of statutes of limitation may be germane:

> A question of the ownership of a coat, a tool, a house, a bale of goods, is a question of the ownership of the concrete results of past labor. We know from the nature of the thing that it must be owned by somebody, but after a lapse of time we cannot from the weakness of human powers undertake in case of a dispute to determine who that may be; and hence, refusing to inquire so far back, we assume the right to be in the possessor, of which we have at least presumptive evidence. But a question of the maintenance or abolition of slavery or private property in land, of the continuance or noncontinuance of a trade monopoly, a hereditary pension, or a protective duty, is a question whether the state shall or shall not in the future lend its power for the wrongful appropriation of

> the results of labor yet to be performed. There is in this no place for the principle of statutes of limitation. No indistinctness as to the past can affect the decision. It is not a question of what has been done in the past, but of what shall be done in the future. And so far from the presumption being that the possessor of this species of property is entitled to it, the moral certainty is the other way.[4]

Although I agree with George's views on land and rent, my purpose here is not to argue for them. Rather, I wish to consider a contrasting parallel which George, to my knowledge, did not directly or explicitly address—to wit, the moral case of interest earned by capital that had its origin in invested wealth derived from rent.

The parallel appears, at least superficially, to be morally correlative: On the one hand, wealth with a clear moral title is exchanged for something to which, according to George, there can be no moral title; and the return to that something—namely, rent—cannot be legitimately appropriated privately, inasmuch as it arises from the effect of public activity and demand upon a passive source that was never legitimately owned privately. On the other hand, the return from something to which there is no clear moral title is exchanged for wealth to which there can be a clear moral title, and this wealth is used to produce more wealth.

How would George respond to this? Assuming, for purposes of discussion, that the drug traffic is not only legally but also morally illicit, should not consistency oblige him to concede that interest originating from invested rent is analogous to laundered drug money, and that the state would be justified in confiscating such interest on the same grounds that it confiscated the houses, automobiles, legitimate businesses, and other assets of convicted drug dealers?

This question would be obviated if we could accept the contention of writers such as Michael Flürscheim in 1891 and Lewis H. Berens in 1903 that pure interest would simply disappear if rent were publicly appropriated (and other types of monopoly income extirpated).[5] The basis for this contention is the observation that the rate of pure interest tends to be driven upward by privately appropriated rent, since wealth will not be invested as capital unless it yields thereby a return at least as high as it would obtain if invested in land, plus a premium ("insurance") for risk and depreciation. In a letter to me, a learned friend has criticized this observation because, as he puts it, "buying land does not per se, abort capital formation; it is a zero-sum transaction: one buys, another sells."[6] But the proceeds from the sale of land do not *usually* go into capital formation. When not consumed, or channeled into such "safe" but often unproductive assets as government bonds, they are likely to be spent to purchase other land (and this not necessarily for speculation), frequently thus putting increased pressure on the margin. If, conversely, more wealth is made available as capital because nothing can any longer be gained by investing it in land, the rate of interest, all other things being equal, will decrease. This seems sound to me, and is supported by the analysis of the 1988 Nobel laureate in economics, Maurice Allais.[7] But the contention based upon it is a non sequitur. That an alternative investment option (land) reduced the supply of capital and thus kept interest rates high does not establish that interest would cease to exist if this option were withdrawn. This, too, is consistent with Allais's analysis.[8]

Flürscheim and Berens did not, of course, maintain that borrowing and lending would cease, or that wealth would be lent with no expectation that it would be restored to the lender. Their position, rather, is that the natural rate of pure interest is zero—an equilibrium between a premium for the use of wealth, and what is technically called "discount"; that is, a premium for the preservation of wealth. That equilibrium, they say, is the return of the value of the principal, and the existence of any premium for either use or preservation signals some maladjustment in the economic structure.

A much earlier economist, known as Jesus of Nazareth, observed in his Parable of the Talents that wealth, when used productively, yields, on the average, a return over and above that represented by its mere preservation.[9]

My own opinion is that even if noncapital avenues for investment were foreclosed, time-preference would still enable disposable wealth, made available by its owners to others, normally to command *some* premium in addition to its replacement value. Otherwise, there would be less incentive to make it available, saving would be discouraged, and disposable wealth would tend to be consumed rather than invested. So I conclude that under a Georgist system, and barring extraneous determinants, the rate of interest would incline to be lower but interest would not disappear.

Granting George's premise that the private appropriation of rent is unjust, and taking as a given the proposition that a thoroughgoing Georgist regime would not bring about the automatic disappearance of interest, what would be his verdict as to the private appropriation of that interest earned by capital which had its origin in invested wealth derived from rent?[10]

This issue may be divided logically into three discrete questions: the question of abstract justice, the question of implementation, and the question of practical necessity. As I indicated earlier, George did not, so far as I know, directly or explicitly address any of these. Yet I shall show that his writings yield implicit answers to all of them.

The answer to the first question of abstract justice is so obvious as to require no demonstration. Even as rent as a social product should be returned to the community, so abstract justice demands that interest from such capital as may stem from rent should also be returned to the community. This is a simple deduction from many statements in George's work.

But abstract justice is one thing, real-life implementation quite another. The fact is that, by and large, there is no feasible way by which to separate interest derived indirectly from private rent from interest with the most Georgistically impeccable antecedents. Land titles may be traced with relative ease, but capital, being as a rule less fixed and subject to fewer legal formalities of transfer, usually undergoes so many combinations and permutations that even to attempt to trace all its titles to their origins would be so complicated and burdensome as to defy the most resourceful and determined efforts. Thus, to this problem, part of the passage quoted earlier from *A Perplexed Philosopher* is surely apposite.

> We know from the nature of the thing that it must be owned by somebody, but, after a lapse of time we cannot from the weakness of human power undertake in cases of dispute to determine who that may be; and hence, refusing to inquire so far back, we assume the right to be in the possessor, of which we have at least presumptive evidence.[11]

Should it be objected that these words are immediately followed by a statement to the effect that statutes of limitation cannot properly apply to property in land or to rent, and the implication be drawn that they cannot apply to wealth derived from invested rent, the response must be that the line between forms of wealth the possession of which initially derived from rent and forms of wealth the possession of which is not so derived is so unclear and indistinct that seldom can it be drawn at all.

The impossibility of implementing the distinction need not disconcert those who are more eager to stop current wrongs and prevent future wrongs than to punish old wrongs. Note the words of George in *Progress and Poverty:*

> if Quirk, Gammon, and Snap can mouse out a technical flaw in your parchments or hunt up some forgotten heir who never dreamed of his rights, not merely the land, but all your improvements, may be taken away from you. And not merely that. According to the common law, when you have surrendered the land and given up your improvements, you may be called upon to account for the profits you derived from the land during the time you had it. . . . But I do not propose, and I do not suppose that anyone else will propose, to go so far. It is sufficient if the people resume the ownership of the land. Let the landowners retain their improvements and personal property in secure possession.[12]

And even more emphatically in *A Perplexed Philosopher:* "We propose to leave to landowners whatever they actually have, even though it be in their hands the fruits of injustice."[13] And again in *The Condition of Labor:*

> We are willing that bygones should be bygones and to leave dead wrongs to bury their dead. We propose to let those who by the past appropriation of land values have taken the fruits of labor to retain what they have thus got. We merely propose that for the future such robbery of labor shall cease—that for the future, not for the past, landholders shall pay to the community the rent that to the community is justly due.[14]

Why does George, that inexorable nemesis of privilege, take in this instance such a mild, irenic stance? Is it merely a matter of expedience, stemming from the realization that to demand compensation for past wrongs would place his program politically forever out of reach? I think not. The answer is that there is no practical necessity for such measures.

Justice for the present and for the future can be fully served without insisting upon reparations for the past. For as George points out in *The Land Question:*

> The right to possess and to pass on the ownership of things that in their nature decay and soon cease to be is a very different thing from the

> right to possess and to pass on the ownership of that which does not decay, but from which each successive generation must live.[15]

Once severed from its landed base, and unsupported by political favoritism that insulates it from competition, the advantage afforded by possession of capital cannot be long sustained except through the *use* of it in ways that redound to the felicity of the public the only way in which such felicity can be really measured, namely, through the choices freely made according to their perceived marginal utility by people in the marketplace. Under such circumstances, accumulations of capital, regardless of how obtained, are soon dissipated unless directed toward the satisfaction of consumers' wants. Lewis Berens does not greatly overstate the case when he says that shares or interest in private undertakings "would only be profitable in exact proportion to the value of the services such undertakings were rendering the community."[16] Otherwise, the adage "from shirt-sleeves to shirt-sleeves in three generations" generally applies.

Let us conclude by returning to the analogy of laundered drug money. It is an analogy that can be pressed only so far. The primary reason for confiscating legitimate assets purchased with drug money is to help stop the drug traffic by removing an incentive for supplying drugs. But George's remedy would already have removed any incentive for the socially harmful activity that was the focus of his concern. A secondary reason for such confiscation is to punish those who flout the law. But the private appropriation of rent is not against the law. Let us by all means seek to make it so. But if we were to do so retroactively, we should be guilty of ex post facto justice, which is no justice at all.

Notes

1. Henry George, *Progress and Poverty* (1879; New York: Robert Schalkenbach Foundation, 1954), 434–436.
2. Ibid., 366–367; Henry George, "The Land Question," in *The Land Question [and Other Essays]* (1881; New York, Robert Schalkenbach Foundation, 1954), 46; and Henry George, *A Perplexed Philosopher* (1892; New York: Robert Schalkenbach Foundation, 1946), 225–232, especially 225–226. "The Land Question" was originally published under the title, "The Irish Land Question." In the Schalkenbach edition cited, each essay is paginated separately.
3. George, *Progress and Poverty,* 364. See also George, "The Land Question," 43–46.

4. George, *A Perplexed Philosopher,* 229.

5. Michael Flürscheim, *Rent, Wages, and Interest* (1891, 3d ed. rev.; London: William Reeves, 1895) and Lewis H. Berens, *Toward the Light* (London: Swan Sonnenschein, 1903).

6. Mason Gaffney, professor of economics, University of California at Riverside.

7. Maurice Allais, *Économie et intérêt* (Paris: Imprimerie Nationale, 1947), 479, 499, 549, 566ff., and *passim.*

8. Ibid. I am indebted to Professor Leland B. Yeager for directing my attention to these passages. See also another Nobel laureate in economics, Paul A. Samuelson, "Land and the Rate of Interest," in Harry I. Greenfield, et al., eds., *Theory for Economic Efficiency: Essays in Honor of Abba P. Lerner* (Cambridge: MIT Press, 1979), 167–185. Cited by Fred Foldvary in *The Georgist Journal* (Fall 1991).

9. Matthew 25: 14–30.

10. Parenthetically, it may be relevant to mention that Marx viewed capital, even in its initial formation, less as the stored-up product of its owner's own labor than as part of the expropriated product of the labor of others. To the extent that he was correct in this, the expropriation, as he shows, may be laid chiefly at the door not of the capitalist but of the landlord, or perhaps of the owner in the capacity of landlord rather than of capitalist. But I shall not pursue this topic here, since Marx's main line of argument against capitalism as a system of exploitation rests upon his theory of surplus value, not upon his opinions regarding initial capital formation. For corroboration of these views, please see: Karl Marx, "Pre-Capitalist Economic Foundations," in *Grundrisse der Kritik der Politischen Ökonomie,* Jack Cohen, trans., and E.J. Hobsbawn, ed. (1857–1858; London: Lawrence & Wishart, 1964), 107, 110–111, 113, and 115; *Capital,* I, Samuel Moore and Edward Aveling, trans., revised by Ernest Untermann according to the fourth edition of 1890, Friedrich Engels, ed. (1867 and 1906; Charles H. Kerr; New York: The Modern Library, n.d.), 651, 787, 805, and 815; and *Capital,* III, Friedrich Engels, ed. (1894; Moscow: Foreign Languages Publishing House, n.d.), 792–801. See *Capital* I, 623–624, for an appropriate admission to the contrary, which is then discounted. See also *Capital* I, 637–640 and 787–805; *Capital* III, 792 and 801; and "Theories of Surplus Value" *(Capital* IV), Emile Burns, trans., and S. Ryazanskaya, ed. (1862–1863; Moscow: Foreign Languages Publishing House, n.d.), part I, 59.

11. George, *A Perplexed Philosopher,* 229.

12. George, *Progress and Poverty,* 366–367.

13. George, *A Perplexed Philosopher,* 240.

14. George, "The Condition of Labor: An Open Letter to Pope Leo XIII" (1881) in *The Land Question [and Other Essays],* 54.

15. George, "The Land Question" in *The Land Question [and Other Essays],* 43ff.

16. Berens, *Toward the Light,* 153.

11

Thomas R. West

Henry George: A Celebration of Land and Labor

Henry George, best known for his land-tax economics, is also familiar as a moralist: No one who reads him can miss the passion with which he attacks the causes of poverty, more especially the privatization and monopolization of land. But apart from the technical merits of his economic thought is the eloquence with which he celebrates two central components of the human enterprise: land, or rather nature as a whole, under the guardianship of the whole human race; and labor, which worked into soil and wood and minerals makes for the things of human sustenance and delight. In defining these as the basis of an economy and a civilization, George did no more than what any sensible economist might do. Separately or together, they have provided the subject of any number of social commentaries. George's way of compounding the two, however, was fresh and distinctively American.

The most recognizable founding statement of the modern capitalist and bourgeois relationship between land and property is the *Essay of Civil Government,* published in 1690 by John Locke (1632–1704). This second of *Two Treatises of Government,* together written in favor of the constitutional settlement that brought William and Mary to the British throne in 1689, considers the grounds of property rights.

Locke, like George, begins with the assumption that nature is for the use of all humanity. But he proceeds to observe that if that common stock does not in some way get divided, it will be of no use to anyone.

The problem, then, can be expressed in a dilemma that Locke only implicitly defines: In order that the common need can benefit, nature must cease to be common.

Locke's explanation of how private property can be carved out of a nature given to the whole of mankind is to assign to labor the just appropriation of some modest portion of it. Mix some natural material with your labor and it becomes an extension of your body and self, belonging to you as your body does. Locke's simple example of an act of labor is the gathering of acorns or other food. The collection is the beginning of an act that will proceed through cooking and eating; it is a preliminary to the body's absorption. By this reasoning, a neighbor's interference with the act of picking the acorns would make no more sense than the neighbor's attempt to interfere in the process of digestion. And lest this be taken as license to the quicker or stronger to gather or grow as much as possible and keep it from others, Locke adds the caveat that the appropriation can be for only as much as the individual can use. If you keep enough food that it will spoil, you have broken the moral rule that nature is for the benefit of the whole of the human race. The extra amount is not yours, and you have taken or kept it by theft.

Up to this point, labor seems to have only a moderate place in the human economy. Allowing it to initiate the business of dividing nature's bounty is no more than a commonsensical, practical way of reconciling the commonness of nature with the need to distribute her riches. The problem is that the formula for the distribution—what is mixed with your labor becomes an extension of your very self—can quickly set up for a completely autonomous, unqualified criterion for uncompromised private property. In that case, it does not matter whether the poor are clamoring at the borders of your property, begging for some scraps of the potatoes rotting in your barn. They are yours as your blood and bones are yours, and the supplicants at the gates of your estate can starve if you so will. Locke does not intend this result. Explaining how a person can legitimately become wealthier than is necessary for self-sustenance, he proposes that the unrestrained accumulation of money is justified by the inability of money to spoil. But with that money, the wealthy can buy land or food or clothing (or a government) and withhold these from the community.

That problem Locke, who means well, does not satisfactorily address. The formula "This is my property because it is mixed with my labor, my body and brain" has twentieth-century expressions that Locke, I am sure, would not have endorsed. It is the conviction of the gun-entranced rancher and right-wing militiaman that he can shoot down anyone who steps onto his property. And it is the conviction among the feminists who, repelled at the archaic view of women as the property of their husbands, now define their bodies in effect as *their* property: not a miraculous and uniquely human locus of thought and will and life, but simply their Property.

But what is wrong with the formula that labor or the activities of the body translate into inalienable private property? If it is right, then let the militiaman and his property-defending kind do as they wish; let the hungry at the door starve, whether the food in the storage bin is spoiling or not. Simply conclude that Locke's correlation of property with labor, or the body, is better than his earnest attempt to qualify it.

The most direct response to such a conclusion is that it offends every notion of decency and right. But in the rhetorical form: "Why is the government taxing me for its so-called humanitarian aid? I worked for my property," the crudest attachment of property rights to work is to much of the public more appealing than offensive. So something beyond moral indignation is called for here. For that, the plainest argument is that no translation of labor into property is possible.

For such a translation to make any moral sense, it would have to presume a quantitative and absolute correlation between a given amount of effort and a given quantity of worth or usefulness within the resulting property. Such a correlation is plainly indefinable. Return to the Lockean world. One person plants a radish seed. That act of labor, according to the formula, earns a property in the one radish. Someone else, expending about the same amount of energy, begins a potato plant, and for the effort gains a vegetable many times more nutritious and filling. Which should the act of planting earn in property: one crisp but fleetingly consumed radish, or the nourishing potatoes? A carpenter expends thirty hours of effort and intensity in making a bench; a farmer, an equally intense thirty hours in growing food, which he exchanges for the bench. It is an obviously fair arrangement. Now suppose the two live on thin land with scrawny wood. The carpenter receives thirty hours of food just sufficient to keep him alive, and the farmer gets a bench weak and lacking beauty of grain. Or they live on rich land with gracefully grained wood, and after the thirty hours of work and the exchange the carpenter feasts while the farmer rejoices in a handsome bench. That each of the two exchanges is unquestionably just within its own circumstances makes it all the clearer that no right, absolute correlation between work and return is possible: Here thirty hours bring comfort and pleasure, elsewhere they bring only a meager survival.

Locke's comments are more about property than about the specific character of labor. He does observe, as will more recent commentators on economics, that labor adds to objects most of their value. The clearest meaning of that is that without the picking, the potato will serve no nutritional value. Wheat, of course, accomplishes its purpose only after the gathering, the grinding, and the baking. But Locke's factual declaration contrasts with George's evocative description of the ingenuity and skill that turn nature's offerings into the useful and beautiful things of civilization, and the vast network of reciprocal effort that accomplishes the transformation.

The formula that renders labor into property, then, fails both to make its case and adequately to examine the interior character of work. In insisting that effort be rewarded, in fact, it draws attention away from the virtues of work as good in themselves. For that closer consideration of work, a good place to look is a discussion that took place among British commentators nearly two centuries after Locke's *Two Treatises*. It gained force with an essay, "The Nature of Gothic," that the great British Victorian art and social critic John Ruskin (1819–1900) included in his mid-century study of architecture, *The Stones of Venice*.

Against the clear and sunny architecture of the Mediterranean, Ruskin sets the massive and, as he perceives them, rude structures hurled toward heaven in the worship offered by the peoples of the frigid north. (Later critics would observe to the contrary that Gothic architects aimed at shaping lightness and space; but that is another issue.) In those gigantic edifices Ruskin detects the innocent imagination and unquestioning faith of simple craftsmen who have been allowed to express in rugged stone all their ingenuity.

From there, Ruskin turns to consider what has become of workmanship under the factory system. It has lessened the act of work, he complains, forcing each attendant to repeat over and over some precise and minute act from which all largeness of intention and inventiveness has been pinched. In comparison he poses handicraft as he believes it to have been practiced in earlier times. Seeking an imagined beauty or comeliness, the worker stumbles from moment to moment, imperfections of hand movements making for nicks and flaws in the material being crafted. These impart to the finished product its real beauty: They mark the presence of free, honest, and eager work—with, Ruskin might have added, some poetry to it in both the modern sense of the phrase and that of the word's Greek origin, a making. George, occupied in the fine craft of printing, begins like Ruskin with a sense of the worker's distinctive and intimate art. But he will welcome as Ruskin would not the advanced technologies and sciences that turn craft from the skilled touches of the hand to the mastery of the more abstract world of machines. The disagreement here is not over what is virtuous in work but over what activities might entexture that virtue.

Ruskin's idea of work more tightly connects the effort and its outcome than does the bourgeois and capitalist connecting of work to property. The object crafted is not merely a quantification of effort demanding monetary compensation, as though there could be no other reason for working. It is instead a specific, unique embodiment and statement of the imaging, exertion, and skill of the worker. Property, indeed, is not even the question. Ruskin's workers find joy and much of their reward in the working. If he romanticized the labors of peasants and craftsmen in the days before industrialization, then be grateful for the romanticizing: What he lost in historical skepticism, he gained in an ability to raise the question of what work, at its best, might be.

What of the other component of an economy that George will identify toward the end of Ruskin's century, the land that the worker elaborates into the treasures of civilization; here, the wood and stones and fibers that come of the land? As the craft ideal developed in the later years of the century, the virtues of honesty and directness that Ruskin (as well as George) insisted on in work itself were demanded of materials. That was partially in protest against the use of machinery to make ugly imitations of natural substances: to decorate walls, for instance, with wooden slabs contrived to look like marble. What a craft romanticist must presume the worker's love of the surfaces of wood, the delicacy of thread, the malleability of clay to imply, in contrast to a coldly possessive bourgeois ownership of objects and money, is an intimate, sensuous partnership between work and nature.

One of the most important critics in the craft lineage is William Morris (1834–1896), who in combination with commentary mastered any number of skills: weaving, surface design, and perhaps most notably printing. That last is a curiosity. The interchangeability of parts, a core principle of industrialism, had in the early modern invention of print possibly its founding instance. Determined to impart taste to his affluent British countrymen, Morris had entered the business of interior decoration. Coming to recognize that far more was needed than refining the sensibilities of the well-to-do, he turned to socialism. Morris, unlike other adherents along with opponents of that doctrine, located socialism in its objectives most enhancing to human dignity. His socialism has a point in conformity with the commonwealth imagined in George's thought: It would not put a government in control of the distribution of goods to a population of consumers. Morris sought to empower workers to articulate their creative capabilities and to shape the conditions of their lives. He took that to mean not only the abolition of capitalism but the relegation of machines to a secondary place in the process of work. In the future depicted in his *News from Nowhere,* everyone will be at liberty to undertake whatever pleasing work is at hand. The worker will not own the product. Knowing that someone into whose hands it comes will take use or pleasure from it should be satisfaction enough.

The land was essential to Morris's politics—the land itself, or more particularly the English countryside. Like others who held to the craft persuasion, he was almost as much a cultural traditionalist as a political radical. The English landscape, carved into shapely fields, he perceived as the work of the centuries. He opposed restorations of old buildings: The ruins should remain for the most part undisturbed, still carrying the imprint of the hands that had nestled them in the English land.

The idea of labor in concert with land had in Lev N. Tolstoi (1828–1910) an advocate who admired Henry George. Like the anarchist Peter A. Kropotkin (1842–1921), the great Russian novelist had been born into the nobility whose power he abhorred. In concert with George and largely through his influence, Tolstoi identified as the cause of all oppression the control of land by anyone other than its workers. In Russia, that control was especially oppressive. A peasantry, which until 1861 had been in legal serfage to landowners, still toiled on fields from which they did not draw the benefit. Tolstoi's demand was not that peasants become owners themselves, able to make money and with it amass property. He did not believe in property in land: Though continuing to live in comfort, he abandoned formal ownership in his estate, turning it over to his family. His objection to the existing system was that in draining away the gain from the soil, the wealthy kept the peasants in poverty and severed them from free and secure management of the land that was their rightful heritage.

In none of this could Morris have disagreed with Tolstoy; and Tolstoy, who detested much of industrialism and urbanism, would have had few quibbles if any with the society depicted in *News from Nowhere.* But there is a difference in sensibility between the two. Tolstoy's deeply Russian feeling was for a pious rural folk, content to work the land, instituting only whatever improvements would not compromise the peasant character of their lives. Of the crafts that thrive in Morris's imagined new age he would surely approve. But while the English land that Morris wished to liberate from capitalism and industrialism was the setting for his society, the bearer of its tradition, and the occasion for agriculture as one craft among others, Tolstoi wanted a peasantry wholly given to a nearly liturgical working of the soil.

Had it not been for the craft idea as Ruskin, Morris, and commentators of the kind as late as the recent counterculture promulgated it, social criticism would have been the poorer, for it has forced a close thinking into the character and virtues of work. But it has one signal failing, an inability fully to define the ways in which work is virtuous precisely in not being spontaneous, celebrative, expressive of sensuous needs and impulses.

This is not to say that the leading advocates and practitioners of craft did not know the difference between work and play. Morris's practical writing on the craft of design makes clear the exquisitely painstaking rigor of good work, and much of his hostility to the labor condition of his time was for the lazy shoddiness it encouraged. Morris himself lived by so strenuous a range and exactitude of projects that his physician judged him to have burned himself out. And the loathing of the craft partisans of the Victorian Era for industrialism itself is an entirely understandable reaction both to the shabbiness of its products and to the dreary factory towns and the exploitation of the labor force. But as industrialism progressed, a different set of qualities was increasingly making itself known: qualities far different from the tactile values of craftsmanship at its best but in that very difference demanding of their own respect. What advanced technology was beginning to reveal was the presence of a mentality trained to mechanics and measurement rather than to a purely physical dexterity, an inner austerity able to impress itself on its machines and buildings.

The requirement that, in their opposition to the crass products of Victorian industrialism, the champions of craftsmanship had established for visible honesty in work and materials actually came to the United States to the aid of industrial technology. By the end of the nineteenth century, the concept was growing in George's homeland that instead of plastering surfaces with Greek or Renaissance façades, the architects of office buildings should make clear that the structures are held up by steel girders and intended for the purposes of modern industry and commerce. This means that the technical and mental demands of machine technology can find an aesthetic form as worthy as the physical flourishes in the slips of the hand that delighted Ruskin, or the exactly executed lines in a design that Morris would admire.

Aside from the honor that functionalist machine design was expected to pay to the slender strength of steel and the cleanness of glass, what notice could the land and its products receive from industrial technology? In time, as that technology continued to refine itself and shed some of the bulk that the heavy, muscular machinery of an earlier day had borne, it was discovered that, as Lewis Mumford (1895–1990) would observe, the unobtrusive wires of electrical power could spread technology over the countryside in ways that fade it into nature. Frank Lloyd Wright (1869–1959) was to discover that steel could define shapes and spaces consonant with a rural setting.

But neither this awareness nor functionalist architecture was available when George formed his ideas of an economics that would do homage to nature as belonging to the whole of the human race, free its materials from monopolization and private ownership, and make them available to whoever is prepared to work them up into objects beneficial to humanity. What he could draw on from his homeland was a culture that had early learned to pride itself on inventive ingenuity and, in the absence of contrary traditions, could unabashedly affirm the virtues of industrialism, combining them with an ethic of neighborly generosity. And he had a land that, sprawled ruggedly across a continent and not yet intricately cultivated into fields traced with hedges, seemed a location fit imaginatively as well as practically for an equally sprawling industrial development.

Perhaps a knowledge of the inviting and unspoiled plenty of the continent, along with a recognition that it was coming under the domination of private and corporate wealth, added to George's perception of what land free of monopoly and private ownership could do for the human race. His solution, to tax away from the land any richness that soil and minerals contribute to the value of a product of work beyond the value of the poorest of their kind, gives respect to God as offering His goods to the whole of mankind, and not to be lowered to the status of private property. That the tax would also deprive the landowner of value that the toil of others had added to the plot—say, an empty lot owned by an indolent speculator and valued because of the thriving city surrounding it—gave moral urgency, so George believed, to the levy upon unearned wealth. The tax, in extracting from the product all that is not of human labor, also honors work as a separate and definable contribution, drawing crops from the earth or imposing on earth's iron ore and sand the complex geometry of a steel-beamed skyscraper. In both ways, George's social project improves on the intentions of Locke, who wished to assert the cooperative character of nature but ended by assigning her in parcels to individuals and, wanting to give to labor its just portion, offered no scheme calibrating possession to degree of effort.

The land tax, to be sure, cannot designate what might actually be the measurably just reward for an act of work. Taxing away the richness of land brings the worker's property only into a ratio with the property of others; it does not bring either into accord with an absolute standard. But no sensible follower of George would claim that it could do so. His scheme has the more modest effect of suggesting the injustices in other systems of appropriation. And beyond that, it pays tribute, as did Ruskin and Morris in another way, to the magnanimity of nature compounded with the dignity of work.

However he might divide use of the land and private possessions, George's ultimate vision is not of capitalist property-owning but of a commonwealth of workers. There exists, he writes, "a force . . . which is the electricity of the moral universe. . . . He who looks may see, as says Plutarch, that 'the soul has a principle of kindness in itself, and is born to love, as well as to perceive, [to] think, or to remember.'"[1]

Here, as in George's evocations of work as enticing natural materials into complex forms and his vision of the cooperative character of that endeavor, is the larger recognition he gives to human effort, beyond the insult that capitalist economics—along with Georgist economists at their most formulaic—inflicts upon work by locating its meaning in the property it happens to fetch, the wealth that cowers under the shelter of the state or its own pseudo-morality.

Note

1. Henry George, *Progress and Poverty* (1879; New York: Robert Schalkenbach Foundation, 1960), 463.

12

Roy Douglas

The Rise of the British Land-Taxing Movement: How It All Began

The 1909 Paradox

The finance bill that Chancellor of the Exchequer David Lloyd George introduced in April 1909 is perhaps the most famous fiscal measure in British history. It inaugurated a titanic struggle between the House of Commons, dominated by Liberals, and the Conservative House of Lords, which was still in full spate when war broke out in 1914.

The so-called People's Budget of 1909 was prompted by the need to raise more money from taxation for two notoriously expensive items: defense and social welfare. A "naval race" was in operation between Britain and Germany; and, in the previous year, the government had introduced the first old-age pensions. Neither naval rearmament nor old-age pensions had been a matter of deep controversy among the main political leaders, though individual M.P.s could be found with deep doubts about each of them.

Most of the measures that Lloyd George proposed in order to provide the money required were of a familiar kind: more income tax, more stamp duties on legal transactions, more legacy duties, more taxes on alcohol and tobacco, taxes on cars and petrol. A new "super tax" was to be charged on very large incomes. People complained about such matters, of course, as they always do. Yet one item soon attracted far more attention than all the rest combined.

The actual land taxes that Lloyd George proposed were odd little duties, which will be discussed later. Nobody, not even the government's most virulent opponents, contended that these land taxes would bring ruin. The total anticipated yield was about £500,000 million a year, only around half a percent of the annual tax burden, even in the tiny budgets of the early twentieth century. The feature that really stirred passion on both sides was not a tax at all, but the proposal to introduce a valuation on all land. This was intended as preliminary to taxation that would be introduced at an unspecified rate when that valuation was complete.

Long before David Lloyd George introduced his budget, everybody with any serious interest in public affairs knew about Henry George, and about the idea of the taxation of land values. Great numbers of radical working men had copies of *Progress and Poverty* on their bookshelves. Lloyd George was appealing not to a naive, unprepared electorate, but to people who had been thinking and talking about this salient notion for many years.

How did it all happen?

The Roots of the Problem

When the Corn Laws were repealed in 1846, Britain moved rapidly forward to free trade—at first in grain crops, but soon in nearly everything else as well. Prophets of doom had foretold the ruin of British agriculture, but they were proved wrong. Thirty years of rising prosperity for farming lay ahead.

But in the late 1870s and early 1880s, some profound economic and social changes were set in motion. The appalling wet summer of 1879 brought ruin to the English grain crop and a return of the potato blight which had been the immediate cause of the Irish famine of the 1840s. In 1876, more than four million tons of potatoes had been produced in Ireland; in 1879, about a quarter of that quantity.[1] In both Britain and Ireland, there was a great demand for foreign food, which was met by importation on a massive scale, largely from the United States. A year or two later, there was widespread disease in livestock, and at almost the same moment the first frozen animal carcasses reached Britain from New Zealand. Food and livestock imports, valued at £143.2 million in 1878, reached £168 million in 1883.[2] From these events enormous consequences flowed, both immediate and long-term.

In Ireland, where poverty was more intense than in Britain, traditional animosity between landlords and their anxious tenants flared into a "land war" which continued in various forms, and under various names, for years to come. There was much violence, and many landlords and their agents were in terror of their lives. The formal objectives of the peasant Land League were moderate indeed, and were largely granted by Parliament in 1881, but agrarian trouble did not end for a long time.

In the very late nineteenth century, a sort of solution emerged, which developed in several stages and culminated in George Wyndham's Land Purchase Act of 1903. Landlords were enabled to sell their land to the government, and tenants were enabled to obtain ownership of their holdings through what were, in effect, very long-term mortgages repayable to the state. Some public money was provided to lubricate the deal.

No doubt landlords and tenants were both pleased by the upshot; but those Irish people who were neither landlords nor tenant farmers gained nothing from the transaction. They received no better title to Irish land than they had possessed before all the fuss began. But it was tenant-farmers, not landless farm laborers or industrial workers, who were the political mainstay of the Irish National Party. The concern of most Irish politicians, and British interest in Irish affairs, moved away from the land question to the vexed political issue of Home Rule, whose echoes yet remain, at the very end of the twentieth century.

Irish Legacies

The Irish "land war" left some remarkable long-term legacies in British politics. While the "land war" was in full progress, two important works of Henry George attracted public attention: *Progress and Poverty* (1879), and then *The Irish Land Question* (1881), later renamed *The Land Question.*

A body called the Land Reform Association was set up in 1883, and reconstituted in the following year as the English Land Restoration League. Its counterpart, the Scottish Land Restoration League, was formed in 1884. Both bodies were soon propagating Henry George's ideas, and lecture tours with George himself as speaker were organized.

Events in a remote part of Scotland played a substantial part in linking the Irish "land war" with the growing British interest in land questions. In 1881, some crofters from the Hebridean island of Skye made landfall in Kinsale, County Cork, and there learned the ideas of the Irish Land League.[3]

People on Skye had good reason to relate Irish problems to those of their own island. The Irish evictions that followed the Famine of the 1840s are notorious; but Skye had its own counterparts. One author has claimed that between 1840 and 1883 something like 35,000 people were driven from Skye.[4] If that figure is correct, approximately twice as many people left the island to make way for Cheviot sheep as still remained there in the early 1880s.

In 1882, crofters at the Braes, on Skye, refused to pay rent and dealt summarily with sheriff officers, and later police, who were sent to evict them. The Hebridean "land war" had begun, and rapidly spread throughout the island. The conflict soon spread to other islands, and to parts of the mainland. Crofters physically resisted the authorities sent to evict them, but few people suffered serious injury. Police were followed by marines, and for much of the 1880s naval gunboats plied the Hebrides. At one point, soldiers were sent to the Outer Hebridean island of Lewis.

These events were treated as being of peripheral interest by most of the English press, but the newspapers of Glasgow and Edinburgh gave them major coverage, appealing—no doubt—to the many people of Hebridean stock who had moved to the Scottish cities. Links were soon made between the ideas of Henry George, events in the Hebrides, and the plight of the Scottish industrial proletariat. As early as 1884, the Glasgow Liberal "Six Hundred" began to press for what was, in effect, a measure of land-value taxation in Scotland. In 1889, the Manchester Conference of the National Liberal Federation came out with a much clearer demand for land-value taxation, which was repeated in the Federation's celebrated Newcastle Program two years later.

Socialism and Land Nationalization

During the last two decades of the nineteenth century, the writings and speeches of Henry George were making a huge impact on radical thought in Britain. Many people like Keir Hardie whom posterity has labeled "socialists" were more Georgists than socialists in the modern meaning of the word. Later, some of these early Georgists, among them George Bernard Shaw, did indeed move toward socialism. Many did not resile to their original opinions, but contrived to hold side by side the very different ideas of Georgism and socialism. Philip Snowden was a famous example. In his standard history, R.C.K. Ensor reflects:

> "Out of Henry George by either Bellamy or Gronlund" was a true pedigree of the convictions held by nearly all the leading propagandists who set socialism on its feet in Great Britain between 1886 and 1900.[5]

An expression that caused much confusion in the nineteenth century, and still causes confusion today, is "nationalization of land." Henry George himself used the term[6] to describe his proposals for the taxation of land values. A Land Nationalization Society was formed in Britain in 1881, under the inspiration of the great biologist Alfred Russel Wallace. In the 1890s it cooperated to an extent with the orthodox Georgist English Land Restoration League. But many people came to understand land nationalization to mean, not the appropriation of land rent through a tax on land values, but rather the direct state control of land use and even actual seizure of land, with or without compensation. Thus Georgists often found themselves linked with doctrines that they did not hold, and the occasional description today of Henry George himself as a land nationalizer seriously misleads people about the opinions he held.

The Single Tax

In *Progress and Poverty,* Henry George declared the objective "to abolish all taxation save that upon land values."[7] This statement must be understood in its historical context. In Henry George's time, a single tax on land values would have been adequate to meet all requirements of the state and probably leave substantial sums for distribution. The enormous growth of public spending during the twentieth century made this objective unrealistic, but it is easy to see how the term "single taxer" came into widespread use to describe George and his followers at the end of his century. Georgists liked the name, because it indicated that they were seeking fewer taxes and not more; while their opponents liked the name as well, because it made Georgists appear eccentric and fanatical in the eyes of people who did not fully understand their doctrines. In 1894, the new monthly organ published by the Glasgow land taxers was accordingly entitled *The Single Tax.*[8]

Local Government

At the same time, the land-taxing movement began to develop other arguments, appealing to large numbers of people, many of whom would have denied indignantly that they had any links with either socialism or single taxing.

During the late 1880s and early 1890s, local government in Britain was largely reconstituted, on a much more democratic base than hitherto. In this period, financial demands of local government formed a very substantial burden on the taxpayer. Thus, in 1889 and 1890, the yield of local rates in England and Wales totaled £27.7 million, almost exactly a third of the taxation revenue of the central government.[9] People began to question the basis on which local government rates were levied. Since Tudor times, these had normally been collected according to the total value of a hereditament—the land added to the superincumbent building and other improvements. Land taxers were quick to suggest that the assessment should be based instead on the value of the land alone. This proposal became known as Site-Value Rating (SVR). SVR, therefore, was simply land-value taxation applied to the needs of local government.

But the organs of local government were not permitted to levy rates on the basis of site values. So pressure was generated for them to receive such powers—or, in the alternative, for Parliament to make SVR the universal basis of local government taxation.

Advocates of SVR for local purposes soon became very influential. The London evening newspaper, *The Star,* reporting the first elections for the new London County Council, declared:

> Taxation of ground rents or values is one of the most popular cries in the election of County Councillors.[10]

In the following year, the Glasgow City Council began to give serious attention to the same problem. In 1894, ninety-four M.P.s signed a memorial to the chancellor of the exchequer, Sir William Harcourt, demanding that municipal councils should be authorized to collect rates on the basis of site values. Twelve years later, another chancellor, H.H. Asquith, received a similar petition, supported by 518 local authorities.

Economic Changes

While these important political developments were taking place, the fundamental character of landownership in much of Britain was undergoing changes no less radical.

Writing in 1881, near the beginning of the present period of study, the earl of Derby, a great landlord who was also politically active, reflected that

> the objects which men aim at when they become possessed of land in the British Isles may, I think, be enumerated as follows: (1) political influence; (2) social importance . . . (3) power exercised over tenantry; the pleasure of managing, directing and improving the estate itself; (4) residential enjoyment, including what is called sport; (5) the money return—the rent.[11]

Thus rent, while no doubt very important, was by no means the exclusive interest, and it is safe to assume that the existence of these other objects meant that the rent collected was often a good deal less than the purely economic rack rent would have been. Most English landlords were resident and usually interested in other aspects of landlordism, while the majority of Irish landlords were absentee and interested only in rent. This fact goes a long way toward explaining the difference that prevailed between English and Irish relations of landlords to tenants.

The massive influx of cheap foreign food in the closing years of the nineteenth century radically changed this position. The first losers from the drop in prices were the farmers, most of whom in those days were tenants. The farmers were usually in no position to reduce wages of their laborers, who could move to alternative work in the towns. But the tenant farmers could no longer survive at all economically if they continued paying the old rents, and so in a short time it was these rents that fell. A recent study has shown that the average annual agricultural rent in three widely separated English counties was 21.3 shillings per acre (£1.065) between 1875 and 1879, but only seventeen shillings

(£.85) twenty years later, following a period of almost continuous decline.[12] As a result, landlords were driven to cut down greatly on their activities, and an increasing proportion of the rent they received went to meet immediate requirements rather than the often colorful and sometimes useful functions they had once discharged. Like the nobles of eighteenth-century France, or the landlords of Ireland at the time, they were seen more and more as mere recipients of rent, who gave little in exchange. Thus not only the economic but also the moral authority of British landlords was seriously undermined.

The Liberal Government

In the early twentieth century, advocates of land taxing were undeniably gaining in strength. When the Conservative government left office at the end of 1905, and the Liberals took over, land taxers had great hopes from the new administration. Some of its members were noted land taxers themselves; few, if any, were opponents. At the beginning of 1906, a general election gave the Liberals a large majority in the House of Commons.

The road now seemed wide open for land taxing. But the House of Lords still retained great power, and was composed overwhelmingly of Conservative landlords.

The first serious move in the land-taxing direction affected Scotland. Scottish land law is markedly different from that of England, and the overwhelming majority of Scottish M.P.s supported less taxing. The time seemed ripe for a pilot scheme in Scotland, which would satisfy at the very least the financial needs of local government.

The natural way of proceeding was first to value the land of Scotland, and then, when valuation was completed, to begin to tax it. In 1907, a government bill was accordingly introduced to that effect. The bill passed the House of Commons with large majorities at all stages, and was then rejected by the House of Lords. In the following year, a similar government bill again passed the House of Commons, but was subjected to wrecking amendments by the House of Lords, and accordingly withdrawn.

The Constitutional Question

At this date, the House of Lords was undoubtedly within its constitutional rights in rejecting or wrecking a valuation bill from the House of

Commons. Many constitutional lawyers, however, were disposed to argue that a "convention" had developed to the effect that the Lords would not interfere with taxation proposals from the House of Commons. This matter soon came to the test.

In 1908, the Liberal Prime Minister Sir Henry Campbell-Bannerman retired, dying shortly afterwards. The new Prime Minister was Herbert Asquith, who had been Chancellor of the Exchequer since the Liberal government was formed at the end of 1905, while David Lloyd George was appointed the new Chancellor of the Exchequer.

Lloyd George had a remarkable background. As a young man in the mid-1880s, he had been an active participant in a Welsh movement that began as a sort of parallel to the Irish and Hebridean "land wars." This movement, however, soon veered off in a different direction, and became largely an attack on the tithes paid to Church incumbents. Lloyd George, however, appears to have picked up enough of the original ideas of land reform to be ready to take action when the opportunity presented itself. The new chancellor's 1909 budget was the occasion.

As has already been seen, the budget called for substantial measures of increased taxation, and there is every reason for thinking that Lloyd George would have been glad to introduce land-value taxation as a major feature. In the previous November, he had received a memorial, signed by 250 M.P.s, calling for him to do so. A general system of land-value taxation, however, was not possible until the valuation basis had been established. The recent Scottish experience suggested that there would be extreme difficulty in getting a valuation bill through Parliament.[13]

Lloyd George, who was much more interested in practical achievements than in heroic gestures, thought that he had a possible way round the difficulty. If the House of Lords could be expected to let government taxation proposals pass, however loudly it might squeal in protest, his course would be to link what he wanted to achieve with the current budget and present taxation.

The chancellor's actual proposals for land taxation were of four kinds. There was to be a tax on half an (old) penny in the pound, or about two-tenths of a percent, on undeveloped land with a value of over £50 an acre. This tax "was designed to make speculation in land bordering upon existing cities unprofitable."[14] An increment tax of 20 percent to collect added land values, was payable when the land changed hands—or, in the case of land owned by a corporation, every fifteen years. There was to be a rather complicated tax aimed at collecting mining royalties. A 10 percent reversion duty would be levied on the value of the benefit accruing to a lessor at the determination of a lease.[15]

This was, to put it mildly, a great deal less than what Henry George suggested. But it was linked with proposals for the valuation of land throughout the country, which were far more important than the taxes that the chancellor proposed to levy. A strong argument exists for the view that Lloyd George had never sought the great struggle with the House of Lords that eventually developed, but had rather hoped to secure his essential requirements without any serious fight at all.

The chancellor's speech in defense of these proposals was long, dull, and hesitant. Initial reactions on both sides were subdued. Then opposition to the budget began to quicken. Conservatives argued that the chancellor should have forsaken free trade finance, and turned to a policy of tariffs—"tariff reform," as it was known. The Irish Nationalists objected to the whiskey duty and the new license duties. A considerable number of Liberal M.P.s, notably the large landowner Sir John Dickson-Poynder, expressed considerable hesitation about the land proposals.

Soon, a great campaign against the budget was set in motion. What did the miscellaneous critics hope to achieve? Possibly they would generate enough of a head of steam to defeat the government, though for reasons of ordinary political arithmetic this seemed unlikely. More likely, they hoped to wring substantial concessions from the government as the budget passed through the House of Commons. More likely still, they hoped to discredit the government in the eyes of erstwhile supporters, and undermine its authority.

Appeal to the Land Taxers

Until the late summer of 1909, the budget looked like a major political liability for the government. It had generated much opposition, but little enthusiastic support, even from land taxers. Then, suddenly everything changed.

Contemporaries understood what happened next far more clearly than many subsequent commentators have done. An explanation comes from C.F.G. Masterman, who worked closely with Lloyd George at the time, and later served in Asquith's Cabinet:

> more by instinct than by reason, Mr. George realized that a controversy on the land question would raise the failing and dispirited forces of the Liberal Party. . . . The critical debate was on the clause authorizing the valuation of all the land of England. The Opposition had assembled to laugh it out of court. The Chancellor of the Exchequer was called away by a domestic bereavement. Mr. Asquith undertook to defend a proposition perhaps as unpopular on the Liberal as on the Conservative side.[16]

On July 30, Lloyd George sprang back in his very best form, at Limehouse, in London's East End. The chancellor's speech was witty rather than passionate, and he concentrated on ridiculing the landed interest's opposition to the budget. Thereafter, enthusiasm grew as if by magic.

The budget passed the Commons—not unscathed, but with its essentials intact. Then it went to the House of Lords. A few months earlier, nobody on either side of the controversy had anticipated that the last-ditch stand against the budget would be made in the Upper House. Had not the Lords permitted the radical budget of Sir William Harcourt to pass in 1894—a budget which struck at their hereditary holdings almost as much as the present measure?[17] But in September 1909 it became clear that the House of Lords would defy any real or imagined constitutional convention to the contrary, and would resist the budget. On November 30, 1909, it was rejected by 350 votes to 75; but at the same time the Lords made it clear that if a new general election gave a majority to the budget's supporters, it would then be allowed to pass.

When polling took place in January 1910, the Liberals and Conservatives were almost exactly balanced: 275 to 273. Labour, with forty seats, could be added to the Liberals' total for most purposes. But the highly fissile Irish Nationalists, with eighty-two seats, held the balance of power.

In the end, John Redmond, leader of the Irish Nationalists, decided to support the government. Little as he liked the budget, he liked still less the prospect of a government defeat, which would necessarily set the Conservatives in office, and destroy all hopes of Home Rule for many years to come. Some Nationalists disagreed with Redmond and voted against the government, while others were absent. But on the critical divisions the government won with substantial majorities. The finance bill enshrining the budget proposals was sent to the Lords, and passed without a division.

That was by no means the end of the story. The valuation took a great deal longer than the land taxers had anticipated, and was still incomplete when war came in August 1914. Many years later, Sir Edgar Harper, who had been chief valuer of the Board of Inland Revenue at the time, was to make a trenchant criticism of the unnecessary complications introduced into the valuation, arguing convincingly that a much simpler system could, and should, have been applied.[18]

Be that as it may, land taxing was still a vital political issue at the outbreak of war, and down to that moment there was every reason for believing that it would soon be brought into effect.

Aftermath

The aftermath really demands a separate essay for itself. When war came in 1914, the government's controversial measures, including the land legislation, in the interest of national unity went swiftly into cold storage for the duration. In the following year, Asquith set up a coalition, incorporating Conservative and Labour members as well as Liberals, and in 1916 a second coalition was formed under Lloyd George. Immediately after the armistice in 1918, a general election was called. This resulted in a large majority for the coalition, but the Conservatives formed much of the largest component. The knives were soon out for land taxing, and by a strange irony Lloyd George was prime minister of the government that formally ended land taxes and valuation alike in 1920.

By this time, other important developments were taking place. The Liberals were becoming increasingly split between Lloyd Georgists and Asquithians. The Labour Party was building up rapidly at the expense of both. In the decade that followed 1914, people who had been keen land taxers before the war migrated in all directions. Some remained in the Liberal Party, and continued to follow Asquith. Others followed Lloyd George. Some went into the Labour Party. One of them established a little, and ephemeral, party of his own. Winston Churchill, to the amazement of many, became a Conservative. Most of these people found themselves associated with colleagues who had different agenda.

The idea of land taxing did not die. Philip Snowden, Labour's first chancellor of the exchequer, was able to make a new land valuation a feature of his 1931 budget; but almost as soon as this became law the

Labour government fell, and was succeeded by a "national government" in which Conservative influence soon dominated all others. The Snowden valuation was first suspended, then abolished. In opposition, the Labour Party remained for a time true to its land-taxing traditions. A bill was introduced in 1938—unsuccessfully, of course—calling for London rates to be collected on the basis of site values.

Then came the 1939 war. Afterward, land taxing was not so much rejected as ignored. The impetus had been lost. Some land taxers certainly remained in the Labour and Liberal Parties, and even Churchill made the occasional nod in their direction; but that was about all. Land taxers themselves are not exempt from blame for this state of affairs. Many of them found it a good deal more pleasant and entertaining to convince themselves and their cronies how right they had always been than to go out into the cold and collect converts.

As the twentieth century draws to a close, British land taxers confront a very different problem from that which had faced their grandfathers and great-grandfathers. In those days, the significance of land taxing had been well understood by sympathizers and opponents alike. The task of the land taxers was to defeat informed, and often interested, opposition. Today there are as few vociferous opponents of land taxing as there are vociferous supporters. Probably fewer than twenty M.P.s could today make a decent case either for or against land taxing. The task facing British land taxers now is to restate their ideas in present-day terms to an audience that is utterly unfamiliar with the arguments of either side.

Notes

1. F.S.L. Lyons, *Ireland Since the Famine* (London: Fontana Press, 1973), 165.
2. Werner Schlote, *British Overseas Trade from 1700 to the 1930s* (Oxford: Basil Blackwell, 1952), 132.
3. Letter, Lord Lovatt, McNeill's Report, Lothian Papers, GD/40/16/32 fo. 21 ff.: National Library of Scotland.
4. Quoted in Frederick C. Sillar and Ruther M. Meyler, *Skye* (Newton Abbot: David and Charles, 1973), 111.
5. R.C.K. Ensor, *England 1870–1914* (Oxford: Clarendon Press, 1966), 334.
6. Henry George, *The Land Question* (1881; New York: Robert Schalkenbach Foundation, 1965), 64.
7. Henry George, *Progress and Poverty* (1879; London: Henry George Foundation of Great Britain, 1943), 288.

8. *The Single Tax,* later called *Land Values* and eventually *Land and Liberty,* is still published, though now as the quarterly publication of the Henry George Foundation in London.

9. Figures are based on those cited in B.R. Mitchell, *British Historical Statistics* (Cambridge: Cambridge University Press, 1980), 609.

10. *The Star,* London, 8.i., 1889.

11. Lord Derby, "Ireland and the Land Act," *Nineteenth Century,* October 1881, 474.

12. M.E. Turner, J.V. Beckett, and B. Afton, *Agricultural Rent in England, 1690–1914* (Cambridge: Cambridge University Press, 1997), 58, using figures from A.D.M. Phillips, *The Underdrainage of Farmland* (Cambridge: Cambridge University Press, 1989), 156–157.

13. Memorandum, David Lloyd George, 13.iii., 1909, CAB 37/98/44, Public Record Office.

14. K.W. Epstein, *The British Constitutional Crisis, 1909–1911* (New York: Garland, 1987), 128.

15. *Liberal Magazine,* June 1909, 280–283. See also Geoffrey Lee, *The People's Budget: An Edwardian Tragedy* (London: Henry George Foundation, 1996).

16. Lucy Masterman, *C.F.G. Masterman* (London: Nicholson and Watson, 1939), 133. The last sentence was an exaggeration, but Lloyd George had certainly encountered considerable difficulties from some of his Cabinet colleagues, and owed largely to Asquith his success in keeping the land taxes in the budget.

17. Harcourt was chancellor of the exchequer in a Liberal government that was sustained by a much smaller majority than the government of 1909. His 1894 budget provided, inter alia, for equalization of death duties on realty and personalty, and for the graduation of the death duties. Lord Salisbury, a Conservative leader and a great landowner, successfully urged his colleagues in the House of Lords, essentially for constitutional reasons, to allow Harcourt's budget to pass.

18. Sir Edgar Harper, *The Lloyd George Finance (1909–1910) Act 1910: Its Errors and How to Correct Them* (International Union for Land Value Taxation and Free Trade, 1929).

13

Damon J. Gross

Comments on the Problem of Public Revenue

Introduction

There are a number of problems with public revenue that merit serious study. One of them is getting sufficient revenue to support the legitimate responsibilities of government without burdening taxpayers counterproductively. The problem taken up in this essay is essentially ethical and prior to other problems with public revenue. What concerns us is how the transfer of even a penny from a person to the government, or from one person to another under the aegis of a government, differs morally from theft. We will examine several ways in which people have sought to justify public revenue.

Consider the sales tax. While there is a growing movement to lower or eliminate tax burdens on international transactions, even amidst controversy about working conditions and environmental policies of some trading partners, most states have no compunction whatsoever about imposing tax burdens on transactions within their own borders, even though intrastate commerce is universally recognized as a good thing. Or consider taxes on buildings. Although hardly any municipality would seriously attempt to entice a firm to locate a new plant or headquarters building in its environs without abating taxes on the proposed new building for a considerable number of years, almost all cities routinely tax the buildings of their long-standing citizens. Or consider the value-added taxes so prevalent in Europe these days. Why not tax in inverse rather than direct proportion to value added, on the grounds that those who add the least value are least deserving of their profits?[1] Or take the income tax. What connection is there between the quantity of an income and some purported right of the government to take it away from the one who earned it?

There are, of course, the many license fees and other taxes that governments impose. For example, many states tax life insurance premiums. In Iowa the tax is 2 percent and, as of January 1, 1998, Tennessee has, in a grandiose gesture, reduced its premium tax from 1.9 to 1.85 percent. Why not tax poor people who do not have life insurance, on the grounds that the state is likely to be stuck with their final expenses? And where do these numbers come from? Imagine the subtle reasoning by which these state legislatures have determined that their citizens owe the states for the privilege of paying life insurance premiums. All of this would be comical if livelihoods were not at stake. There must be a reason why it is morally permissible for the government to take money from a citizen in each of these cases—otherwise the taking is theft. The mere fact that the government needs revenue will not suffice as justification, because some of the most vile robberies are surely committed out of genuine need.

It seems plausible that public revenue could be justified by any one of four elements.

1. The nature of the monetary transfer between a taxpayer and a government; that is, it is voluntary, like a market transaction. (We will discuss user fees and revenues from gambling in this light.)
2. The type of the government that collects the revenue. (In this vein we will discuss democracy.)
3. The use to which the revenue is put. (Here we will discuss what can be termed the "bully theory.")
4. The source of the money to be transferred to the government. (Here we will examine the distinction between earned and unearned income, and the contention that we owe a portion of our earnings to the public, roughly in proportion to our ability to pay, on the grounds that it collaborates as a sort of silent partner.)

Finally we will consider the moral arguments for land-value taxation.

Not all attempts to justify public revenue fit easily into these categories. Because much of the argument of this paper is negative, our investigation starts with two examples of public revenue that are justifiable.

Pollution

Most people would probably agree that a nation is justified in holding polluters liable for the damage they inflict on the environment and in assessing them the cost of cleaning up. I do not wish to suggest that pollution abatement taxes are voluntary on the grounds that if the polluter wants to avoid them he may simply stop doing so. Of course he may, but this does not make them voluntary in any useful sense. If it did, then every conceivable tax, except perhaps some bizarre possibility like one on infants (I say on the infants, not on their parents), would be voluntary. A pollution tax is an example of the recovery by the public of a cost incurred.

User Fees

The city picks up my garbage on a weekly basis and properly disposes of it. For this service it charges a fee. If the choice of private haulers were allowed, then the charge would be a straightforward market transaction, whether a private provider or the city made it. Presumably because of public health concerns, such a choice is not allowed. Nonetheless it is still possible to determine a market value close enough that garbage fees can be conceived as a payment for benefits received.

These two examples, pollution tax and garbage collection, should provide sufficiently clear notions of reimbursing the government for a cost and paying it for benefits received.

Gambling

Various states have recently turned increasingly to proceeds from gambling for revenue. As of this writing, some thirty-six states run lotteries. The relatively unpopulous state of Iowa collects revenue from gambling on at least half-a-dozen riverboats docked on its shores on the Mississippi and Missouri Rivers. Pari-mutuel betting on horse and dog racing is springing up everywhere, even where there are no horse or dog tracks, through simulcasting. Apparently some American Indian tribes (viewed as nations within the nation) support themselves entirely through the operation of casinos. This is done to create jobs, and to obtain public revenue voluntarily for any number of laudable causes, of which economic development is usually the most prominent. Are these justifications adequate?

Gambling is an extremely inefficient way of raising public revenue. All sources of revenue require administrative overhead, but gambling receipts are always more wasteful than other taxes because they require not only the administrative overhead but also the cost of running the games themselves; such as slot and lottery machines in gas stations or grocery stores, stables of horses or dogs as well as the special structures in which to race them, the riverboats and huge casinos, and the labor to run these endeavors. The more resources that are wasted passing currency from one hand to another, the less they are available for the production of goods and services. This raises the hurdle that must be overcome by those who would advocate that the government encourage or engage in gambling for the sake of the economy. It is surely doubtful that the devotion to economic development of what little money the government collects from gambling could offset the effects of this waste over a long period of time and throughout a broad geographic area.

Gambling does, of course, create jobs. So does war. So would dumping all of the computers in the world into the Pacific Ocean. The creation of jobs that do not provide goods or services is the very reverse of economic development. Of course, gambling is entertainment and that is a service to those who partake of it voluntarily, which is just the point of the gambling promoters.

There would, however, need to be some justification for government to conduct that particular form of entertainment as opposed, say, to being in the movie business. And there would need to be a justification to burden that particular form of entertainment with a tax. That gambling is voluntary will not help the advocate of gambling taxes because every form of entertainment is voluntary. So is eating. No justification is forthcoming for the government to be in the entertainment business in the form of gambling or any other, but there might be a justification for the public to tax gambling. It is often alleged that legalized gambling in fact attracts or generates a criminal element that other forms of entertainment do not. If this is the case—and this is a big if—then the state might be justified in taxing gambling establishments to generate the revenue necessary to abate the "social pollution" that this criminal element constitutes, as taxation to abate environmental pollution is justified.

If we look closely at a particular gambling operation, we will see a source of revenue that is even more clearly justified. One year, the operators of the riverboat docked at Marquette, Iowa (called the *Miss Marquette,* appropriately enough), paid the city $958,510 in gambling taxes, a lease for the dock site, and admission taxes.[2] The gambling and admission taxes require no comment beyond what has been said above. But the assessment for the dock site is really three charges, all justified. It is a fee for the construction and maintenance of the dock itself by the city. This is a market transaction. It is also a charge for the special privilege of docking at this particular location, a privilege that cannot be granted to any more than one ship of this size. This is a special benefit. It is also a charge for the roads, police and fire protection, parking areas, and general use of the town adjoining the dock site. This is also a benefit for which the city may charge. Of course, this justification for the city's revenue from the dock site lease is not peculiar to gambling. The *Miss Marquette* could be a floating furniture store and the city would be entitled to the same revenue.

There is another way in which the public could generate revenue from gambling if it chose to do so. The state prohibits conducting gambling without a license and chooses to grant fewer licenses than are applied for. Indeed, there is now a bill before the Iowa state legislature that would impose a five-year moratorium on new licenses. The freedom to operate a gambling establishment without legal repercussions is therefore a special privilege created by the government, with a market value the government would be entitled to collect. It is a kind of benefit created by the government.

Democracy

It is sometimes said that citizenship—bringing an entitlement to vote, hold elected office, attempt to influence the political process, and enjoy the constitutional protections of free speech, equality before the law, unbiased courts, and the like—entails a moral obligation to obey whatever laws are enacted as the outcome of that political interaction. These laws would of course include the tax legislation. And if a citizen is paying what he is morally obligated to pay, then the payment is not theft. But will this do?

If the many protections enjoyed by citizens in a democracy implied that unanimous consent was required to pass laws, then of course everyone should be bound by them, but this is not the case. Citizens who do not vote and perhaps even people who vote lackadaisically, with little knowledge of the issues or the positions of the candidates, may be said to have given their tacit consent. This still does not add up to unanimous consent. Why should those who dissent conscientiously feel bound by laws to which they object just because they were enacted democratically?

Clearly many laws under any form of government are simply codifications of what is morally right and wrong independently of the government. Laws concerning theft and fraud are good examples. But an advocate of democracy theory must also hold that democratically derived laws entail an obligation to obey them even if they are not codifications of what would otherwise be morally obligatory. There are a number of very good reasons to obey laws no matter how they are enacted. For one, disobeying a law is nearly always highly imprudent. Normally we also have a variety of moral obligations to family, friends, employers, creditors, and others that we would risk not being in a position to discharge if we acted so imprudently as to violate a law. And to many, patriotism is a virtue, so it is our duty to be law-abiding citizens. All these reasons to obey the law are good in themselves. But of course they tend to dispel the notion that it is the democratic derivation of laws that obligates us to obey them.

An intuitive feeling may linger that we still have some special relationship to the law under democracy that we would not have under any other form of government. The basis for this intuition may be that, in the light of democratic safeguards and such rights as constitutional protection, equal freedom before the law, free speech, and unbiased courts, the likelihood of political persecution for expressing dissenting views is considerably reduced. If an individual ever has a prima facie duty to speak out against injustice, then in lessening a major prudential consideration to the contrary, democracy increases the reason for attending to this duty. Thus it is not an obligation to obey the law peculiar to democracy that we sense intuitively, but a duty to share our insights concerning what laws should or should not prevail. It is the fulfillment of this duty that democracy enables in the right to vote and seeks to protect with constitutional safeguards.

Nozick's Twist on the Democracy Theory

Robert Nozick has made an ingenious suggestion that, if tenable, might give a majority vote the moral force of unanimity, thus rescuing the democracy theory. Suppose that citizenship amounted to voluntarily exchanging shares in an individual's own rights for an equal amount of shares in the rights of others. If there are n people in a given society, each person would trade one of the shares in his rights with each of the other $n - 1$ people for one share in the other's rights. Each person would obtain a $1/n$th share in the rights of each of the other $n - 1$ people in the society, and of course each would retain a $1/n$th share in his own rights. The consequence would be that if more than half the population voted for a proposition in an election, then more than half the shares in each person's rights would have been cast for the winning side. In this way a simple majority would have the morally binding impact of unanimity. Nozick proudly announces

> In elaborating this eldritch tale we have arrived, finally, at what is recognizable as a modern state, with its vast panoply of powers over its citizens. Indeed, we have arrived at a *democratic state.*[3]

The problem with Nozick's tale, as he even points out, is that it depends on the tenability of the notion of a person's selling shares in his rights. An alternative claim might be that rights adhere to an individual unconditionally. That is part of the notion of having rights, and any example that might be adduced to show otherwise is not a case of selling rights, or shares in them, but a case of entering into a contract, which is an example of exercising one of the rights an individual has. Which conception of rights is correct?

While it would take us too far afield to examine the notion of rights thoroughly, there is at least one right that cannot be transferred in a voluntary transaction. It is the right itself to enter into transactions voluntarily. Suppose a society consists of two people. They agree to exchange their rights to engage in transactions. After they do so, do they then have the right to engage voluntarily in transactions? If so, then nothing has changed and no exchange has occurred. If not, what has occurred is not an exchange but a revocation of rights. Nozick's strange scenario is thus necessarily mere fantasy.

Biggest Bully on the Block

Some calamities are so horrendous that we would do almost anything to avert them. The most obvious one would be to allow our country to be conquered by a foreign power. Accordingly, when so threatened we turn to the biggest bully we can recruit to our aid. It is, of course, the government. In this case taxes that would otherwise be confiscatory—that is, government theft—are justified simply because the alternative is even worse. This justification has two limits. It is temporary and it applies only to threats of the most severe nature. The reason for its legitimacy, moreover, is not only that the government is the only bully big enough to protect us but also that anyone in his right mind would voluntarily agree to special taxes in such circumstances. The legitimacy of the bully justification explains why the Johnson administration sought to declare "war" on poverty and why the Clinton administration insists that the state of health care in the United States today is a "national emergency." The limitation of the government's scope gives the lie to these excuses for confiscatory taxation.

Earned Versus Unearned Income

If we can distinguish between earned and unearned income, then we might have a way to determine what citizens are entitled to keep and what the government may collect. This approach would seem promising. The idea is that income is either earned or—what is the alternative here?—stolen, or something much like that. Of course, each individual may keep what he earns. In its role of protector of rights the government is not only entitled but obligated to collect the unearned portion and return it to its rightful owner—the public at large perhaps? The idea sounds simple, fair, and quite justifiable. In fact it is a minefield.

These items, and probably more, have been advanced as candidates for the status of unearned income:

1. Gifts (over a certain amount, from anyone who is not a relative, from outside the nuclear family; the variations go on and on)
2. Inheritances (over a certain amount, from such sources as non-relatives)
3. The appreciation of art treasures (over what the present holder paid; over what the first purchaser paid, and so forth)

4. The temporarily high market values of certain commodities that a natural disaster has placed in short supply
5. The appreciation of anything whatsoever that has gone up in price since it last changed hands
6. The multimillion-dollar-per-year compensation of the CEOs of large corporations (or the excess of their compensation over what is received by lower -evel executives who are just as smart and work just as hard)
7. The salaries of sports heroes (or the excess of their salaries over what an "ordinary" person who worked just as hard could make)
8. Excess profits
9. Interest
10. Land values, but particularly the appreciation of land since it last changed hands

The length of this list might arouse suspicions that in our quest for unearned income something may have gotten a bit out of hand.

The first two items on the list, gifts and inheritances, deserve special comment. If the donor earned *x* and gives *x* to the recipient, then if the government takes it from the recipient, even on the grounds that he did not earn it, which is true, it would seem that the government has violated the donor's right to dispose of what he did earn. Thus we see a difficulty already in an idea that seemed so innocent: It is not clear that the government can collect all unearned income and at the same time leave the harmless disposition of earned incomes to those who are entitled to them.

This difficulty aside, a single criterion is surely needed by which all holdings can be sorted into the two classes of earned and unearned.

The criterion implicit in the intellectual exercise that generated the long list here is that what is acquired by exertion is earned and what is acquired without exertion is unearned. No less a figure than John Stuart Mill has written approvingly of "that equitable principle, of proportion between remuneration and exertion."[4] An apparent consequence is that genuine earnings are limited to what would be made by "the typical day laborer"[5] with the same effort. Let us call this "the exertion view of earning." If the excess over earnings were spent by the government on social welfare, this view would lead to socialism. If it were spent on palaces for the rulers, or something of the sort, the result would be worse. Other consequences are absurd. One is that if a person works very hard doing nothing of any value (repeatedly digging a hole in the backyard and filling it in again could be an example), he may have *earned* more than the very productive person who does his job with ease. It is also important to note what status land would have in relation to this view. Suppose that I save $10,000 from my earnings at day labor and buy a lot with it. Because the land was purchased with the proceeds from my earnings, it would fall on the earned side of the distinction. But if it appreciated after I purchased it, its appreciation and only its appreciation would be unearned.

The way out of these difficulties is to recognize that exertion is meritorious not for its own sake but for the sake of what is produced. It is not the input to human endeavor but its output that matters. Mill applauds "the recognition, in each person, of a right to the exclusive disposal of what he or she has produced."[6] The measure of earning is how much the rest of the world wants what the producer makes, and that is its value on the market. The producer is entitled to the market value of his product, not because he worked so hard, but because it would not have existed had he not done so. Call this "the production view of earning."

With this view the list of unearned incomes dwindles to almost nothing. For lack of a standard that profits and prices are in excess of, they cannot be excessive. The items that we produce go up and down in price as they become rare or plentiful, but that is just the way the market rewards and punishes those who produce and sell goods that are wanted more or less by the rest of us. Interest is simply the market value of a certain class of goods that have been produced.

Gifts, inheritances, and land remain alone on the unearned side of the distinction. The recipients of gifts and inheritances are entitled to them because the donor has the right to dispose of his earnings as he wishes. That leaves land. It is not just that the holder of a particular piece of land did not produce it, for land is not the kind of thing that can be produced.[7] It, and its rent, differ not in degree but in kind from earnings.

Rent, however, is as much a market phenomenon as are the sources of income that are on the earned side of the distinction. It is not stolen. The explanation of why the government may and must collect unearned income therefore collapses. This way of looking at matters throws light on why the government's taking of things other than rent is theft. It does not provide a positive reason for government collection of rent, but at least we have come through the minefield with limbs intact. The positive arguments must wait until we have considered one more very prominent theory of public revenue.

Ability to Pay

Much popular discussion concerning the appropriateness of various schemes for obtaining public revenue centers around the "ability to pay." In the absence of some theory about what an individual's liability is in the first place, one person's superior ability to pay does not make him any more liable for higher taxes than another less liable.

The notion of ability to pay is so ambiguous as to be nearly incoherent. So we must distinguish between "actual ability to pay" and "potential ability to pay." This distinction will help only a little but it will bring out the problem.

Suppose we made a serious attempt to tax people on the basis of what they could actually pay. First we must decide whether all of a person's assets make him able to pay or whether only liquid assets count. Suppose we opt for all assets. Then each tax year we determine how much revenue is needed and we reduce the wealth of as many of the wealthiest people as necessary until enough revenue is obtained. To picture this, we lop off the top of the pyramid each year. Of course, each year the people who believe that they may be subject to taxes try to guess how much will be taken and they spend that amount on frivolous pleasures. Pretty soon there is no top of the pyramid to lop off. Would anyone really want to base taxation on actual ability to pay? On the other hand, suppose we attempt to tax people on the basis of their potential ability to pay. To do this we must estimate for each person how much he would be able to pay given all of his abilities, all of his life circumstances, and all of his obligations whether they be formal or informal. We must know him better than he knows himself so as not to overlook some hidden potentiality or weakness. Is it humanly, never mind bureaucratically, possible to make this estimate accurately for everyone?

The most colossal attempt to implement ability to pay is the United States income tax. The entire, endless debate that occupies the most brilliant minds in Congress session after session is merely fruitless vacillation between something we don't want, actual ability to pay, and something we can't have, potential ability to pay.[8]

Suppose, contrary to fact, that the notion of ability to pay is clear enough to be the basis for tax liability. Can it be supported morally? While some of us may secretly harbor a larcenous sympathy with Robin Hood, if such a person existed he was, after all, a thief. Some argument must be produced to show that we have some sort of obligation to the public that is somehow not magically connected to our relative abilities to pay. In transactions between individuals, financial obligations and claims spring from goods and services provided and received. It must be shown that when the government is one of the parties to the transaction, or even the absence of anything resembling a transaction, for that matter, your mere possession of more wealth or a higher income is justification enough for the government to take more from you.

Of course, there are arguments that purport to show just this. The most important historically and the most formidable is based on an appeal to the notion of society as a "silent partner."

The conception of society as a silent partner is often brought in to buttress the idea that much wealth is unearned, and indeed the portion of wealth that is allegedly attributable to the collaboration of society is sometimes labeled "unearned." But we have already examined the distinction between earned and unearned wealth and identified a portion that is unearned. What is at stake here is whether the contribution of society to the production of *earned wealth* justifies the government's taking some of that.

It can be said that in an advanced state of society in which the production of considerable wealth is possible, wealth is not produced by individuals in isolation. Indeed it takes remarkable ingenuity and perseverance for a Robinson Crusoe merely to survive. An individual's production of wealth is due in large part to the contribution society makes to the ability to produce. Society is a silent partner working in concert with individuals to help them produce more wealth than they could have in isolation. Society is, therefore, justified in claiming some part of the wealth people produce, and it will be in proportion to ability to pay because the people who have produced the most, those who have lifted themselves the farthest above the level of a Robinson Crusoe, have obviously benefited the most from the partnership with society at large.

Consider a brain surgeon. Presume he has a high income. He is surely a recipient of the utmost benefit from society. Without the last couple of centuries of medical advances, the profession that supports him so amply could not even have existed. Without the vast network of emergency providers that exists, potential patients for his craft would not live long enough for his skills to be of any service to them. Without a division of labor sufficiently advanced, he could not have spent so many years concentrating exclusively on the development of his surgical skills to become a brain surgeon. Surely he owes society for all these benefits. So he has no legitimate complaint when his silent partner, society, comes calling once a year to collect its portion of his earnings.

But he does have a legitimate complaint. Let it be granted that over the last couple of centuries the occupation of brain surgery has benefited more from the advancement of society than has that of ditchdigging. After all, brain surgery as we know it today did not exist two centuries ago. Let it be granted that in general the most remunerative occupations benefit more from the social environments in which they are practiced than ditchdigging does. Should society expect more from the brain surgeon than from the ditchdigger? Yes. Is the government justified in taking more in taxes from the brain surgeon than from the ditchdigger? No. The brain surgeon has already paid more than the ditchdigger. He has put more value onto the market than the ditchdigger. Someone has been saved from a stroke by the brain surgeon, whereas from the ditchdigger's efforts, someone else has only a hole in the ground.

To make the matter clearer, consider the surgeon's patients. It would be absurd for the government to tax each of his patients for having received treatment that would not have existed were it not for the current state of the medical arts, the contribution of our silent partner, society. It is no less absurd to ask the brain surgeon to compensate society for contributing as a silent partner.

The advancement and organization of society makes it possible for some people to earn exceptional wealth, but only by putting into the exchange goods or services that are of exceptional value, those goods and services that other members of society have received. The exceptional people have already paid, and society has already received, what is owed to society as a silent partner. The market value of the goods and services an individual puts into the exchange is not merely the basis on which he is paid but is also the measure of the value to society of what he has provided. If the market value of what a person puts into the exchange is higher because society has been a silent partner, then the market value of what society receives is higher by exactly the same amount. The ledger is even. No justification for taxation on ability to pay is provided by the concept of society as a silent partner.

Let us pause for a moment to speculate on the pathology of the ability-to-pay fetish. Jealousy may be one motivation for it. Another may be the failure to distinguish between tax liability and the personal duty of private charity. Those who have more may well have the duty to share more with those less fortunate, but to coerce them to do so is theft, plain and simple. Finally, the reliance on ability to pay as a criterion for taxation indicates a lack of awareness of a clear alternative. The alternative, of course, is cost-benefit. We have already seen examples of benefits and costs for which some individuals owe the public. We turn now to the most pervasive form of cost-benefit from which government revenue can be justified.

Land-Value Taxation

The classic statement of the moral and economic justification of government collection of land rent is Henry George's *Progress and Poverty.*[9] George defines three fundamental categories of existence. There is land, which includes not just the dry parts of the surface of the earth, but all of nature in its original state unmodified by human endeavor. There is man. And there are the things people craft from the resources of our universe, irrespective of whether they are improvements attached to land, such as buildings and crops, or movable artifacts. On this tripartite ontology George constructed his single-tax system, according to which all public revenue should be obtained from land-value taxation.

> The moral rationale for George's system rests upon two logically independent but complementary arguments, one primary and the other secondary. The first of these is the argument that since God created the earth for the use of all men, no one has the right to arrogate to himself exclusive access to any portion of it without indemnifying those thereby denied access. The indemnity, amounting to the market value of the advantage, namely, ground rent, is seen as a divinely provided fund that should be used by the community to meet general social needs.
>
> The secondary argument is that inasmuch as the market value of raw

> land is wholly a social product, that value should be appropriated by society as the most "natural" and equitable source of public revenue.[10]

First consider the second of these arguments, and call it the benefit argument. The measure of the benefit to be expected is the market value of land. The value of all things that are bought and sold depends partly on social demand, but land is unique in not being produced; its market value is entirely a social product.

The territorial nature of many of the legitimate functions of government, such as police and fire protection, makes this clear. Whoever lives in the jurisdiction of a government that provides such services cannot help but be the benefactor. Charging the possessor of a site the market value of the benefits accruing to its position in the nexus of commercial and governmental interactions is simply a fee for these benefits, of which land rent is the economic manifestation. The site lease the owners of the *Miss Marquette* pay is a thinly disguised form of land-value taxation. The city would have the same justification for it even if the *Miss Marquette* were based on land in the narrow sense, although the amount might be less because then it would not enjoy the luxury of cruising on the Mississippi.

Because government makes land valuable by its beneficial action, it should always be possible to fund government programs by collecting this value unless the program is not worth what it costs. That a government program fails to produce land value sufficient to pay for itself is because the public does not want it enough to pay for it. In this way using land-value taxation as the sole source of government revenue would check wasteful spending.

A fee for municipal garbage collection seems to be an exception because it is justified independently of these considerations. Of course, if no charge were made for garbage collection its value would accrue to land, but there are good environmental reasons for charging separately for garbage collection by the amount of garbage each resident sets out for pickup. But charging by the bag, so to speak, may be viewed as land-value taxation from a different point of view. It is rental of space in a landfill, that is, land-value taxation. Thus the example of charging a user fee for garbage collection may not be an exception to the rule that land-value taxation is the most appropriate way of financing all government services.

It will be objected that all government revenue must come from what is produced, because that is all there is, and that the silent-partner argument is also based on government collection of benefits people derive from society. How can the silent-partner argument fall while the reasoning under consideration here stands? The answer is that land value, the market phenomenon of rent, definitively separates out that exact quantity of what is produced that is directly attributable to the one factor of production that is not produced, land, whose value can only come from society. The silent-partner argument, on the other hand, provides no clue as to just what part of something produced is due to society and what to individual enterprise. It is worth noting here that land-value taxation is the only form of public revenue whose quantity is determined by the market rather than by government fiat.

The primary argument, called here the cost argument, is equally unassailable. What is crucial to it is the assertion that we have a right to use land. Can there really be any doubt about this? It is only by the use of land that we can satisfy our most basic needs. The process of obtaining the requisites of life through the application of our industry on the earth is the indispensable condition of human existence. George's vision of the three fundamental components of the material world is compelling here.

If all of us have the right to use land, and if this right is equal (as rights of this fundamental nature must surely be), then whoever excludes others from land with any value whatsoever must indemnify the public for its loss. Land value is a measure of the cost to the rest of us from being excluded from its use. Aside from aesthetic concerns, is not the justification the same as for taxes on polluters? We are entitled morally to require polluters to pay precisely because we have a right to land, and economically that of course includes the sky, streams, and the rest of nature. If we can demand indemnification for damage to the environment, may we not equally demand indemnification for deprivation of access to land? The answer seems clearly positive.

Final Comment

We have sought justification for the public, through its legal arm the government, to collect revenue from individual citizens. We have seen that there is a clear justification for land-value taxation and for other taxes under extreme circumstances. It might be objected that the question of justification has been posed exactly backwards, that the real question should be: What is the justification for the government not to confiscate what there is and distribute it in a far fairer manner? The response is that market-based distribution is fair. One argument that has been given here for the fairness of market-based distribution is that it rests on the production view of earning, and throughout the remainder of what has preceded this comment the fairness of market-based distribution has been assumed implicitly.

Skeptics of the fairness of market-based distribution generally express their discomfort with it by raising examples of distribution that is ostensibly based on the market and apparently quite unfair. While it would be beyond the scope of this paper to consider all such examples, the response to a large class of them may be illustrated by considering one member of this class. Suppose that one summer a remote village suffers a drought and all of the wells in town go dry except for one. Since water is necessary for life, the market will allow the person who has the working well to charge his fellow villagers what it would cost to truck water in from the nearest place where it is readily available, or an amount that would reduce their living standards to no better than bare subsistence, whichever is less. But this is not fair.

The example is well chosen for its appearance of utter simplicity masking considerable complications, but we are now in position to address it. The well that is working, just like all the dry wells, actually consists of two components. It is a combination of a structure, both above and more importantly below the ground, that is man-made, and a location that is not produced and is in fact land. If it does not differ from the dry wells in structure but has water only because of its location, then all of the villagers have equal rights to the water because they have equal rights to land. Whether they choose to allow the market to reign free and collect the rent or assert their equal rights simply by insisting that everyone be allowed to use the well free of charge is immaterial morally. On the other hand, if the water in the good well is due to a structural difference that could be replicated in the other wells, then the person who has the good well is entitled to whatever he can obtain for the water. The more outrageous his charges, the more reward to those who are first to modify their wells so that they can get in on the bounty, and the better for the public in general. In this case the old expression "the cure for high prices is high prices" is apt. If the productivity of the good well is due to a structural difference that cannot or may not be replicated in other wells, such as patent protection, for example, then the price its holder can charge is due to monopoly, and monopoly charges are not based on the market. In any case, the recognition of equal rights to land coupled with individual rights to what is produced unravels the puzzle.

Notes

1. Also see Jesus' parable of the talents, Matthew 25: 14–30. (A talent is a unit of weight of gold or silver used as money.)
2. *Des Moines Register,* February 19, 1998.
3. Robert Nozick, *Anarchy, State and Utopia* (New York: Basic Books, 1974), 290.
4. John Stuart Mill, *Principles of Political Economy* (1848; New York: D. Appleton, 1884), 160.
5. Barbara Fried, "Wilt Chamberlain Revisited: Nozick's 'Justice in Transfer' and the Problem of Market-Based Distribution," *Philosophy and Public Affairs* 24, no. 3 (Summer 1995), 242. Also see my rejoinder, "Land and Human Endowments," *Reason Papers* 22 (Fall 1997).
6. Mill, *Principles,* 171. The proximity of the two passages quoted in the work of an author of Mill's stature illustrates my calling the distinction between earned and unearned income a "minefield."
7. "Land cannot be produced" is admittedly a tautology because of the economic definition of "land." That there exists such a thing as land, however, is a fact of the utmost importance: I do not have the foggiest notion of what it would be like if it were otherwise.
8. I submit that we should also not want to tax according to potential ability to pay, even if it were possible.
9. Henry George, *Progress and Poverty* (1879; New York: Robert Schalkenbach Foundation, 1966).
10. Robert V. Andelson and Mason Gaffney, "Seligman and His Critique from Social Utility," in *Critics of Henry George,* Robert V. Andelson, ed. (Rutherford, NJ: Fairleigh Dickinson University Press, 1979), 275–276.

14

Fred E. Foldvary

The Ethics of Rent

Rent is a source of public revenue that does not engender any economic damage. But is it morally right to take revenue for government from only one class of owners? And is there a conflict or is there harmony between what is morally right and what is economically sound?

What Rent Is

The term "rent" has several meanings. The classical meaning is the return on land as a factor or resource of production. Since it was recognized that landowners as landowners receive rent without having to do anything for it but have title to land, the term became extended to "economic rent," meaning any income beyond that which is needed to put a factor into production. More recently, the term "rent seeking" was introduced to mean the economic rents taken by whoever receives government privileges, subsidies, and other transfers.[1] Popularly, "rent" also means a payment for the use of property owned by others, as in renting a car or apartment; a synonym for this meaning is "rental." Unless otherwise qualified, the term "rent" in this chapter refers specifically to land rent. "Economic rent" will take the definition just given, and "rental" will refer to payments for the use of any property and (as discussed below) to land rent due to the presence of public or civic works.

"Land" in economics includes all natural resources, everything prior to alteration by human action. The narrower meaning is the solid surface of the earth. Here, "land" will refer to economic land, which embraces all natural resources and opportunities, including those not traditionally associated with land. The various forms of land include sites on the surface of the earth (whether solid or water); all minerals, oil, water, virgin soil, and other material resources beneath the surface; air space; the spectrum of radio and television; the earth's wildlife, the genetic stock of the planet (all the genetic information present in life); and usable locations in outer space, such as satellite orbits.

Material land becomes a capital good after it is extracted, since it is then altered by the process of production. But some forms of land do not get altered. Space, whether the three-dimensional space around the earth or radio frequencies, does not become changed when it is used. Space therefore remains land regardless of the alterations of the matter in that space.

Rent is the return on land, the income the owner receives in the role of landowner, aside from the parts of the income due to the owner's role of manager receiving wages and the return from being also the owner of the capital goods on the land. What determines the rent of a particular plot of land or amount of material resource? Beginning economics students would respond "supply and demand," but that is no answer; these are only the tools used to determine the answer. What we really want to know is what determines the supply and demand.

The supply of land is fixed by nature, and the demand depends on the productivity of the land and the population. Consider two cornfields of equal size. Upon application of the same amount and quality of labor and capital goods to either, one produces a hundred bushels per season and the other produces eighty bushels. If you can get the eighty-bushel land for free, then you would pay twenty bushels to use the hundred-bushel land, so that the returns to labor after rent are the same. Competition will equalize the returns after rent, and the extra product is land rent. The market rent is thus twenty bushels.

Rent, then, is due to the difference or differential between the productivity of better and worse lands. The least productive land in use for a particular product is called the "extensive margin of production." If the margin has free land, then all the productivity above that of the margin is rent. There is also an "intensive margin" with land that is used more intensely; more workers are hired to work a plot of land until the productivity of the last worker is the same as that of the worker at the extensive margin. The margins of production apply to all products and types of land. Economists say that the rent can also be the "marginal product" of land, or the extra product obtained from using a bit more land with equivalent tools and other means.

In the case of material land such as minerals and oil, the rent is the annualized value of the resources in the ground, before extraction or preparation. The value of material resources is based on the regional market (such as for water) or global market (such as for oil) for the resources, and the rent is also based on the location, which determines the cost of extraction and delivery.

We can see with a simple agricultural model the dynamic economic impact of site rents, those due to location. Picture an unpopulated island where we are going to produce one good—corn. There are ten grades of land. On the best land, we can grow ten bushels of corn per week; the second land grows nine bushels; and so on to the worst land, where the output is zero. How will site rents affect the settlers?

The first settlers go to the best land. While there is free ten-bushel land, rent is zero, so wages are ten. When the ten-bushel land is all settled, immigrants go to the nine-bushel land. Wages in the nine-bushel land equal nine while free land is available. Wages in the ten-bushel land must also be ten, since labor is mobile. If you offer less, nobody will come, and if you offer a bit more than nine, everybody in the nine-bushel land will want to work for the higher bidder. Competition among workers makes wages the same all over (we assume all workers are alike). So that extra bushel in the ten-bushel land, after paying nine for labor, is rent.

When the margin of production moves to the eight-bushel land, wages drop to eight. Rent is now one on the nine-bushel land and two on the ten-bushel land. As the population grows and the margin moves to less productive lands, wages keep going down and rent goes up. When the margin is rather unproductive, wages are at poverty or subsistence levels, and all the extra production goes to the landowners as rent. This illustration explains how there can be poverty in the midst of wealth.

We can also now see that wages are determined at the margin of production. That is the "law of wages." The wage at the margin sets the wage for all lands. The production in the better lands, that which is left after paying wages, goes to rent. That is the "law of rent." If settlers can get land to rent and sell for higher prices later rather than using it now, land speculation will claim additional lands and make the margin move further out than without speculation, lowering wages and raising rent even more.

Capital goods and technology increase the productivity of land, but do not affect the relation of rent to wages. Both wages and rent increase with increasing productivity, but the worker must pay for the capital goods out of his increased wages. At a rent-free margin, wages will not rise as much as productivity after paying for the capital goods, yet rent in the superior lands will rise in proportion to productivity, since the capital goods are paid for out of the wages, which are the same everywhere. Technology, capital goods, and an increase in productivity through growth in trade and a decrease in interference in trade thus do not alter the basic relationship between wages and rent, except possibly to change the relative share taken by rent.

Governments can and do compound the inequality of income with heavy taxes on wage income and lighter taxes on rent. But even if the rates of taxation were the same, taxation makes labor income that much poorer. A progressive income tax would take higher percentages of both wage and rent income, but in practice much explicit rental income is offset by costs, whether real or legal fictions, that offset the revenue. Also, implicit rental income on land occupied by the owner generally escapes taxation.

This explanation describes natural rents, those due to the opportunities provided by nature. A second source of rent, complementary to natural rent, is human activity. Activity rents derive from population, commerce, and technology, which increase the demand for space by making space more productive. Population growth may have increasing returns, such as when a city of greater density is more productive per worker because of more efficient transportation or the division of labor becomes more productive, and these increasing returns can offset somewhat the decreasing returns due to the movement of the extensive margin to less productive lands. Better technology has made the electromagnetic spectrum more useful for radio, television, communication, and remote controls. A larger population and more commerce place a greater demand on the limited amount of such spectra. But the people and technology still use those frequencies provided by nature.

The third source of rent (or rental, since it is not economic rent, which will be discussed below) is territorial infrastructure, that is, the civic goods that government typically provides, although private communities also provide them (these three categories of rent are recognized also by Nicolaus Tideman).[2] Streets, highways, outdoor lighting, water delivery, security, fire protection, parks, and other public works make land more desirable and increase the demand for its use, increasing the rent and land value. Civic rentals complement activity rents, since the public works enable population and commerce to be more productive.

Deriving a Rational Ethic

Besides an understanding of rent, the ethics of rent requires that there be a moral standard by which to make ethical judgments. For there to be objective, universal propositions about the ethics of rent, the ethic they are based on needs to be objective, rational, and universal. It must be independent of cultural and personal viewpoints. It should be derived from reason. And the ethic also must be universally applicable to all human action.

Such a universal ethic will be traced out here briefly, on the basis and by extension of my presentation in *The Soul of Liberty*.[3] It may be possible to derive the ethic in other ways, such as from the framework of Aristotle's ethics. My approach is based on the framework set up by John Locke in his *Two Treatises on Government*.[4]

Locke's basic statement on natural law is stated in his *Second Treatise:*

> The state of nature has a law of nature to govern it which obliges every one; and reason, which is that law, teaches all mankind who will but consult it that, being all equal and independent, no one ought to harm another in his life, health, liberty, or possessions.[5]

The "state of nature" is human society apart from government. It also refers to human nature, apart from any culture. Locke is saying that human nature generates a moral "law of nature" or natural moral law. How do we know what it is? When Locke says "reason, which is that law," he means that natural law is based on reason. Natural law is thus distinguished from laws that are derived from authority, such as tradition, power, or whim. Critics of natural law claim that those who derive it are really just basing it on their own personal views, but Locke says that reason "teaches all mankind who will but consult it." He means that any person who "consults it" by examining the derivation will be either taught the law, or able to teach others if they discover flaws in this reasoning.

From what aspects of human nature does the moral law of nature derive? Locke says that natural law flows from a fact universal among persons: "being all equal and independent."

What does it mean for individuals to be "independent," when human beings are socially and economically dependent on others? The premise of independence is not economic or social, but biological. Each person is a self-directing biological unit; thinking and feeling occur individually. Henry George also based "the right of a man to himself" on "the fact that each particular pair of hands obey a particular brain . . . that each man is a definite, coherent, independent whole."[6]

The premise of independence is foundational for methodological individualism, a cornerstone of economics. As James Buchanan and Gordon Tullock state the case, "all theorizing, all analysis, is resolved finally into considerations faced by the individual person as decision maker."[7] Additionally, the independence premise implies subjectivism in values. Each person has his own personal values, interests, feelings, and views, and there is no basis in nature for values other than those held by individuals from their desires, beliefs, and circumstances. As Carl Menger put it: "Value is thus nothing inherent in goods."[8]

What could Locke have meant by saying that people are "all equal"? Again, the premise cannot be economic or social, but is biological (or anthropological). Human beings are biologically endowed with the capacity for volition, self-awareness, and reason. Each one is an attribute of the human species, as a capacity or capability, whether or not actualized at some moment. Such an ability is not the same as intelligence, which is a matter of degree. It is the ability of each individual to have conscious control over his acts, be aware of his being, imagine the consequences of his and others' acts, and be able to make conscious choices on the basis of such imagined consequences. Choice, so central to economic and political theory and practice, is a common attribute of people, and therefore an attribute equally possessed by everyone. It is this capacity to choose, in purposeful and rational action, that makes people equal. As Buchanan put it, "each person counts for one, and for as much as any other."[9] Henry George also held that nature endows humanity with equality:

> She makes no discriminations among men, but is to all absolutely impartial. She knows no distinction between master and slave, king and subject, saint and sinner. All men to her stand upon an equal footing, and have equal rights.[10]

On the premises of independence and equality, Locke concludes with a statement of natural moral law: "[N]o one ought to harm another in his life, health, liberty, or possessions." In this passage, however, Locke does not provide the derivation, nor does he deduce natural law in any of his writing. It is nevertheless possible to construct such a derivation. The following is a brief summary of the deduction I presented in *The Soul of Liberty.* This ethic, formulating natural law into a set of rules, I term the "universal ethic" (UE).[11]

First, consider acts with only beneficial external effects. A "benefit" is defined as a direct, welcomed ingress or entering into the domain of another person. Benefits are acts that not only make others better off from their viewpoint, but involve some transfer into the property of the recipients, such as giving people a gift or helping them do something. If you do something that someone else likes, but there is no transfer or ingress, then the act is an incidental gain rather than a direct benefit.

Since all values are subjective and originate in personal ethics, the values assigned by the UE originate with personal goods, evils, and neutrals. Hence, for external benefits, the UE must assign such acts the value "good." If the UE assigned the value "evil" to benefits, it would contradict the premise of independence. The act cannot be neutral since neutrality implies the absence of "good." Only an assignment of "good" is consistent with the premises.

It is possible, of course, for some particular financial benefit to be tied to conditions that the recipient feels are unfavorable or even coercive. Thus, the whole situation may not be a benefit, but given the other elements of a situation, a particular benefit is good in being preferred to not having it.

Note that we now have a UE rule for "good": Acts that benefit others are morally good. The values are taken from personal values, but the rule itself is independent of personal views. The UE itself has not created or constructed any values. This assignment of good is consistent with the principles of normative individualism. As Viktor Vanberg put it: "From the perspective of normative individualism social states are judged to be 'good' to the extent that the individuals concerned judge them to be good."[12] (This holds for pure good not mixed with aspects that are evil for others, as explained below.)

The second case to be examined is an act that does not affect others. From a social point of view, there is no logical basis for assigning to such acts a moral value of evil, since that would be a purely subjective, individual value. There is also no logical basis for necessarily judging such acts as good. They are, therefore, assigned a value of neutral, meaning neither morally good nor evil. It is least arbitrary to assign the value of neutral to an act that only affects the actor. If doing damage to the actor also hurts others, the act is judged according to how it affects them.

We commonly regard some self-directed activities such as spiritual improvement as inherently good, and other activities, such as ingesting unhealthy substances or having some negative prejudice against some group, as inherently bad. These values reflect widely shared intersubjective sentiments, but an objective universal ethic is by premise independent of such personal and cultural views. One person, for example, might regard another's spiritual quest as a waste of time. There is no objective ground for assigning the value "good" to any particular type of activity or thought. The independence of minds thus results in the rule for moral good as giving welcomed benefits; it precludes categorizing activities as good or bad. This does not invalidate any cultural or personal standard for good; the designation of neutral is for the universal ethic, whose application is for social policy and social justice, rather than for personal or religious values. By extension, if there are two people and they both choose to perform an act with no outside effect beyond the two, it is neutral with respect to the others.

To generalize: Acts that are performed among consenting persons and with no external effects on others cannot be assigned the value of evil. If the acts are perceived as mutually beneficial within the group, or by at least one recipient of another's acts as a benefit, then the acts are good; otherwise they are neutral.

The remaining case is when others suffer an injury, feeling that they are left worse off. Injuries are of two types. One is an "offense," an injury that depends entirely on the subjective values of the recipient—on his beliefs, biases, interests, attitudes, and culture or worldview. The other type, "harms" (explained below), are injuries that do not depend entirely on personal views.

If the UE assigned offensive acts a value of evil, then evils would depend on personal views, and the UE would depend on personal and cultural values. But this would contradict the criterion that the UE as a rational ethic must be nonarbitrary, and independent of any personal or cultural values. In order to be logically consistent with this criterion, the UE must assign to offenses a value of neutral. They may be evil by some people's personal values, but the UE neutralizes the acts in order for the UE rules to remain independent of purely subjective values and rules.

The incidental gains mentioned here, acts that others find pleasing but do not involve an ingress such as a gift or direct aid, are also assigned the value "neutral," for the same reason. Suppose some act is offensive to some people, but regarded as pleasing by others. In either case, there is no invasion or ingress, so the moral value is neutral, since whether the act is pleasing or displeasing depends entirely on a personal view.

Other injuries, not dependent for their effect on the mental views of the victim, have some origin external to the recipient. The act consists of a penetration or intrusion from the outside into the person, domain, or property of the recipient. Such an act is an invasion, taking or destroying the property of another.

Since an invasion consists of a harm that is coercively imposed, it will be called a "coercive harm." It is possible to do physical harm to someone with the person's consent, in which case it is not a coercive harm. Physical harm done to the actor is, by definition, not coercive. The only acts eligible for the value "evil" are acts of coercive harm, which are invasions.

The universal ethic can now be summarized by three rules:

1. An act is good if and only if it benefits others.
2. An act is evil if and only if it coercively harms others by invading their domains.
3. All other acts are neutral.

If some situation contains a mixture of good and evil, the good does not cancel out the evil. If a thief, for example, steals money and gives it to charity, the theft is still an evil. Similarly, government persecution of some people is evil even if that government also does things that some people find pleasing.

After derivation of the universal ethic, the concept of a "right" can now be given some meaning. The right to do or have *X* means that it is evil to negate *X*, such as by destroying or taking it away. The right to own property means that taking away property is evil. A right is therefore the correlative of a moral wrong; if something is morally wrong, then doing it violates someone's right. Murder is evil, so doing it violates the right of someone to live.

The right to liberty implies that arbitrary restrictions on the possession and income of justly acquired property is evil. An oppressive government violates the right to liberty by restricting and taxing peaceful and honest action.

An aggressor who invades and coerces another person puts himself in a superior position to his victim, upsetting the equal status of human beings. It is, therefore, not evil for the victim to defend himself, since the defense restores moral equality. The defender may thus properly use force to resist aggression. But it is wrong to injure or punish an attacker for revenge, beyond what is needed for defense and restitution. ("To me belongeth vengeance. . . ."—Deut. 32:35; "Vengeance is mine; I will repay. . . ."—Romans 12:19.)

Ethics Applied to Natural Rent

The universal ethic will now be applied to the ownership of natural rent, rents derived purely from nature. The primary question is, how is proper ownership of property determined?

Let us first examine property to determine its basic categories.

The classical factors or resources of production are land, labor, and capital goods. The ultimate and original factors are land and labor. Labor is human exertion in the production of wealth. The ownership of wages implies the ownership of labor, which in turn implies the ownership of the worker, that is, his time and body. If one person can properly own another person, they are not in a position of equality. The Lockean premise of equality implies that there are no inherently inferior and superior individuals. If no one owns another, then each person equally owns his or her own self.[13]

Self-ownership extends to labor, its wages, and its products. A worker therefore has complete rights to his wages; it is morally evil forcibly to take away any part of someone's wages. But self-ownership does not extend to land, since land is not produced by labor. The premise of equality implies that human beings are in an equal moral position with respect to land. For one person rightfully to claim more than others would put him in a superior, unequal status.

Suppose workers are getting low wages, while the owner of a firm is making a large profit. Does this violate equality? If there is a pure free market, then the worker is typically receiving what he contributes to production. That other workers earn higher wages does not violate moral equality, which involves the equal right to apply labor and keep wages. Moral equality is an equality of opportunity, not of outcomes. Likewise, in a pure free market, that some owners of firms are making large profits does not violate equality, since the profits are the result of production and innovation, bringing new goods to market.

Property is anything that can be controlled or claimed, and ownership consists of rights to property. Ownership is a bundle of rights. The ownership of land is separable into rights of control (meaning use and exchange) and rights to the rent. The benefit of land is its return or rent. Control is only a means to the benefit. Equal benefits from land can therefore be established by an equal ownership of its natural rent.

Henry George wrote that morality required making land common property[14] and "abolish[ing] private property in land."[15] This could only mean the abolition of the individual ownership of its rent, not the abolition of rights of control, for George also declared that "The equal right of all men to the use of land is as clear as their equal right to breathe the air."[16] Rights of use are a strand of rights of control, along with the right to transfer possession. George also recognized that the right of labor is tied to the right of land use, hence control: "The denial of the equal right to the use of land is necessarily the denial of the right of labor to its own produce."[17] Security of tenure is needed to maintain the incentive to invest labor in capital goods for future yields.[18]

George identifies "the fundamental wrong" not as a control but as "the continuous increase of rent" in the hands of those "who do nothing to earn it."[19] This is made clear by George's statement that "the value of land expresses in exact and tangible form the right of the community in land held by an individual."[20] The land value is its capitalized rent. The rights of the community are to its rent; this leaves to the individual the holding of land, which is control. As George stated, individual and collective rights are reconciled by making the "fixity of tenure"—rights of control—conditional on paying "rent for the benefit of the community." This accomplishes and is what George means by "the equal rights of all to the use of land."[21] George refers to the East Indian grant of land that says, "To whomsoever the soil at any time belongs, to him belong the fruits of it."[22] The fruits refer to the yield of the soil, the "soil" being a metaphor for the rights to yields that attach to land. It is the rent, the fruit of the soil, that is the rightful common property. Having paid the community, the proper owner, its due, the title holder may exercise full rights of control, so long as the use does not coercively harm others.

Title to lots of equal value is therefore not needed to satisfy equality, and indeed such a condition is impossible and would be wasteful if tried. Population is a flow as well as a stock, as babies are born and people die. Continuous repossession is infeasible and not necessary when the rent is equally shared. As noted above, capital goods are ultimately produced from land and labor. Once the rent of land is shared, then the possessor's moral obligation with respect to the land is paid. A worker is then entitled to keep what he produces with labor on that land. After applying labor to material land, the property is no longer land, and others no longer have any rights to that property. Hence, to the creator belong the rights of his creation.

Since it is morally wrong or evil to deprive someone of what is properly his, the unequal sharing of natural rents by humanity violates the natural right to an equal share of the rent. The benefit of rent, however, need not be manifest in money payments, but can be satisfied in kind, in common services, if the subjective value of the services is regarded by most as a reasonable or necessary substitute for the money.

If the rent were all distributed in cash, it would be a simple matter to pay each person an equal rent dividend each year. When it comes to services, however, different people not only have different views on which ones are optimal, but benefit in different degrees and ways. Who is to decide? As described below, moral equality is best met when the governance is voluntary.

Civic Rentals

Civic rentals are generated by civic goods, public works such as streets, parks, and security, both in cities and in rural areas. Civic rental is the marginal or extra rental that people are willing to pay, relative to payment for areas without these goods.

The rental generated by civic goods attaches to the land but is actually created by capital goods. Since the return on capital goods properly belongs to its creator, the site rentals due to the capital goods belong not equally to humanity, but to the owner of the capital goods. Civic rentals are not only not natural land rents; they are also not economic rents, hence they are really a rental rather than a true rent. Economic rent is a return not needed to put a factor into production, but civic rentals are needed by the producers of civic goods, since without the return, the goods would not be produced.

A clear case of civic rentals arises with private communities, such as condominiums, homeowner associations, housing cooperatives, and land trusts. The association owns community facilities such as grounds, streets, parking spaces, common elements of buildings, recreation facilities, meeting rooms, utilities, and security services. These amenities increase the rental value of land, and the civic rentals are proper returns to the organization that provides them.

Though, conceptually, the distinction between civic rentals and natural rents is clear, the separation of site rent into the two categories can be fuzzy in practice. By comparing sites that have various different goods, it is possible to determine the rental generated by various civic works, especially its capitalization into land value.

The capitalization of civic goods generating land values has been tested in several studies. One early test by Wallace Oates concluded that services and property taxes were indeed capitalized.[23] Walter Rybeck reports that the Washington, D.C., subway (Metro) caused a growth of land values of over $3.5 billion.[24] Stuart Gabriel, Joseph Mattey, and William Wascher found evidence for the capitalization of several significant variables, including highways and public schools, that add to the quality of life.[25] Jon Sonstelie and Paul Portney, using gross rentals and amount of tax rather than tax rates, found empirical evidence for a significant favorable effect of community services on rent; these services include public safety, fire protection, streets, reduction of pollution, and education.[26] The general findings are that civic goods increase land rent and land value, while taxes on real estate reduce land rent and land value.

Proprietary real estate such as hotels, marinas, shopping centers, and industrial estates provide services to the guests or tenants, paying for them from the rentals. Besides generating internal rentals, these activities as well as commerce in general can result in spillovers, in which land value created by one party increases the value of other title holders. A shopping center, for example, might increase the rental value of the surrounding residential sites. A new shopping center thus creates a windfall gain for those owners. Suppose a landlord near the shopping center rents real estate to a tenant, and after the shopping center is built, the rent increases by $20 per month. Does the rental properly belong to the owner of the shopping center, or is this an incidental benefit that the landlord does not have to compensate for? After all, the landlord did not enter into any contract with the owner of the shopping center.

The deeper problem actually is that there is no contract at all. There is no contract between the owner of the shopping center and the city government, and no contract between the landlord and the city. Government is imposed over some territory, whether individuals and property owners agree or not. If many residents do not vote, the government might not even be able to claim backing by a majority. In the extreme case, if only half the eligible voters cast ballots, and barely over half of them elect the government, then only one-fourth of the voters elect the representatives. If the political system, furthermore, is such that the candidates are selected by political party leaders, and the election is funded by special interests in exchange for privileges and special benefits, then democracy may be more in form than in substance. Even legitimately obtained revenues are then wrongfully taken from the proper recipients, the public.

The solution can be more clearly seen if the entire governance is contractual. Real estate owners then belong to neighborhood or civic associations, which federate into higher-level associations, up to the city level.

If the shopping center and the neighboring homes belong to the same group, the contractual agreement can then specify that the rental generated by the shopping center belongs to the association, since the public works created by the association outside the shopping center in turn increase the rental value of the center. Shoppers who are also nearby residents receive this rent in dividends or benefits from the association. Alternatively, the contract can specify that the rental goes to the owner of the shopping center. The resolution of mutual spillovers becomes a matter of contractual agreement among property owners. In voluntary agreements, those who would otherwise lose from some arrangement can be compensated. These agreements then precede the building, and negotiations as well as competition will tend adequately to compensate the parties. If the shopping center and the landlord belong to separate associations, then they can create agreements among the various local groups, possibly in conjunction with membership in a higher-level association, again a contractual solution.

This logic implies that by the universal ethic, governance should be by individual consent; otherwise government becomes a wrongful imposition. Those individuals and groups who do not abide by the universal ethic may be forcibly brought into compliance, and that is not an imposition but a maintenance of moral equality.

Thus what is at first sight an ethical problem regarding civic rentals is really a problem of governance and self-ownership. When government is imposed on unwilling subjects, equality is violated. Equality implies that a majority may not impose its will on a minority, even when a majority designates itself a government. The ethical problem arises when the owner of the shopping center is not in a contractual relationship with the landlord, but both are under a city that imposes the rules.

An imposed government, in the absence of contracting strict application of ethics, would require that those who generate rentals are the rightful owners and are due those rentals from others. In practice, however, there is a web of mutually generated rentals. Each building and item of public works generates some rent (possibly negative for unwelcomed works), and it can become difficult to sort out exactly what the net rental is for any particular plot. The costs of the sorting and the fuzziness of the estimates may preclude any compensation, and if the waste of resources in the attempt would outweigh the compensation, the government may as well simply treat the civic rentals as activity rent, the third type discussed in the next section.

Activity Rents

Human activity such as housing and commerce creates a demand for land, apart from the civic works. Unlike that for civic works, the demand cannot be traced to particular people or activities, but is the sum result of the population and its enterprises. Activity rent, unlike civic rentals, is an economic rent, since the rent is not a return to the activity itself, which instead obtains its returns from labor and capital goods. This land rent is centered in the community in which the activity is located, and thus is generated by the residents. Under the moral principle that "to the creator belongs its creation," the community as a whole is the proper owner of activity rents, and the governing agency covering a local market area such as a city or metropolitan area is the one most suitable to obtain the rent.

Government, Policy, and Rent

The ethics of rent stipulate that natural rents belong to humanity as a whole for the equal benefit of each person, that activity rents belong to the local communities, and that civic rentals belong to the agency providing them.

The separation of activity rent from civic rental and natural rents is fuzzy, but not impossible to discern. One of the problems is that an infrastructure is typically accompanied by activity. But when the public works are provided by a citywide agency, the separation is not a problem since the same agency will collect the activity rents and the civic rentals.

Global comparison of site rents can determine the relative influence of natural features such as harbors, sunlight, and rain, and other natural locational advantages, as opposed to the influences affecting the locally generated rents. The techniques for doing so are a study in themselves, and would be developed much further were policy to shift to the collection of rents.

One general principle for policy is that users pay the marginal costs of their particular usage, while the fixed costs are paid out of rent. In a transit system, for example, there is a cost for providing the service to one more user. The cost is not only the fuel and maintenance, but also the extra crowding imposed on others. The fees paid by the user would compensate the provider both for the marginal physical costs and for the crowding costs. The congestion fee is typically an extra charge during the most crowded times. The rental generated by the transit system would then fund the fixed costs, those which remain the same in the short run regardless of how many riders there are. Whatever rent generated by the service is less than the fixed costs is an indication that the service is not economical and should not be produced.

The ethics of rent include the expenditure side as well as the collecting side. If the natural and the activity rent belong equally to the global and the local communities, and if the funds are wasted or spent in ways that do not provide well being, then the rents have been unjustly taken from their owners. Government is properly an agent for the members of a community.

The paradigm or model of democracy as it exists in the world today is that of masses of people electing representatives who then determine the policy agenda. The branch of economics known as "public choice" studies this political process. Public choice has identified the "disease of democracy" as rent seeking, the seeking of economic rents in what Richard Wagner calls a "market for legislation."[27] Rent seeking or transfer seeking involves special interests that finance political campaigns in exchange for transfers of wealth, protection from competition, laws prohibiting unapproved activities, and other transfers and privileges. Besides taking funds from taxpayers and consumers, rent seeking further wastes resources in the campaigns to obtain the transfers and also when taxes that fund them impose a burden on the economy.

So even if all public revenue came from user fees and rents in accord with the universal ethic, if they go to special interests the rent is still stolen from the people. Since the ethics of rent include its proper distribution to the rightful owners, the members of the community, it is not sufficient for justice that the rents be collected. The implementation of justice requires a governmental structure that assures that the rents will not be siphoned to pressure groups.

Mass democracy is inherently dysfunctional, since candidates require massive funds to wage media campaigns. We have seen in the United States that campaign finance reforms have not solved the problem. The root lies in the very structure of the democratic process. The problem needs to be remedied by confronting the cause rather than only treating the effects. One alternative to having masses elect officials is confining elections to small groups. Mancur Olson describes how in small groups the dynamic changes. When the group is small enough, the voters personally know the candidates, and media campaigns become redundant. An activist can easily run for office, and the electorate has ready access to its representatives. Olson also noted that services can be provided by federations of small groups rather than by large agencies.[28]

Small-group democracy is centered in neighborhood associations of about 500 persons, small enough for the voters personally to know their representatives, but large enough so that there are usually enough people willing to sit on the boards or councils. Gordon Tullock theorizes that many urban services can be delegated to the neighborhood level, as is demonstrated by many villages as well as local associations, condominiums, and land trusts.[29] Case studies of two such communities, Arden Village in Delaware (a land trust founded by followers of Henry George) and the Fort Ellsworth Condominium Association in Virginia, show that communities of that size can provide for local civic goods and also the volunteers for their governance.[30]

The neighborhood associations would then federate to form higher-level groupings for services that affect a greater territory. The neighborhood association boards would elect the representatives from its members, keeping that election in a small group. The second-level grouping would in turn elect representatives to the next higher level, and the multilevel structure would extend to cities, states, countries, and finally an association for the planet.

Each level of association would provide services most economically provided at that level. Tullock also proposes "associations with quasi-governmental power" which, like churches, would not necessarily have a unique geographical jurisdiction.[31] They would supplement the multilevel territorial associations. Where activity rents are shared among the various levels of association, special boards with representatives from all levels can be set up to assess the rent fairly. Small-group voting and voluntary associations would avoid much of the rent-seeking disease of mass democracy, with its larger groups, and also provide for a more diverse range of local communities and greater choice. Associations would provide for economic justice in the distribution of rents for all society.

Association governance would also provide for justice in law. The universal ethic mandates the prohibition and punishment of acts that are evil, those that coercively harm others, and would be implemented by all associations. All other acts, those that are neutral and good, would not be mandated. Government would force people not to do good, but only to avoid evil. There would be no laws prohibiting voluntary victimless acts. Associations, however, would be free to have whatever internal rules they agree to, and they could, for example, prohibit gambling or require that no business be done on the Sabbath. These rules would apply only to those families that voluntarily agreed to join the community.

When government imposes such rules on all, it is engaged in a form of rent seeking, since the state not only restricts behavior but reduces the value of sites, some users not being able to make the best use of them according to their personal values. Each local association would be able to have local rules conformable to its culture, and this would maximize both local and global liberties and land rents.

Conclusion and Summary

The universal ethic endows individuals with the right to their labor and the products of labor, and it is therefore morally wrong for government to tax wages and returns to capital goods. Moral equality endows all human beings with an equal claim to natural rents. Rents due to local activity belong to those communities, and rentals due to infrastructure belong to its providers. It is therefore just to derive public revenues from individual user fees as well as rents. Revenue is then not redistributed from the owners of factors but instead consists of returns to the proper owners of the rents.

The ownership of rents includes the receipt of the rents either in cash funds or in services that are wanted. The governance structure thus needs to serve the public rather than special interests, which can be better implemented when the voters are in small groups rather than in massive electorates. Multilevel associations elected from lower-level groups can then serve territories of larger size to provide collective services, supplemented by nonterritorial associations.

The ethics of rent are thus tied to the ethics of governance and of law. Economic theory and practice have shown that land rent is the most efficient source of general revenues, in addition to user fees paying for particular services and marginal costs.[32] While taxes on labor, capital, goods, and transactions impose a burden and reduce incentives, rent payments are at worst neutral and at best induce a more efficient use of land.

As Henry George wrote, "economic law and moral law are essentially one."[33] It would be the greatest of dilemmas if the economics of rent indicated one policy while ethics indicated another. There is evidently a profound law that creates the unified universal moral and economic principles of rent. The policies for rent that are just also provide for economic efficiency.

Notes

1. The term "rent seeking" was coined by Ann Krueger in 1974. Gordon Tullock had previously developed the consequences of the long-known concept of the capture of government by special interests. See his "Rent Seeking," in *The World of Economics,* John Eatwell, Murray Millgate, and Peter Newman, eds. (1987; New York: W.W. Norton, 1991), 604–609.

2. Nicolaus Tideman, "The Economics of Efficient Taxes on Land," in *Land and Taxation,* Nicolaus Tideman, ed. (London: Shepheard-Walwyn, 1994), 103–140.

3. Fred Foldvary, *The Soul of Liberty* (San Francisco: Gutenberg Press, 1980).

4. John Locke, *Two Treatises of Government* (1690; New York: Hafner Press, 1947).

5. Ibid., 123.

6. Henry George, *Progress and Poverty* (1879; New York: Robert Schalkenbach Foundation, 1975), 334.

7. James M. Buchanan and Gordon Tullock, *The Calculus of Consent* (Ann Arbor: University of Michigan Press, 1965), 315.

8. Carl Menger, *Principles of Economics* (1871; New York: New York University Press, 1976), 120.

9. James M. Buchanan, *The Limits of Liberty: Between Anarchy and Leviathan* (Chicago: University of Chicago Press, 1975), 11.

10. George, *Progress and Poverty,* 335.

11. The ethic derived here is confined to acts affecting human beings. The application of morality to animals would take the discussion beyond the employment of the ethics of rent, since it is human beings who pay and receive rent. The relationship of ethics to children is also not considered here. See *The Soul of Liberty* (note 4) for the applications to these topics.

12. Viktor Vanberg, "Individual Choice and Institutional Constraints—The Normative Element in Classical and Contractarian Liberalism," *Analyse & Kritik* 8 (1986): 115.

13. Note that this presentation does not begin with the concept of self-ownership. After the derivation of the universal ethic and natural rights, they can be applied to labor. Since ownership is a bundle of rights, self-ownership means that one has the right to control one's labor and retain wages.

14. George, *Progress and Poverty,* 328.

15. Ibid., 333.

16. Ibid., 338.

17. Ibid., 341.

18. Legally, "possession" means control. The law recognizes "actual" and "constructive" possession: The former means physical control while the latter refers to the power to control. The ancient French legal term *droit-droit* meant a double right, that is, the right to possession of property and also the right of property. A complete title to land included both rights, indicating that the right of possession was not the plenary right or the whole bundle of rights to land. Today, those who possess real estate still have to pay property taxes, which signifies that in current law, the rights of possession also do include the right to keep all the rent. But since Henry George used the term "possession" in ways that indicate plenary rights, including the right to the rent, to keep the meaning clear the term "control" is used here for the bundle of rights other than to rent.

19. George, *Progress and Poverty,* 342.

20. Ibid., 344.

21. Ibid.

22. Ibid., 262 (cited) and 346.

23. Wallace E. Oates, "The Effects of Property Taxes and Public Spending on Property Values: An Empirical Study of Tax Capitalization and the Tiebout Hypothesis," *Journal of Political Economy* 77 (November-December 1969).

24. Walter Rybeck, "The Property Tax as a Super User Charge," in *The Property Tax and Local Finance,* C. Lowell Harris, ed. (New York: Academy of Political Science, 1983), 133.

25. Stuart A. Gabriel, Joe P. Mattey, and William L. Wascher, "Compensating Differentials and Evolution of the Quality-of-Life Among U.S. States," *Federal Reserve Bank of San Francisco Working Paper* (June 1996), 96–107.

26. Jon C. Sonstelie and Paul R. Portney, "Gross Rents and Market Values:

Testing the Implications of Tiebout's Hypothesis," *Journal of Urban Economics* 7, no. 1 (January 1980).

27. Richard E. Wagner, *To Promote the General Welfare* (San Francisco: Pacific Research Institute for Public Policy, 1989), 179.

28. Mancur Olson, *The Logic of Collective Action* (Cambridge: Harvard University Press, 1971).

29. Gordon Tullock, *The New Federalist* (Vancouver: Fraser Institute, 1994).

30. Fred Foldvary, *Public Goods and Private Communities* (Aldershot, UK: Edward Elgar, 1994).

31. Gordon Tullock, "A New Proposal for Decentralizing Government Activity," in *Rationale Wirtschaftspolitik in komplexen Gesellschaften,* Hellmuth Milde and Hans Monissen, eds. (Stuttgart: Verlag W. Kohlhammer, 1985).

32. The literature on how rent can be an efficient revenue source for providing collective goods includes: Kris Feder, "Geo-Economics," in *Beyond Neoclassical Economics* (Aldershot, U.K.: Edward Elgar, 1996), 41–60; Mason Gaffney, "Land as a Distinctive Factor of Production," in *Land and Taxation,* Nicolaus Tideman, ed. (London: Shepheard-Walwyn, 1994), 39–102; Nicolaus Tideman, "The Economics of Efficient Taxes on Land," 103–140; and William Vickrey, "The City as a Firm," in *Economics of Public Services,* Martin Feldstein and Robert Inman, eds. (London: Macmillan, 1977), 334–343.

33. George, *Progress and Poverty,* 560.

15

Hanno T. Beck

Land-Value Taxation and Ecological-Tax Reform

Introduction

This essay seeks to approximate a theme of popular television shows: to find and reintroduce two adults who were born twins, but separated at birth. I will argue that land-value taxation, although not commonly considered a "green tax" or "ecotax," nevertheless matches the structural and practical characteristics of such taxes. The two-rate property tax, moreover, is the most commonly used political implementation of land-value taxation, and is a perfectly normal example of ecological-tax reform, the latest mechanism for advancing ecotaxes.[1]

The first three sections consider ecotaxes and ecological-tax reform, and outline their structural and practical characteristics. The following three sections do the same for land-value taxation including the two-rate property tax. The last section summarizes our exploration.

The Ecotax and Ecological-Tax Reform

What is an ecotax?[2] I will not be considering here such questions as whether any taxation at all is justifiable, whether government uses money wisely, or what its proper functions at its various levels might be, but will rather begin from the situation we find ourselves living in the late 1990s. We have governments and they levy taxes. What does it take for one of these taxes to be considered an ecotax?

Taxes have varied impacts: A sales tax discourages buying, a tax on tobacco discourages smoking, a high business tax causes businesses to move away, and so on. It is important to recognize that every tax has effects, that every tax constitutes conscious or unconscious social engineering, and that wise tax reform must recognize these impacts.

It might be tempting to define an ecotax by its effects: "An ecotax is a tax that discourages environmentally bad activities." That would mean, however, that a tax that has such effects only on an occasional or random basis would sometimes be an ecotax, sometimes not. It seems clear that a more stable definition, which still captures the environmental point, would be based on how it is levied. I suggest that an ecotax is a tax that is raised from a thing or process that imposes costs on the natural environment, particularly when those costs are not already being paid or taken into account by the imposer.[3]

A simple example of an ecotax would be a tax on fuel based on petroleum; such a tax would discourage air pollution by discouraging the use of such fuels. It does not mean that we can point to any particular vehicle and be certain that it will adjust to the tax by consuming less fuel—but across the entire economy, we can indeed be sure that increasing its cost will cut fuel consumption in the short run and stimulate the production of cleaner substitutes and other substitute arrangements.

Similarly, a tax on site-holding (owning parcels of land) is an ecotax because it discourages idle speculation, underuse, waste, and sprawling development of sites.[4] We cannot point to any particular parcel of land and be certain that it will adjust to the tax by being developed in a more efficient way—but across the entire economy, increasing the cost of site-holding will most definitely reduce idle speculation in the short run and cause less land-intensive sprawl development, more infill and redevelopment of urban areas, and the restoration and rehabilitation of buildings and existing neighborhoods.

Notice that whether an ecotax is defined by its effects or by how it is raised, no reliance is placed on how the resulting revenue is spent. So in the past there have been ecotax proposals urging a variety of different priorities for the revenue. Some suggest spending the revenue on environmental cleanup projects, some recommend educational projects to increase environmental awareness and sensitivity, and others would prefer the revenue to be used for general government expenses.[5]

But there is an additional possible use for ecotax revenue, and it is this use that has become the keystone of recent ecotax proposals: Why not assign the ecotax revenue to offset some existing tax on productive activity? It would permit the cutting or removal of some deleterious taxes. In this way, government revenue can be maintained, while by virtue of the introduction of the ecotax some groups of taxpayers get a distinct benefit in the form of a tax cut. This approach—shifting the burden of taxation away from productive activity and onto consumption of natural resources—is called ecological-tax reform, or ETR.[6] Let us look in some detail at ETR and what it offers.

Structural Characteristics of Ecological-Tax Reform

How will it become convincing that an ecological-tax reform is a good idea? By examining the way in which a good argument for ETR is constituted, we can learn much about its strengths.

Imagine an argument in favor of a particular ecotax—we'll call it a tax on *K*. In its simplest form, the argument's structure would run:

1. A tax on *K* would provide good effects. . . .
2. Therefore, let us tax *K*.

There are missing premises in this argument, however, and opponents would be quick to point them out. To make a useful argument we must "unpack" the first premise into components. Every tax has some effects, but not all are likely to be good. A persuasive case, moreover, will not focus on "good" effects measured by some absolute scale, since such a scale is impossible to construct, but will show that the ecotax's effects are merely *better than those of the current system.* Hence a more explicit logical structure would be:

1. The current tax configuration has effects *A, B,* and *C*. . . .
2. The tax configuration including a tax on *K* has effects *P, Q,* and *R*. . . .
3. *P, Q,* and *R are preferable to A, B,* and *C*. . . .
4. Therefore, let us tax *K*.

Now the argument is more explicit in its logic, although it is also difficult to make it convincing in practice. Even if strong evidence exists for the first two premises, the third is most questionable. It is not sufficient to show that a tax on *K* would have some positive effects; the argument must also demonstrate that a tax on *K* would have no effects that are bad; or if it would, that they are less bad than the tax on *K* is good.[7]

So a convincing argument, to demonstrate premise three, must make an apples-to-apples comparison of two bundles of effects—*A, B,* and *C* versus *P, Q,* and *R*—bundles that might not be comparable in any straightforward way. If a tax on coal burning reduces air pollution and pays for better public schools, while forcing coal companies to downsize, who is to say which effects are preferable? The third premise expresses not only a value judgment, but a difficult and complex one at that.

Any tax, if enacted, will have winners and losers as their fate is measured against that under the current system. Losers will claim that their loss is more important than the gains of the winners. The separation between winners and losers makes any beneficial change very difficult. Proponents of the ecotax have only one known (or reasonably assumable) effect that they can point to that the current tax configuration does not have: the eventual environmental benefit that will result. (They can have also considerable benefits such as spending the revenue on environmental education programs or on cleaning up toxic waste dumps, but such projects, if they have not already justified a tax increase, do little to energize the argument in favor of one.) How else could ecotax proponents increase their support or decrease the level of their opposition? Proposing a stronger or weaker ecotax may alter the volume of the debate, but still does not change the roster of winners and losers. Unless proponents have a tool that can transform some losers into nonlosers or nonwinners into winners, there will be little room for change and few ecotaxes will be implemented.

Here an innovation can greatly strengthen the arguments in favor of the ecotax. This innovation provides a new factor that ecotaxes can offer, in addition to environmental benefits. Suppose we stipulate that a proposed ecotax will not change overall revenue to the government. For every dollar raised by the new tax, some existing bad tax can be cut by a dollar. Now, when presenting the third premise, ecotax advocates can point to at least two favorable items, effects that are not offered by the current tax system: The environment will be better off, and *some group of taxpayers will enjoy a tax cut.* That, in a nutshell, is ecological-tax reform.[8]

There is no nationwide consensus that more revenue for government is a good thing, or that global warming is an urgent problem, or even that fewer trees should be destroyed; but there are many taxes for which we enjoy a nationwide consensus that they should be cut. The core strength of the ETR concept is that it offers two benefits, not just one, and it is precisely this that makes a mere ecotax proposal into a dynamic ETR proposal.

A further theoretical point is in order. The structural hallmark of ETR is that it offers a second benefit set, in addition to environmental relief, and can actually be achieved in more than one way. Two techniques might strengthen the third premise to ensure that *P, Q,* and *R* are indeed "preferable" in at least two ways to *A, B,* and *C.* The obvious means is to assign the ecotax revenue to a tax cut for some overtaxed group not already supportive of the ecotax, adding more constituencies to the list of "winners" in virtue of the ETR proposal. A second theoretical way, however, would be *to decrease the list of complaining "losers."*[9]

This approach has, in fact been done: in the case of Sweden's taxation of nitrogen oxides, air pollutants that cause acid rain. That nation started a tax on nitrogen oxides in 1992. The largest power and heating plants were concerned that such a tax would reduce their international competitiveness as well as their ability to compete domestically against smaller plants, which were exempt from the tax by reason of the high monitoring costs that such taxation would bring.[10] So the Swedish government assigned the revenue from this ecotax to go back to the polluters. The trick? Rebates would be in inverse proportion to their polluting. The industry as a whole would break even and thus lose no international competitiveness, but plants that were high polluters might find themselves paying out more than they received while relatively clean plants received more than they paid out.

The British Petroleum Economics Unit reported that fine-tuning the revenue assignment in this way would keep from harming in general the competitive position of large Swedish plants in relation to smaller domestic and international firms.[11] Sweden achieved revenue neutrality for the government and the industry, yet still successfully introduced environmental incentives via the tax. (We might add that the tax succeeded: According to the BP Economics Unit report, "the aim was to reduce NO_x emissions by 30 percent over three years. Instead, emissions were reduced by 35 percent in the first year alone."[12] No business wants to subsidize its competitors.)

To recapitulate: The same group of taxpayers who are losers can become the recipients of a tax cut. This assignment of the ecotax's revenue sounds strange at first, like a pointless juggling of money, but the main point of an ecotax is to send *long-term signals* throughout an economy. It is those signals that bring about improvements in efficiency of resources and in cleanup technology. Today's polluters do not have to be recklessly penalized in order for them to be sent.

Theoretically, the political strength of an ETR proposal is increased by a measurement of what interest group would offer the most support, or decrease its opposition the most—and focus the tax rebate onto that constituency, though not necessarily uniformly. That results in the ETR proposal most likely to succeed. So the argument structure for proponents of ecotaxes is made more favorable not only by their ability to cite that environmental benefits will ensue—the "intrinsic" advantage—but also by their ability to offer and adjust rewards from the tax's revenue—the advantage in assignment of revenue—so as to mitigate opposition, cultivate new allies and supporters, or do both.

In this section we have made explicit the logical structure of ecotax proposals and considered its strengths and weaknesses. We have then demonstrated how ecological-tax reform is an enhanced mechanism for proposing an ecotax, embodying not only environmental benefits but a tax cut or rebate that can be used to decrease some bad tax and to provide short-term relief to polluters without disturbing the long-term incentives for environmental conservation.

Practical Characteristics of Ecological-Tax Reform

We have considered the form that ETR takes, and the form of arguments in favor and against it. Here we will survey the most common specific points made during consideration of ETR proposals. Their adequacy or inadequacy will be only lightly discussed. Instead, we will focus on giving the reader an impression of the political and economic landscape an actual ETR proposal can be expected to present.

General Distributional Effects

Obvious Winners and Losers

Ecological-tax reform can be said in general to favor relatively clean industries, such as electronics, software, and service sectors, while penalizing dirty industries such as coal and petroleum production. Cleaner enterprises will not feel much burdened by a tax on pollution, while those that pollute more will be asked to pay more, either directly or indirectly.

Ecological-tax reform can also be expected to stimulate a new sector of the economy that is already growing—businesses that specialize in waste prevention, recycling, and creative reuse of resources.[13] Reducing an enterprise's waste output, or finding ways to draw on such waste as a valuable input, already makes money for the modern entrepreneur.

Although it is obviously in society's interest to minimize environmental deterioration, moving away from polluting industries and toward a more high-tech economy oriented to service provides relatively little comfort to the polluters themselves. They can be expected normally to oppose ETR.

Size and Number

A second important generalization about the distributional effects of an ETR program is that its establishment would be likely to bring about a small number of heavy losers—recipients of a net tax increase—and a much larger number of small-scale "winners," who receive a net tax decrease. Such is not necessarily the case—an ETR can be designed to have the opposite effect—but in general, where ETR proposals have been implemented, the new pollution costs hit large polluters, and tax cuts are often applied to broad-based levies such as payroll taxes.[14] The opponents of an ETR will therefore likely feel more strongly about it than the immediate beneficiaries. We commonly see this political situation, in which ETR supporters must try to build a coalition of small, diverse winners and environmentalists to overcome opposition from a small band of large polluters.

Specific Distributional Effects

Regressivity?

An often-heard claim is that most ETR programs would be regressive. If people, for example, are taxed on their consumption of gasoline, or if a fuel tax is levied earlier in the production process but is passed along to consumers, the result is considered regressive because poor people spend a higher portion of their income on gasoline than do rich people.

That claim is a holdover from the days when ecotaxes were proposed outside the context of ecological-tax reform, and has little merit in the 1990s. While virtually any tax system can be designed to be regressive, ETRs can be retooled comfortably without regressivity. Robert Herendeen and Farzaneh Fazel's research focused on several ETR scenarios embodying a large tax on energy.[15] They noted that such a tax, in the absence of a rebate scheme, would be regressive, but nearly any plausible rebate scheme, even a simple equal sharing per capita of the revenue raised, would make the ETR program progressive. Jean Hanson and Margaret Walls examined an ecotax consisting of vehicle fees, levied in various ways.[16] The ecotaxes considered alone were regressive, but when they were part of a tax shift, the regressivity was easily eliminated.

Certainly, if taxes are levied against energy use, poor people would pay a greater percentage of their income for the tax than would rich people. But that is a point only against an ecotax scheme that does not embody ETR. The beauty of the ETR program is the ability to design a program that gives relief to the injured, to protect them from immediate shocks while sending the proper long-terms signals into the economy as a whole. When used against ETR, the argument concerning regressivity is out of date.

Special Cases

In any change in tax laws, certain unlucky individuals will find themselves injured. And so opponents of the change will find whatever victims they can, preferably elderly widows, and loudly parade them about.

Every attempt at change in tax laws meets this form of resistance; it is not in any way peculiar to ETR. And the counterarguments are also not peculiar to ETR. Special relief programs can be arranged. Are we to stay forever with our current, inferior tax laws simply because they are what we have today? Is no change ever justified? Are victims of today's tax laws less deserving of relief than those who would be affected by new ones?

Time and Rate of Change

Long-Term Is Essential

An ETR program has two types of effect—the initial, distributional effects that make some pay more and others less, and also a group of effects on long-range planning. A business, whether receiving a tax cut or getting a tax increase by an ETR program, will be motivated to minimize its tax burdens in the future. If those burdens are related mostly to pollution and waste, then it will make efforts to cut pollution and waste. For some industries, such motivations could take many years to emerge into measurable results.[17]

These longer-term effects are the motivation behind ETR; they are the real goal to be sought. ETR proponents have no special interest in rewarding or penalizing today's taxpayers except to enhance the attractiveness of bringing about a future that poses fewer environmental risks and dangers.

Opponents of ETR programs downplay these long-term effects. Proponents of ETR commonly experience the challenge of selling vague, future benefits in a world concerned with short-term gratifications.

Autonomy

Ecological-tax reform does not ban polluting activities, nor does it tell any particular plant to reduce its pollution by amount *X*. Rather, it specifies tax rates and allows normal market forces to adjust without interference. Allowing this freedom of choice in the marketplace, rather than decreeing specific outcomes, enables maximally efficient adjustments by polluters. This factor has emerged as a leading point in favor of ETR over "command-and-control" approaches to environmental degradation.[18]

Other Considerations

The "It's a Wash" Claim

A very superficial objection to ETR, which is nevertheless heard often enough to warrant attention, is "you want to tax Joe a little less, and

Sam a little more, but you're still collecting the same money from the economy. So what difference does it make? Why all this hot air about nothing?"

People are not passive—they react, especially to taxes, and so the things and processes on which taxes are levied do make a great deal of difference. As Henry George wrote, "The mode of taxation is, in fact, quite as important as the amount. As a small burden badly placed may distress a horse that could carry with ease a much larger one properly adjusted, so a people may be impoverished and their power of producing wealth destroyed by taxation, which, if levied in another way, could be borne with ease."[19]

Pain Versus Gain: Tradeoffs

Another common concern about ETR, voiced often by sympathetic politicians, is purely practical. It is claimed that to establish an ETR program takes the same political work as raising taxes; that ETR elicits heavy opposition; and that if enacted, the government gains no new spending authority and no surplus revenue. So is it worth the trouble?

Politicians, like any other group, will be staunch advocates of ETR only if they are persuaded that long-term environmental protection is needed. The ETR proponent must often spend as much effort educating supportive politicians, who focus by habit on short-term considerations, as they do on the wider public.

Past as Property

One more issue that often comes up in discussions of ETR is the concept of a vested interest in pollution, a claim that people have property rights in the perpetual continuation of their past actions. If Sam's factory has polluted in the past, without paying taxes; if Sam invested in factory expansion, expecting that situation to continue; and now Sam faces new taxes on pollution, isn't something unfair or unjust?

This issue, to be taken seriously, requires us to imagine that someone who repeatedly imposes costs on others will be owed something by those others, rather than owing them. Although on immediate presentation this seems absurd, the concern arises often enough to make it a customary feature of the ETR debate.

This survey of the main features and issues surrounding ETR is now complete. Now we will turn our attention to a tax not always regarded as oriented to the environment at all, yet has impressive potential.

Land-Value Taxation and the Two-Rate Property Tax

What is land-value taxation?[20] It is a tax levied on the rental value of land or its equivalent. For example, here is a parcel of land that rents for $1,000 per annum; if that parcel is taxed at $100 per annum, there is then a 10 percent land-value tax in place.

Land-value taxation is actually quite common. It is normally one component of the property tax. Property taxes fall on both land value and the value of improvements—the portion that falls on land value is a land-value tax. Such a tax is normally levied not on the rental value of land directly, but rather on the land's assessed market value; but that market value is simply the current capitalized value of the stream of future rents it is anticipated to yield, so unless the rate were to grow high, the normal practice of taxing the price of land is an excellent surrogate for a pure land-value tax.

Proponents of the land-value tax point out that it has the effect of encouraging more compact development of sites, which leads to more efficient use of urban infrastructure and decreases pressure for suburban sprawl.[21] Indeed, failing to tax land value is seen as a form of subsidy, and this is especially evident in cases such as the announcement of a new subway station or park, where surrounding land values escalate overnight simply by virtue of government plans, not by individual initiative.

From the beginning of agitation for land-value taxation in the 1880s,[22] the argument for it has been embedded within a broader argument, including a tax shift from buildings or improvements to land. Henry George's recommendation for economic justice did not entail a tax shift but a single tax combined with the elimination of all other taxes. George explicitly proposes "to abolish all taxation save that upon land values."[23] He develops at length the argument that "The advantages which would be gained by substituting for the numerous taxes by which the public revenues are now raised, a single tax levied upon the value of land, will appear more and more important the more they are considered."[24] The notion of a tax shift, has, nevertheless, been incorporated into the advancement of land-value taxation.

Although at times variants of land-value taxation different from the single tax have been proposed as a new revenue source,[25] or as the least disruptive source for revenue when a tax increase is necessary, the canonical form of a land-value tax proposal has been revenue neutral—simultaneously to urge the reduction or elimination of other taxes with the introduction of the land-value tax with identical yield. It has also usually meant reducing the property tax rate on improvement value, and increasing the property tax rate on land value, rather than artificially holding those two taxes to a single rate. Such an arrangement is what we call the two-rate property tax, or 2R.[26]

Land-value taxation has enjoyed nontrivial success when proposed in the context of a two-rate property tax. Local or regional property taxes in the United States, South Africa, Australia, New Zealand, and elsewhere have in many cases been modernized in this way.

Structural Characteristics of Two-Rate Property Taxation

The two important aspects of ecological-tax reform, then, were the intrinsic effects (long-term environmental benefits) and the revenue assignment (a tax cut or relief)—also essential features of 2R. The intrinsic effects are the desirable results that the proponents of the tax shift view as favorable—less sprawl, more jobs and housing in urban areas, and lower infrastructure costs. The revenue assignment, normally used to reduce the portion of the property tax that falls on improvement value, serves to reward property users with a tax cut and also to offer the reduced tax rate to all others as a "carrot" encouraging efficient development.

The two-rate property tax shift thus already embodies the basic innovation of ecological-tax reform, since it assigns revenue as a second positive ingredient, in addition to the tax's promotion of long-term efficiency. By allocating the revenue to holders of property improvements, the 2R proposal makes the class of property owners the group that both pays more taxes and receives the rebate; because of this, relatively large tax shifts can be made without resulting in large tax shifts in *burden*. Many property owners who pay more land-value tax pay less improvements tax and wind up with trivial increases or decreases in burden. Only property owners whose development of their sites, as measured by improvement value compared to site value, is relatively high receive a tax break, and those whose development is relatively low receive a tax increase.

Is there a 2R equivalent to the Swedish NO_x tax innovation, the Swedish invention of a new tax solely for the purpose of refunding it to the payers by an environmental criterion? The answer is no, not in any straightforward way, because most areas already have a land-value tax collection infrastructure in place and it would be inefficient to add a second mechanism for tax collection. The pre-existence of a land-value tax in most communities, however, does allow another strategy by its proponents—an attack on whatever local taxes are least popular, a call for their termination, the municipality to maintain its revenues by adding to the land-value tax. The most recent case of such a program implemented was in 1996 in Allentown, Pennsylvania.[27]

Practical Characteristics of Two-Rate Property Taxation

General Distributional Effects

Obvious Winners and Losers

The clearest general claim to be made about 2R's distributional effects is that efficient use of land is rewarded and wasteful use penalized. By land in this context, we mean land value, not land acreage. Like ETR programs, 2R favors reuse of existing materials or infrastructures. Who, then, will be the obvious losers? The occupiers of large values (not necessarily large acreages) of land with relatively little improvement value. Those people would be idle land speculators, owners of rundown or abandoned structures, and owners of obsolete one-level parking lots in downtown areas. Other extensive land uses, such as for junkyards and car dealerships, would also be losers if they were located on valuable sites. The winners in nearly every case studied tend to be property owners with well-kept homes on modest lots or efficiently developed structures such as apartment dwellings.

Size and Number

What commonly occurred was another main distributional generalization for ETR: a small number of large losers and many small winners. This phenomenon has also emerged in the campaign for 2R. Most often it is speculators with large tracts of valuable downtown land who will have to pay more, while homeowners on average sites typically receive small tax cuts. As with ETR, the same political scenario unfolds—supporters of 2R must try to build a coalition of small-scale winners to overcome opposition from a minority of land speculators.

Specific Distributional Effects

Regressivity?

The claim of regressivity, it might seem, cannot be made against a 2R system; after all, ownership of property is more concentrated than income ownership, and land-value ownership is more concentrated than either.[28] A shift toward taxing land value will therefore be progressive.

Questions, however, have been raised about who ultimately pays the land-value tax. Little evidence exists for it, but if renters and shoppers and other nonowners of land value have the tax passed on to them, then regressivity is at least a possibility.

Special Cases

The 2R approach has at times been accused of bearing disproportionately against farmers, and at other times of threatening to throw elderly widows out of their homes.

Our remarks made above in the case of ETR apply equally here.

Time and Rate of Change

Long-Term Is Essential

Like ecological tax reform mentioned above, the two-rate property tax innovation does not make a priority out of rewarding current land-value users or penalizing land-value wasters, except to motivate all land-use decisions toward efficiency in the future. When a 2R tax shift is implemented, its effects are measured not during the ensuing days, but over the course of years. This tax has the same drawback as ETR, that there is little urgency for a long-term change and much complaint over any short-term inconvenience.

Autonomy

The two-rate property tax does not ban land speculation, nor does it tell any landholder to develop more efficiently or sell the site. It merely specifies tax rates and allows normal market forces to adjust without interference. Again, this tax parallels perfectly the situation with ETR.

Allowing this freedom of choice in the marketplace results in flexible outcomes. Some landholders pay the extra tax; some develop their properties and take advantage of the reduced tax on improvements; and some sell their sites to entrepreneurs.

Other Considerations

The "It's a Wash" Claim

Because 2R is usually proposed in a configuration that assigns the revenue to property owners, who are also the payers of the land-value tax, its proponents have frequently heard this objection: "You're just trying to take money from property owners and give it back to them, so where's the benefit?"

But this, like the matter of the ETR, requires dramatizing to people the point that they are not passive pincushions when it comes to taxation. People react. When a 2R reform is put in place, the community may receive no net benefit on that day, but future decisions will be stimulated toward more efficient land use and fuller use of the existing infrastructure. They will boost the creation of jobs and housing, yield more tax revenue and ease the demand for new infrastructure investments, while cutting the pressure to convert more wilderness into suburban sprawl.

The confusion and the method of clearing it up are the same as those encountered by ETR supporters.

Pain Versus Gain: Tradeoffs

When a proposal is made for a tax change that increases and lessens the same group's taxes, without enabling the government to enjoy any new authority, politicians will be reluctant, as in the case just discussed, to exert much energy to promote 2R unless the long-term effects can be made clear to them. It can be quite a challenge.

The 2R approach has the beauty of being appropriate for local levels of government, while ETR ideas have typically been attempting to deal with nonpoint pollution and other environmental hazards that require policy on the national or international level. But this has its downside. A local politician who favors the 2R approach will receive phone calls and visits from local land speculators, slum landlords, and others who would pay more under this approach; local elected officials can be made to feel the heat. In the author's view, such opposition is the biggest problem faced by 2R. Even when people are convinced of its advantages, a concrete political cost remains to favoring 2R and a more vague, less clear benefit that might accrue only after the politician has left office.

Past as Property

When objecting to 2R, a land speculator or slum landlord might assert any number of things. Claiming that he has had a perpetual property right in the past and that any tax increase is therefore unfair is, however, very difficult to sustain. Unlike a new ecotax, land-value taxation is in most communities already in place. An argument against its increase is therefore no stronger than an argument against all increases in any tax. If a property right in the past is recognized, then no tax change is ever justified, and a community that once drew its revenue from taxes on slaves and wagon wheels must continue to do so forever.

Despite its weakness, the argument that past is property is often heard, and in this respect makes for yet another parallelism between campaigns for 2R and efforts for ETR.

Summary and Conclusion

It has been shown that ecotaxes, carried forward in the form of ETR proposals, and land-value taxation, carried forward in the form of 2R proposals, share a wide range of structural and practical characteristics. It should be clear that they are members of the same species.

Why point this out, if it is so obvious? The proponents of 2R and the proponents of ETR have not, until fairly recently, overlapped to any significant degree. *They have been constructing the same arguments, enjoying the same strengths, shoring up the same weaknesses, hearing the same objections, and countering the same challenges—without doing so together.*

ETR proponents have, as their main priority, the well-being and sustainability of our environment. Two-rate proponents have, as their main priority, justice in taxation and a fair economy. These are not identical goals, but I reject the idea that they conflict.

Proponents of 2R have shortchanged themselves by not making more explicit the desirable environmental results of land-value taxation; tools for urban redevelopment are in many ways the best friends environmental protectors could want.[29] ETR proponents have also shortchanged themselves by not making more explicit the simple opportunities inherent in ecotaxes for justice and economic growth; constituencies that support fairness need to be made more aware of ETR.

Additionally, 2R proposals, which are generally local, dovetail superbly with ETR proposals, which are more often made at higher levels of government. ETR is properly understood to be the class of environmental tax shifts that includes 2R, while 2R is the easy, local ETR.

As the drive for ETR continues to expand, it becomes increasingly important for ETR proponents to find outlets for local activism; to be able to point to a track record of successful implementations; and to attract the support and appreciation not only of dedicated environmentalists but of additional constituencies. The two-rate property tax offers all these, and so, once properly recognized, it may rightly be called the cutting edge of ecological-tax reform.

Notes

1. This paper assumes a little familiarity with the two-rate property tax and ecological-tax reform. For more information on land-value taxation and the two-rate property tax, see the other articles in this volume. To learn more about ecotaxes and ecological-tax reform, see the thorough report by M. Jeff Hamond, *Tax Waste, Not Work: How Changing What We Tax Can Lead to a Stronger Economy and a Cleaner Environment* (San Francisco: Redefining Progress, 1997).

2. "Ecotax" is one of several commonly used terms. It is intended as a synonym for "green tax," "ecological tax," "environmental tax," and "envirotax."

3. When a polluter dumps toxic wastes at no cost to himself, but imposes a multimillion-dollar cleanup cost on the surrounding community's taxpayers, we have an example of a cost not being paid or accounted for by the polluter.

4. See "Compact Cities: Energy Saving Strategies for the Eighties," Subcommittee on the City, Committee on Banking, Finance, and Urban Affairs, U.S. House of Representatives, 96th Congress, July 1980. This report details land-value taxation's role in sprawl containment policy.

5. Nel van Dijk, *Ecotax: An Introduction to the Ecotax* (Brussels: Greens in

the European Parliament, 1991) gives a variety of such spending ideas in chapter 4, "Ecotax Proposals in Europe," 31–44.

6. It has also been called "the green tax shift" or "environmental tax shifting."

7. Politically, the case must be made that the plan put forward is better than another proposed plan, upholds American values, and so forth, but here we are only looking at structural characteristics.

8. It is clear when ecological-tax reform first became a technique. The booklet *Ecotax: An Introduction to the Ecotax* was published in the spring of 1991 and shows no awareness of ETR strategy. On the other hand, Sweden in that same year began levying a carbon dioxide tax and, in conjunction with it, cut the income tax. The notion of levying an environmental tax and rebating the revenue goes back at least to the 1970s; see, for example, R. Herendeen, B. Hannon, and C. Ford, "An Energy Conserving Tax: How Large Should the Rebate Be?" in R. Fazzolare and C. Smith, eds., *Changing Energy Futures: Proceedings of the Second International Conference on Energy Use Management,* Los Angeles, California, October 22–26, 1979 (New York: Pergamon). In another early work, Davies and Davies mention pollution fees and incentives to influence the marketplace, but do not bring these two together as a strategy or concept. See J. Clarence Davies III and Barbara S. Davies, *The Politics of Pollution* (Indianapolis: Bobbs-Merrill, 1970; 2d ed., 1975), 199–203. When the ETR idea started to become adopted as a conscious promotional strategy is uncertain. This spotty evidence suggests that the strategy began in the early 1990s.

9. This technique is also mentioned in David Malin Roodman, *Getting the Signals Right: Tax Reform to Protect the Environment and the Economy* (Washington, DC: Worldwatch Institute, 1997), 50.

10. Information on this Swedish tax comes from Hanno T. Beck, *Citizens' Guide to Environmental Tax Shifting* (Washington, DC: Friends of the Earth, 1998) and "Economic Instruments for Environmental Regulation," 8 (London: BP Economics Unit, 1995). The former book will be published shortly.

11. "Economic Instruments," 8.

12. Ibid.

13. For dozens of examples of this new entrepreneurial frontier and its surprising profitability, see Wayne Roberts and Susan Brandum, *Get a Life* (Toronto: Get a Life Publishing House, 1995). Also see Curtis Moore, "Snooze, We Lose," *Friends of the Earth Magazine* (September/October 1995) and Curtis Moore and Alan Miller, *Green Gold: Japan, Germany, the United States, and the Race for Environmental Technology* (Boston: Beacon Press, 1995). The former citation is published by Friends of the Earth (Washington, DC).

14. Roodman, *Getting the Signals Right,* 47–48.

15. Robert Herendeen and Farzaneh Fazel, "Distributional Aspects of an Energy Conserving Tax and Rebate," *Resource and Energy* 6 (1984): 277–303. North-Holland: Elsevier Science.

16. Jean Hanson and Margaret Walls, "Distributional Aspects of an Environmental Tax Shift: The Case of Motor Vehicle Emissions Taxes" (Wellington, New Zealand: Victoria University of Wellington, Graduate School of Business and Government Management, 1996).

17. Such a gradual transformation is claimed by some proponents to be prefer-

able. That places less stress on economic and social patterns. Consult Roodman, *Getting the Signals Right,* 8–9.

18. "Economic Instruments," 3.

19. Henry George, *Progress and Poverty* (1879; New York: Robert Schalkenbach Foundation, 1981), 409.

20. The term "land-value taxation" is one of several commonly used. We intend it as a synonym of "site-value taxation," "site-value revenue," and "location-value charge."

21. For a brief summary of the connection between taxes and sprawl, see "Taxes and Sprawl," *Friends of the Earth Magazine* (Spring 1997): 13.

22. Land-value taxation had been proposed well before the 1880s, but the modern era of LVT advocacy began with the enormous international popularity of *Progress and Poverty* in the early 1880s.

23. George, *Progress and Poverty,* 406.

24. Ibid., 433.

25. In a recent and notable case in 1996 carried out by the Pittsburgh Downtown Business Improvement District, it was decided to raise funds for its operation by means of a land-value tax.

26. The two-rate property tax has also been called "split rate," "two-tier," "site-value rating," the "graded tax," "property tax reform," and "property-tax modernization."

27. On April 23, 1996, the citizens of Allentown, Pennsylvania, voted to freeze the city's deed transfer tax, earned income tax, business privilege tax, occupational privilege tax, amusement devices tax, and residence tax at their 1996 levels. Additionally, the property tax on improvement value would be reduced. The city's revenue needs would be met by increases in land-value taxation. Consult Josh Vincent, "Allentown Voters Approve LVT," *Henry George News* 60, no. 5 (New York: Henry George School of Social Science, 1996), 8.

28. Harvey S. Rosen, *Public Finance,* 2d ed. (Homewood, IL: Irwin Press, 1988), 483–489; Mason Gaffney, "The Property Tax Is a Progressive Tax," Proceedings, National Tax Association, Sixty-Fourth Annual Conference, Kansas City, 1971, 408–426.

29. There are encouraging signs of a convergence between the ETR and the 2R community. In 1996, the Sierra Club, Chesapeake Bay Foundation, Maryland Public Interest Research Group, and ETR leader Friends of the Earth (all heavyweight environmental organizations) registered support for the two-rate property-tax approach.

16

Herbert Barry III

Psychological Perspective on the Land-Value Tax

Introduction

Psychology is the scientific study of human behavior, including social behavior. The psychological perspective on social behavior includes the study of mental activities, which are inferred from observable behavior. Among important mental activities are motivations, perceptions, and attitudes.

A psychological perspective can help to answer two persistent questions about land-value taxation, which includes the original single tax, proposed by Henry George. The first question is why this proposal is a constructive tax reform. The second question is why most people oppose it.

Diverse taxation changes have been labeled tax reform by their advocates. Steven Forbes in the Republican presidential primary elections of 1996 proposed the flat income tax as a substitute for the graduated income tax. The Pennsylvania state legislature in 1998 proposed a shift of local taxes from real estate to a sales or income tax. A psychological perspective, however, analyzing the effects of taxes on motivations, supports the Georgist tax reform. Henry George advocated abolition of all taxes on products of human labor. All government revenue should be obtained by solely taxing unimproved land value. The purpose of this proposal can be summarized by the slogan, "Tax Bads Not Goods."

The first major publication by Henry George was *Progress and Poverty* in 1879.[1] This book was bought by millions of people throughout the world and attracted many supporters for land-value taxation. Some partial tax reforms, known as the two-rate tax in the United States, that have been enacted and are still in force were inspired by Henry George's proposal for the single tax. Most people are unaware of this effective tax reform in spite of its success in many places, including Australia[2] and Pittsburgh,[3] the second largest city in Pennsylvania.

Rewarding Desirable Behavior

A fundamental principle of psychology is the importance of reward on behavior. It applies to human beings and all other species of animals. A response with a pleasurable outcome is repeated. Habits are established and strengthened. A response with a painful outcome is subsequently avoided. The unpleasant experience usually inhibits a habitual action and thereby results in a new response and a different habit.

People learn and repeat behavior that satisfies physical and social desires; and they inhibit behavior that is punished or ignored. Most habits have previously been rewarded by a pleasurable feeling. The pleasurable feeling results from satisfaction of a biological or social need. Social needs include money, status, and approval.

A psychological taxation policy should tax undesirable and destructive behavior and relieve from taxation the desirable behavior. Most taxation does the opposite. Most taxes take away part of the rewards for desirable activity. The income tax detracts from the reward for diligence. The capital gains tax detracts from the reward for careful management and patience. The sales tax takes away part of the price received by the seller and adds to the cost for the buyer. This tax therefore detracts from the reward both for buying and for selling.

An exception is the "sin tax" on products that can be harmful, such as tobacco and alcoholic beverages. The tax is limited to a few products that harm the person who consumes too much. The revenue for the government decreases if the "sin tax" has the desired effect of decreasing consumption.

A more effective tax is on ownership of excessive unimproved land

and other natural resources. A high tax on the value of land does not decrease consumption and government revenue, for the supply is fixed and everybody needs a place to live and work. People who own more than their fair share of land either pay for the privilege or sell part of the land to other people who need it.

Real estate has two components: unimproved land and buildings or other construction. The two components are generally taxed together at the same millage rate. Homeowners usually describe themselves as owning a house and paying taxes on it rather than on the combination of a house with plot of land.

A house or other structure is a product of human labor. The building yields income if rented. If it is the residence of the owner, it substitutes for the expense of renting. A lower tax on the building makes the constructive activity less costly and more probable. The constructive response benefits both the owner and the community. A new or enlarged building can accommodate more people. An improved or renovated building increases the value of the property and improves the attractiveness of the neighborhood.

Contrary to psychological principles, buildings are generally overtaxed and land is generally undertaxed. Assessments are generally too high on the building and too low on the plot of land. Assessments lag behind the depreciation of the building and the increase in value of the land. Even if the neighborhood is not becoming more populous or prosperous, the steady progress of inflation causes land values to rise in relation to the value of the dollar.

An increase in the taxation of land enables governments to reduce the undesirable taxes on buildings, income, and other products of human labor. This tax shift thereby rewards "goods" instead of "bads." An adequate tax on the value of land also increases the opportunity for property ownership. More land is available for purchase at a lower price because the tax increases the cost of holding it for a future increase in value. The lower sale price may disappoint the owner but it is beneficial for the purchaser. Lowering the purchase price of land benefits the community by making landownership affordable for more people. The more numerous new owners develop their property, thereby enriching the community and themselves. There are fewer vacant lots and dilapidated buildings. Cities become more compact, which minimizes undesirable urban sprawl. Wealthy owners of extensive land in a growing city pay adequately for the privilege so that they support the community instead of becoming richer at its expense.

Henry George emphasized the theme of social justice rather than the advantage of taxing "bads rather than goods." He stated as a physical law "that men seek to gratify their desires with the least exertion."[4] A more valid psychological principle is that desirable rewards should exceed the effort required. People willingly exert themselves greatly if the rewards are correspondingly greater.[5]

Three Sources of Opposition to Land-Value Tax

The land-value tax is the only stable source of government revenue that detracts from undesirable rather than desirable behavior. This advantage of the land-value tax appears to be a sufficient reason for its adoption. Some people ask why it is not more prevalent since it is so beneficial. Three psychological motivations account for opposition to this rational tax. These sources of opposition are identified in this passage from Friedrich Nietzsche. "We will seldom go wrong if we trace extreme actions back to vanity, middling ones to habit, and petty ones to fear."[6] Vanity induces in people the hope to become rich from their ownership of a house with its plot of land. Habit is indicated by acceptance of traditional taxation that falls more heavily on the house than on the land. Fear causes people to oppose higher taxation on their plot of land.

Vanity

Two different forms of vanity contribute to the opposition to the land-value tax. Greedy vanity motivates people to inflate their own wealth. Envious vanity motivates people to diminish the superiority of people who have greater wealth.

Greedy vanity causes the homeowner to overvalue the potential for wealth from property. People are aware that great fortunes have been made by owners of land that becomes highly valuable because a great city is nearby. The owners of houses on small plots of land in residential areas likewise hope that their property will enrich them or their descendants. People who buy a house are delighted and feel proud when its value has multiplied two or three decades later.

Most homeowners do not realize that the increased market price of property is not due to the higher value of the house they have maintained and improved. It is due to the increased price of the plot of land, attributable to inflation that decreases the value of money and in some cases developments and facilities that increase the value of the neighborhood. Most homeowners also are not aware that the principal beneficiaries from a low tax on land are the wealthy individuals and corporations who own large amounts of underdeveloped land. The homeowners pay for the profits of the wealthy owners by other higher taxes. Studies have shown that when the same tax revenue is obtained from a shift to a lower tax rate on buildings and a higher tax rate on land, the average homeowners pay less tax. Most homeowners live in a well-maintained house on a small plot of land in a residential area where the land values are relatively low.

Another expression of this type of vanity was when George McGovern, the 1972 Democratic candidate for president, proposed that inheritance should be limited to a maximum of $500,000. A press spokesman for McGovern commented that "it would wipe out the dream factor—every slob in the street thinks that if he hits the lottery big, he may be able to leave half a million to his family; it wipes out dreams."[7]

Envious vanity induces people to support the income tax and other taxes on products of human labor. Envy blocks the awareness that equalizing incomes inhibits the constructive activities that benefit everybody. Winston Churchill made this observation eloquently: "The inherent vice of capitalism is the unequal sharing of blessings; the inherent virtue of socialism is the equal sharing of miseries."[8]

An extreme expression of envy is the graduated income tax. People with higher income automatically pay more with a fixed percentage tax. The graduated income tax, by exaggerating this effect, induces many wealthy people to find tax shelters for their income. It is more rational to impose a high tax on land values. Extraordinarily high incomes and capital gains, however, are more visible and better publicized than ownership of valuable land, which will gradually become more valuable in the future.

Fear

In common with vanity, fear has two different forms. Fear of novelty is a desire to cling to safe, traditional customs and resist change and unfamiliar ideas. Fear of bankruptcy perceives that the taxes might exceed the income.

Fear of novelty expresses the rational recognition that the world is a dangerous place. Fear is a necessary emotion to enable survival. This form of fear induces people to cling to traditional ideas and reject novel proposals. The desire for a familiar environment is expressed by the frequently repeated sentiment: "Be it ever so humble, there's no place like home."[9]

The traditional policy has been heavier taxation on buildings than on land. Beginning early in the twentieth century, the national policy has taxed income and sales rather than property. The land-value tax advocates a reversal of this traditional policy. The prospect of a fundamental change in taxation arouses fear of novelty.

An adequate tax on land values induces fear of bankruptcy because the land does not directly generate income. Taxation of a proportion of income or capital gains seems to be a safe tax because it takes only part of the money that has been received. People prefer to be taxed on the basis of their ability to pay. This preference was recognized in a statement attributed to J.B. Colbert, the finance minister of Louis XIV: "The art of taxation consists in so plucking the goose as to obtain the largest amount of feathers with the least possible amount of hissing."[10] From this point of view the sales tax is advantageous because a small percentage can raise more money than a higher rate on income or property. The sales tax, though, has a pervasive though generally unrecognized inhibitory effect on all buying and selling.

The land-value tax is on capital resources rather than on income. People who own land might not have the money needed to pay the tax on the land value. The term "land poor" was commonly applied to owners of large estates in North America before and after the American War of Independence. Many of them were land speculators who overextended their financial resources in the effort to become rich. Instead, some became bankrupt. Others accumulated great wealth for their descendants, free of any high tax rate on land. Their profits were at the expense of people who, in the absence of sufficient taxes from the valuable land, paid too much in other taxes.

A prominent source of fear for homeowners is that the rising value of their property will result in more taxation than they can pay. Many local governments provide tax relief for homeowners so that they will not be required to move to a less expensive location. It is morally questionable to give tax relief to owners of expensive property, some of whom are very wealthy, rather than to the larger number of less fortunate people. An additional drawback of tax relief for homeowners is that it helps them to withhold their valuable property from people who need it and wish to use it in a way that benefits the community.

Habit

People tend to accept traditional policies. Since human beings are born helpless, initial learning is to affiliate with the parents and other sources of nourishment and protection. Rebellion and striving for self-reliance are later responses. The tendency to conform and obey is earlier, and for most people remains stronger.

For many centuries, real estate taxes have been lower on the value of unimproved land than on buildings. Beginning in the twentieth century in the United States, federal taxes on income have generally exceeded local real estate taxes. These taxation policies are beneficial for most political and business leaders, who own valuable land and can use tax shelters to minimize the tax on their income. In the book *Escape from Freedom,* Erich Fromm described "automation conformity" as a typical response of individuals to the increasing power of monopolistic capital in the United States in the twentieth century.[11]

Habit motivates repetition of a behavior that is adaptive and therefore is rewarded. If the behavior continues to be adaptive and rewarded, habit is a useful way to ensure its repetition. It is usually easier to repeat previous behavior than to make novel choices that will establish new habits. Repeated habitual action enables the person to focus attention elsewhere. Habitual behavior is more comfortable because it precludes hesitation and doubt.

The habit of accepting traditional practices induces people to ignore the maladaptive taxation policies and to oppose constructive tax reform. Vanity contributes to habitual acceptance because most citizens of the United States feel proud of their country and are inclined to accept national policies. Fear of novelty also contributes to this repetitive behavior because it perpetuates habitual attitudes even when they are no longer adaptive and rewarded.

Habitual acceptance, augmented by vanity and fear, explains why many people ignore taxation policies. Most homeowners, for example, are probably unaware that they are taxed more heavily on the true value of their house than on their plot of land underneath it. They want to avoid the unpleasant recognition that the tax policy is fundamentally flawed.

Motivations of Henry George

The extensive publication of speeches, letters, and books by Henry George provides useful information on his motivations for proposing the single tax. Three biographies each contribute some different items of information on his personality.[12] The motivations for opposition to the land-value tax, which includes this single tax and the two-rate tax, can be clarified and verified by identifying the differences between them and his motivations, which initially evoked them.

Vanity is a prominent motive for many opponents of the land-value tax. Vanity also was a motive for many of George's extreme actions, but they were usually directed toward service for humanity rather than accumulation of personal wealth. Social justice and freedom were the two most prominent themes in his writings. His vanity included pride in his insight that high land prices have destructive effects, and pride in his single-tax proposal on land values. This ingenious idea reconciled his support of social justice with his commitment to freedom. Vanity was also a motivation for his energetic and persistent writing and speaking that made him the principal advocate of this constructive tax reform.

More than two decades before publication of *Progress and Poverty,* George when he was not yet twenty had desired to enrich himself by participating in the Canadian Gold Rush. Instead, he lost his small amount of money. George subsequently manifested little vanity or envy concerning financial status, and in spite of his great success in writing and lecturing did not become wealthy.

The motivation of fear, which is an important reason for opposition to the land-value tax, appeared to be a weak influence on George. He showed little fear of financial deprivation or personal harm. He was not afraid of the possible adverse effects of individual liberty or the excessive growth of human population. His fear was centered on the consequences of misguided taxation policies. His personality manifested more hope than fear; he was optimistic about the ultimate acceptance of his proposals.

Habit is another motivational difference between George and the opponents of his proposal. Against the prevalent habit of supporting traditional policies, George had a strong habit of rebelling against tradition. He enthusiastically devised and advocated an unorthodox scheme.

The rebellious inclination of George may have originated from his position in his family during childhood. He was the second born and the first boy in a family of ten children. His affiliations were mainly with his younger brothers and sisters rather than with a sister who was a year older. Frank Sulloway has reported evidence that later-born children are more likely to support novel and unorthodox opinions in science, politics, and religion.[13] Although George was the oldest son, he might have selected the path of conformity because of rivalry with his older sister. An additional motivation for affiliating with the younger children was his physical appearance. He was described as being small and with a complexion delicate as a girl's before he grew a beard.[14]

The rebellious tendency of George was expressed by his behavior in youth and maturity. He accepted very little formal education but was an avid reader. At a young age he left home to become a crew member of a ship on a long voyage. He settled in San Francisco, far away from his childhood home in Philadelphia. His love of liberty was an expression of his hatred of authoritarian rule and monopoly. He did not affiliate with a church although his father was an active Episcopalian.

George did not totally rebel against his family antecedents. He maintained affectionate correspondence with his parents and other family members. His advocacy of social justice and freedom was partly motivated by his acceptance of the ethical orientation of his parents. A recurrent phrase in his writings and speeches was "the fatherhood of God, the brotherhood of man."[15]

All human beings have a combination of opposite traits, such as conformity and rebellion. Henry George was more a rebel than a conformist, but his prevalent attitude was positive, optimistic, and constructive. An expression of his predominant attitude appears to be his response to his fatal stroke in 1897. His last word, repeated loudly many times, was "Yes."[16]

Motivations of Georgists

Henry George was a highly persuasive writer and speaker. Many of his supporters were convinced by his outstanding intellect and eloquence. Their vanity, in common with George's, was expressed by pride in the advocacy of tax reform for the benefit of all humanity. Their fear was minimized by his courage and by the growing number of supporters. They acquired the habit of advocating the single tax rather than destructive traditional policies.

The personal influence of Henry George has waned during the century since his death in 1897. Present-day Georgists are a diverse group, with various motivations for their support of the single tax and the two-rate tax.

Some Georgists emphasize social justice rather than freedom. They are drawn to the proposal that the land should be a common resource, shared by everybody. They view a tax on land as a method of sharing rather than of taking away personal wealth. An implication is that owners of extensive or expensive land hold wealth that should belong to the community rather than to any individual. This way of thinking is suggestive of socialism. It also implies that the inequalities in landownership should be quickly and completely abolished. If individuals continue to use land, taxation of the full rental value is required to abolish inequities.

Other supporters of the land-value tax emphasize protection of individual freedom and the free market. This view implies preference for a partial, gradual change in tax policies rather than immediate abolition of the privileges of landownership. George recognized the merits of partial and gradual change. In an article that argued against compensation to landowners, he advocated stopping short of collecting the full amount of economic rent on unimproved land.[17] In a letter that argued in favor of the single tax rather than land nationalization, he stated: "Either method must be a gradual one."[18] The higher tax rates on land than on buildings in several cities in Pennsylvania are examples of limited but definite progress toward the single tax, although he did not advocate them.

In spite of progress in the promotion of land-value taxation, it continues to be an unorthodox rather than traditional proposal. Most Georgists, therefore, have an unusual ability to accept untraditional ideas. Many of them, in common with George, have strong rebellious feelings.

Some Georgists have responded to other influences. A substantial number are children or grandchildren of Georgists. Some receive financial support from foundations established by an earlier generation of Georgists. Others were attracted by the passionate and eloquent arguments in George's *Progress and Poverty* and his other writings. A cult of uncritical admirers has centered on some charismatic individuals, such as Karl Marx and Sigmund Freud. Such cultists are rare among Georgists, however, because George consistently advocated intellectual inquiry and individual freedom.

Redirecting Vanity, Fear, and Habit

It is difficult to counteract the motivations of vanity, fear, and habit. Vanity, a form of pride, is the basis for many admirable actions. Fear mediates the cautious and prudent actions that are often necessary for survival. Habit enables persistent and consistent behavior. People can be converted from opponents to supporters of land-value taxation by redirecting their vanity, fear, and habit. It is not, however, necessary to diminish these motivations.

Two types of vanity can be redirected so that they motivate support for the land-value tax. Reduction of taxation on products of human labor magnifies the rewards for personal accomplishments and therefore encourages achievements motivated by vanity. The motivation of envy can be expressed by advocating this constructive tax reform, which counteracts the privilege of owning large amounts of valuable land.

The land-value tax enables lowering or abolishing all taxes on products of human labor. The person's productions and earnings are not shared with the tax collector. The land-value tax therefore strengthens the vanity of individual accomplishment while diminishing the wealth obtained by landownership. The same type of vanity can be redirected to subordinate selfishness to the interests of the community and even of all humanity. This type of vanity is emphasized in religious precepts and is consistent with social affiliation as an important human motive. The land-value tax benefits the community and therefore satisfies this communal vanity. The land-value tax in particular helps the poor and underprivileged by making landownership more affordable and more widely accessible.

The land-value tax also is an adaptive response to envy of wealthy individuals. It is preferable to improve opportunities for people who are poor and deprived rather than to impair the economy by an insistence on abolishing great wealth for some individuals. The long-range effect of the land-value tax is to decrease differences in wealth because the greatest family fortunes are based on the privilege of owning large amounts of valuable, undertaxed land.

Fear could be redirected to the threat that revolution is the alternative to a beneficial tax reform. The technological advances that have brought great wealth to some individuals have been accompanied by an increasing mass of urban poor who feel hopelessly confined to an environment of joblessness, violence, and drug addiction. There is special present-day relevance to a statement by George—"Whence shall come the new barbarians? Go through the squalid quarters of great cities, and you may see, even now, their gathering hordes!"[19]

An alternative redirection of fear is to emphasize the benefits of land-value taxation and the danger that the opportunity will be lost. Fear of losing the opportunity for a gain may induce more rational responses than fear of disaster if the traditional policies are continued.

Habit is a basis for opposition to the land-value tax because the proposal appears to be novel and radical. Habit can be redirected with the help of rational examination of the issues. In many cities the beneficial effect of putting lower tax rates on buildings than on land is an effective way to redirect habit from opposition to support of the land-value tax.

Habits are not limited to a continuation of traditional policies. Progress and improvement can become habits. People who support new ideas have not renounced habit but instead have redirected it to seeking better policies. This acceptance of change is especially appropriate in today's civilization, where technological advancements have mediated many beneficial changes.

The opposition due to fear and habit can be minimized by introducing the land-value tax gradually. Mark Twain vividly expressed this necessity: "Habit is habit, and not to be flung out of the window by any man, but coaxed downstairs a step at a time."[20] Evolution is usually preferable to revolution. For many centuries, land value has been grossly undertaxed. Property values are based partly on the speculation over a span of many years, since the increase in land value will exceed the cumulative annual tax on it. Gradual progress toward this tax reform would minimize the disruptive effects of the change.

A successful example of a gradual shift of taxation policies is the decrease in tax rate on buildings combined with the increase in tax rate on unimproved land in Pittsburgh and in more than a dozen cities in Pennsylvania. The differential taxation rates can be extended to other governmental units, such as towns and counties, and to other states. More extensive reform, such as limiting taxation to a levy on land values without other taxes, can follow after most people have recognized the benefits of lowering taxes on buildings rather than on land.

Fear and habit induce most people to ignore the destructive effects of the traditional taxation policies. The initial program of advocacy therefore should be designed to increase people's awareness of the issue. Communications should appeal to rationality and desire for knowledge. Universal education provides citizens who are potentially receptive to this appeal. The proposal for this constructive tax reform should emphasize the benefits rather than concentrate on denouncing the traditional policies.

Conclusions

There are important advantages of land-value taxation and severe disadvantages of traditional taxation. Today, an equitable tax reform is needed more than in Henry George's time, when the total taxation rate was much lower and a larger proportion of taxes was on real estate, which included value of unimproved land.

Some people regard George's proposal or the two-rate tax as outdated. Although there has been great technological change, the same principles apply. Taxation should be on the undesirable behavior of owning more of the earth's surface and resources than a fair share and not on the desirable behavior of constructing buildings, earning and accumulating money, buying and selling, and trading with foreign countries.

In some ways location has become more extensive and flexible. People can be rapidly transported long distances from home to business. In spite of these changes, certain residence and business locations continue to be preferable. Close proximity to facilities is still a great advantage since a limited amount of land and resources is shared with an increasing population.

The principal motivations for opposition to the land-value tax are two types of vanity, two types of fear, and habit. These motives are universal, but they can be redirected. Biographical information on George and characteristics of Georgists show ways in which these motivations can induce advocacy of the land-value tax. Most people have a greater fear of new ideas than did Henry George and his followers, and a stronger habit of accepting traditional policies. The success of a shift from tax on buildings to tax on land values can help induce people to accept as beneficial the two-rate tax with its successful track record.

The principal initial obstacle to acceptance of land-value tax by the public is the desire to ignore taxation issues. People are also unwilling to recognize the fundamental defect in the traditional taxation policies. They do not desire to learn about the distinction between land and buildings. The initial effort therefore should be to describe and propose tax reform in a rational and reassuring manner that emphasizes that the change in tax policies would be gradual.

The advocates of land-value taxation need to counteract the influence of the wealthy, powerful opponents who are the main beneficiaries of insufficient taxation on land values. But they are greatly outnumbered by residents who will benefit from the shift to land-value tax. The supporters of constructive tax reform have the advantage of periodic democratic elections. When the majority of voters learn to recognize the issue and to advocate land-value taxation, each subsequent election will increase the support among elected government officials.

Notes

1. Henry George, *Progress and Poverty* (1879; New York: Robert Schalkenbach Foundation, 1981).
2. Fred Harrison, *The Power in the Land; Unemployment, the Profits Crisis and the Land Speculator* (New York: Universe Books, 1983), 230–242.
3. Wallace E. Oates and Robert M. Schwab, "The Impact of Urban Land Taxation: The Pittsburgh Experience," *National Tax Journal* 50 (1997): 1–21.
4. Henry George, *Progress and Poverty,* 12.
5. Henry George died in 1897, before psychology became a recognized field in the United States. The American Psychological Association was founded in 1892. For many years after this date, psychology was generally considered a division of philosophy rather than a separate social science.
6. Friedrich Nietzsche, *Human, All Too Human,* Gary Handwerk, trans. (Stanford: Stanford University Press,1997), 65.
7. Theodore H. White, *The Making of the President, 1972* (New York: Atheneum, 1973), 119.
8. Winston Churchill, speech in the House of Commons on October 22, 1945. From "The Wisdom of Winston Churchill," F.B. Czarnomski, ed. (London: George Allen & Unwin, 1956), 60.
9. John Howard Payne, "Home, Sweet Home," from the 1823 opera *Clair, the*

Maid of Milan, quoted in *Bartlett's Familiar Quotations,* 14th ed. (Boston: Little, Brown, 1968), 804.

10. Quoted in Bergen Evans, ed., *Dictionary of Quotations* (New York: Delacorte Press, 1968), 680.

11. Erich Fromm, *Escape from Freedom* (New York: Holt, Rinehart & Winston, 1941), 123 and 185.

12. Henry George Jr., *Henry George* (1900; New York: Chelsea House, 1981); Anna George de Mille, *Henry George: Citizen of the World* (originally entitled *The Life of Henry George*) (1950; Westport, CT: Greenwood Press, 1972); and Charles Albro Barker, *Henry George* (1955; New York: Robert Schalkenbach Foundation, 1991).

13. Frank J. Sulloway, *Born to Rebel: Birth Order, Family Dynamics, and Creative Lives* (New York: Pantheon Books, 1996).

14. de Mille, *Henry George,* 11.

15. Henry George, quoted in Kenneth C. Wenzer, ed., *An Anthology of Henry George's Thought* (Rochester: University of Rochester Press, 1997). This work is volume I of *The Henry George Centennial Trilogy.*

16. George Jr., *Henry George,* 607.

17. Henry George, "Different Interpretations of the Single Tax," *The Standard* (August 17, 1998), reprinted in Wenzer, *An Anthology of Henry George's Thought,* 84.

18. Henry George, Letter to Thomas Walker, September 25, 1890, reprinted in Wenzer, *An Anthology of Henry George's Thought,* 77.

19. George, *Progress and Poverty,* 538.

20. Mark Twain, *Pudd'nhead Wilson* (New York: Harper and Brothers, 1899), 56.

17

Alanna Hartzok

Pennsylvania Farmers and the Split-Rate Tax

Introduction

Pennsylvania has been experimenting with an approach to local tax reform which offers an angle entirely different from that of other current reform proposals that attempt to reduce the use of property taxes while introducing sales or income taxes. This approach, known as the "split-rate" or "two-tier" tax, reforms the property tax itself in a way that appears beneficial on a number of indicators.

The property tax is actually two types of taxes—one on building values, and the other on land values. This distinction is important, as these taxes differ significantly in their impacts on incentive motives, development results, and economic consequences.

Because buildings must be constructed and maintained in order to have value, a tax on building values is a cost of production. Such a tax results in lower production, higher prices, or both.

The other part of the property tax is on the value of land. Land is most certainly not a product of human labor but a gift of nature. A tax on land cannot be avoided by producing less land, or by moving land from one jurisdiction to another. Unlike a levy on capital items, a tax on land values is not a cost of production in itself but functions as a type of user fee which has the added advantage of encouraging efficient land use while curbing land speculation. And since land value is enhanced by public expenditures for roads and other improvements of the infrastructure, the taxation of land values recaptures this publicly created value and places government on a firmer footing without burdening private enterprise.[1]

Pennsylvania's pioneering use of the split-rate tax makes this important distinction between land and building values. The tax is decreased on buildings, which gives property owners the incentive to maintain and improve their properties, while an increase in the levy on land values encourages good site utilization. It should be kept clearly in mind that land-value taxation (LVT) is not proposed as an additional tax burden, but should be implemented in tandem with significant tax reductions on productive labor and capital.

The split-rate tax, now in place in varying degrees in sixteen cities in Pennsylvania, encourages improvements and renovations, promotes a more efficient use of urban infrastructure such as roads and sewers, and discourages land speculation and urban sprawl.[2] The split-rate tax reform provides a strong incentive for infill development, as indicated by comparing the increase in building permits in cities using it with stagnation in cities imposing the traditional property tax. This approach fosters more downtown jobs and improvements in residential and commercial buildings. By correctly harnessing market forces and private incentives and at the same time providing a solid source of financing for the public sector, the split-rate tax reform also assures a broader spread of the benefits of development to the community as a whole. Legislative efforts are now under way to extend the split-rate tax option to the boroughs, school districts, and townships of Pennsylvania.

The possibility of extending the split-rate tax to jurisdictions that include agricultural lands raises the important question of *what might be its impact on the farmers of Pennsylvania.*

To answer this question, we will summarize recent research on the overall impact of property taxes on agriculture and also report on the effect that land-value-based taxes have had on farmers in places where similar split-rate or pure land-value tax policies have been in force. Knowledge of the precise impact of this policy approach on farmland in any particular county, township, or region, however, requires research and analysis as applied to that particular area.

Property Taxes in Agriculture

On average in the United States, 60 percent of the private land in the forty-eight contiguous states is in farms and ranches.[3] Although farming and ranching cover a lot of territory, agricultural real estate represents only 5 percent of all real estate value in the United States, according to the National Realty Committee. The Federal Reserve Bulletin estimates the 1994 farm business real estate at $772 billion, which is 6 percent of the nation's real-estate value. Farm business land alone was estimated at $593 billion, 14 percent of American land value. The $5 billion of agricultural real property taxes is only about 3 percent of total real property taxes.[4]

As currently applied, agriculture pays a relatively small part of America's total real property taxes and thus the property tax on farmlands is not critical fiscal policy. The real property tax is more important at the local level, where such taxes constitute 76 percent of the tax revenue, 48 percent of town revenues, and 30 percent of all local government revenue.[5]

The research of Gene Wunderlich of the USDA Economic Research Service revealed that as currently administered, the real property tax appears to be regressive in relation to the value of holdings.[6] Landowners whose value of farmland was $5 million or more paid one-third the rate of landowners with farmland holdings valued at less than $70,000. The owners whose estimated market value of farmland holdings was less than $70,000 paid $1.45 per $100 and owners of $5 million or more paid $.47 per $100. Holdings between these extremes graded regressively.[7]

Property tax policy, with all its partial exemptions, preferential assessments, and levels of rates and classifications, may be excessively complex, Wunderlich says. His findings lead him to recommend that before the real property tax can become an effective instrument of land policy, some of its administrative shortcomings must be addressed. Exemptions, partial and total, based on features of the owners distort the incidence of the tax. Multiple classes and rates further complicate the legal structure and administration. Reform of the real property tax to support effective land use policy requires changes in law and management. Wunderlich's extensive research led him to this conclusion:

> Exercised differently and more vigorously than at present, the real property tax might complement other land use policies or become a strong policy instrument in its own right, but without the concerns about "takings" under eminent domain or regulation. Its influence would be reflected in land values and land prices. The value of land, therefore, is the key ingredient in tax policy pertaining to resource use.[8]

Rising Inequality and Falling Property-Tax Rates

A meticulous study conducted by Mason Gaffney and titled "Rising Inequality and Falling Property Tax Rates" refutes the common belief that property-tax relief would be good for farmers.[9] This research showed that property-tax relief for agricultural land increases the likelihood that it will attract those looking primarily for tax shelters and speculative investments. Such nonproductive incentives ultimately inflate land values overall, making it increasingly difficult for working farmers to acquire and maintain acreage for viable agricultural enterprise. Lower farm-property taxes were also found to be associated with lower ratios of capital to land, and labor to land, both over time and among states. States with lower property taxes also had larger mean farm size and less equal distribution of farm sizes along with underuse and underimprovement of land. Conversely, a positive relationship was found between higher property-tax rates and more intensive use of farmland, which in turn is associated with its more equal distribution.

Gaffney's research made a clear distinction between building values and land values in agricultural holdings. This aspect of the study permits property taxes levied on buildings and land combined or separately to be compared with lower tax rates placed on buildings and higher rates on land values, as would be the case with the two-rate property tax on Pennsylvania agricultural lands.

The study showed that smaller farmers had a higher ratio of building to land than bigger farmers. Property taxes on buildings therefore penalize the former and work to suppress improvements. Indicating that a property tax on land values promoted a more intensive and efficient use of agricultural land, the finding supported the overall viability of smaller farming operations.

Gaffney found that the national average of farm property-tax rates peaked in 1930 at 1.32 percent. It fell to 0.77 percent in 1945, and stabilized at about that level in 1987 (0.85 percent). From 1870 to 1935 mean acres to a farm remained fairly constant at about 155 acres. After 1935 the mean took off and by 1987 it had tripled to 462 acres. Since 1955 real wage rates have not risen as fast as real land prices, and since about 1975 they have not risen at all. This situation, coupled with rising acres, to a farm meant that the labor-price of a farm roughly tripled, from about six years' wages (before payroll deductions) in 1954 to around seventeen years' wages in 1987. Consequently, farms became unaffordable to the average person while concentration in their holdings proceeded.

In 1900 the Census Bureau began publishing farm data ranked by the ratio of acres to farm. Using those data, the Gini Ratio (GR) was calculated for several decades. The GR is a measure of unequal distribution. A rise in GR means that the big became bigger, the small became smaller, or both. It ranges from 0.00 (complete equality) to 1.00 (complete inequality). The GR was 0.58 in 1900, rose only slowly, to 0.63 in 1930, climbed faster, to 0.70 by 1950, plateaued there for fifteen years, then increased again to 0.76 by 1987. The accelerated rise since 1930 coincided with the rise of mean acres per farm; both followed the fall of property-tax rates.

The GR deals only with concentration among existing farms and normally does not reflect their loss. In his research Gaffney modified the GR to combine both effects by adding to the lowest bracket—farms with no acres in 1988—the 4.5 million farms that had died out between 1935 and 1988. Calculating the GR this way gives a better sense of how concentration shot up after the years between 1930 and 1935. This increases the GR for 1988 from 0.76 to 0.92, a radical rise of inequality since 1930, when it was 0.63. "In the Great Depression (1930–1941), millions of small farms provided a refuge for the jobless and homeless," states Gaffney. "Today, that refuge is closed, with explosive social consequences in urban slums."[10] Gaffney also found that during most of this century the concentration of the value of farm real estate has been growing faster than that of farm acres, and that the "land share of real estate value" (LSREV) in the top bracket, 1,000 acres and over, appears to have risen faster than the share held by building values. Higher LSREV means a higher ratio of farm price to cash flow (P/C), which is another barrier to farm entry. A high P/C ratio shows a higher share of land value ($L) in farm wealth.

The common belief that high "capital costs of machinery and equipment" ($M&E) are the main obstacle to farm entry is therefore erroneous. At the time of this study, capital costs were only about 10 percent of all farm assets, much smaller than the costs of land and buildings.

To sum up these essential points from this *Landownership and Taxation in American Agriculture* study:

1. Rising acreages mean there are fewer farms overall.
2. Rising labor prices per farm mean aspiring farmers who lack prior wealth can no longer afford to acquire farms.
3. Acreage is less equally shared among a given number of farms.
4. The higher quality of land is moving into bigger farms.

The combination of these factors means that "the agricultural ladder has been pulled up. Entry is nearly impossible for farmers lacking outside finance."[11] Smaller farms have been forced to sell out as larger farms increase their holdings. These changes accompanied and followed a 40 percent drop in farm property-tax rates.

This study also showed that as the concentration in both acreage and real-estate value of agricultural lands proceeds, land increasingly separates itself from capital. Large farms are for the most part lands without buildings while buildings cluster on smaller farms, many without enough land. The biggest landlord holdings in dollar value, moreover, were found to be 99 percent pure land.[12]

Lack of buildings reveals a dearth of family labor, because so many farm buildings are operator dwellings. In 1988 operators' dwellings were 48 percent of farm real-estate assets in the smallest acreage bracket, 16.4 percent for all farms, and falling steadily to 4.4 percent on farms 2,000 acres and over. For family-held corporate farms of all sizes the share is 6.3 percent; for other corporate farms, 3.2 percent.

These data support the common impression that smaller and unincorporated farms are better supplied with operator family labor. Additional statistical analysis in the Gaffney study clearly indicates that farmland values are much more concentrated than farm-building values.

Such statistics suggest at least three points:

1. Building wealth is more equally distributed than land wealth.
2. The property tax would be more progressive if changed to a pure land tax, exempting buildings.
3. Many large farms are not being used to their potential while capital on some small farms is undercomplemented with land.

Yet another component of the Gaffney study bears mentioning since it concerns how the split-rate property tax might affect the farmers of Pennsylvania. It suggests that "the effect of urban land speculation is toward higher concentration of landholdings . . . observable today around growing cities."[13]

Evidence further supports the understanding that higher property taxes are actually to the benefit of smaller farming operations with more intensive capital and labor. Wisconsin had the highest "building share of real estate value" (BSREV) in 1988 (0.47), while Florida had the lowest (0.15); yet Wisconsin's farm "property-tax rate" (PTR) exceeded Florida's 4 : 1. Wisconsin, the high-tax state, led Florida 3 : 1 in farm output per dollar of farmland value, 5 : 1 in farm buildings for each dollar of farmland value, and 7 : 3 in machinery and livestock. The agricultural landholdings in Florida, the low-tax state, were twice as concentrated as holdings in Wisconsin. Florida, according to the GR, had a 5.5 higher ratio of land value for a farm, had more acres to a farm (3 : 2) and more land value to an acre (4 : 1), and led in total assets (11 : 8).

Extending his data to the eight low property tax states below Florida and to the eight above Wisconsin, Gaffney found that the differences persisted and accumulated consistently. The states lower in property tax were Florida, Arizona, New Mexico, Hawaii, Montana, North Dakota, Wyoming, California, and Texas. At the other extreme were Wisconsin, Delaware, Maine, Pennsylvania, New York, New Hampshire, North Carolina, Oklahoma, and Ohio.

It was found that higher property-tax rates were associated with higher building values, smaller farms (lower land values per farm and per acre), and lower GR values, which indicates a broader distribution of farmland ownership. Higher ratios of capital investment in machinery and equipment as compared to real estate, lower share of leased land, and fuller land usage as measured by sales in relation to land value, were also apparent. From these state comparisons, Gaffney contends that

> The egalitarian effects of a high property tax rate seem stronger than its negative incentive effects, even though buildings are part of the tax base. These egalitarian effects would be stronger if the tax base was limited to land value only, because the land share of real estate value rises steeply with size of farm. Untaxing buildings would also eliminate negative incentive effects.[14]

Gaffney concludes that large farm units are less improved and less peopled than small- and medium-sized farms. They get less production in relation to land value and are possibly being held for long-term land speculation. Large farm units appear to be, in his words:

> oversized stores of value, held first to park slack money and only secondly to produce food and fiber, and complement owner's workmanship. . . . If they are less efficient, heavier property tax rates will induce them to release surplus land for others.[15]

Preferential Assessments, Zoning, and Other Farmland Protection Policies

In all fifty states, agricultural land receives some preferential treatment in assessment. The level and form vary among states, but generally, the preference is in the assessment of value in current use rather than at some higher-valued use rendered by the market. Under the pressure of residential development, for example, the assessed market value of a farmland tract might be multiples of the value for farming, but under preferential assessment law the tract would be taxed only for its value in agricultural use. With some preferential assessment contracts, penalties in the form of fees or taxes are charged for changes in land use.[16] In Pennsylvania, for instance, the corresponding statutes declare:

> Counties may covenant with owners of land in farm, forest, water supply, or open space use. Assessments reflect fair market value of land so restricted. Such agreements may be negotiated to conform with more recent provisions of preferential use assessment described below.[17]
>
> Upon application, qualifying agricultural land, agricultural reserve, and/or forest reserve may be given preferential use assessments. Requirements include ten-acre minimum size for agricultural land, an anticipated annual gross income of $2,000, and qualification for compensation under a soil conservation program for at least three years. Rollback taxes may extend for up to seven previous tax years, and include 6 percent interest.[18]

A USDA Economic Research Service survey found that, as expected, higher taxes were levied on farmland without a preferential assessment than with it, but it was a very small difference.[19] Although a relatively large change in taxes attends a change in preferential status, the evidence suggests that preferential assessments, in aggregate, do not make much difference in tax rates. In 1992, for instance, the average tax for an acre of agricultural land with an assessment preference was $5.12 and without it the amount was $5.93. In 1993, the figures were $5.39 with assessment preference and $5.94 without it.

While it is sometimes assumed that preferential assessments which lower property taxes on farmland can help keep land in agricultural use and protect it from more intensive development, a survey of the literature shows that the opposite may be true:

> There is general consensus from extensive research over a twenty year period that the economic incentive offered by lower property taxes has had minimal effect in preventing conversion of farmland to more intensive uses. In urbanizing areas, the tax reductions have not matched the profits available from subdivision and development, and in some areas may have fueled land speculation.[20]

Since most agricultural land does not encounter competition from urbanization, preferential assessments have little overall effect on changes in land use. In areas affected by urban pressures and land speculation, the effect of the preference is so slight, compared with value increments for more intensive uses, that it is not an effective deterrent to development. Says Wunderlich:

> Only where landowners and local government have a long-term contract agreement, with severe penalties for breaking the contract, are tax preference programs likely to have some effect. A capture of all the increase in land value due to a change in land use likewise could be a deterrent to land use change.[21]

Preferential assessments based on value of agricultural use can be highly lucrative for rural landowners and yet may not guarantee long-term retention of prime farmland. In general, the tax savings for maintaining agricultural uses are insufficient to outbid sale prices offered by developers. As a result, farmland owners often can simply take advantage of sizable tax savings while speculatively waiting for land values to appreciate. Where rollback requirements or transfer taxes are in effect, the farmland owner may simply enjoy the equivalent of a low-interest or interest-free loan while holding property for later conversion.[22] Time is simply being bought through the use of an indirect subsidy but state differential taxation laws do not ensure the continuation of prime farmland in perpetuity.

Another problem for agricultural, open space, and forest land is that preferential assessment usually applies only to land, and not buildings and improvements. The preferential tax laws for agriculture thus favor land and penalize buildings, which then must carry a larger share of the tax burden. When higher tax rates are applied to capital investments such as buildings, the economic incentive is to construct and maintain them less. Yet by raising conversion costs, erecting farm buildings and maintaining their value may do more to discourage land conversion than subsidizing land values does. Wunderlich concludes that "as a measure to preserve agricultural land use the real property tax is weak . . . the preferential assessment is shallow . . . and the taxes carry little or no penalty for land use change."[23] He instead recommends, as a better way to keep land in agricultural use, a shift to property taxes that would fall primarily on land values.

Zoning can be a bigger determinant of value than land use. If after investigating possibilities for implementing the split-rate tax in rural areas the community decides to award special protection to ensure the viability of farming, it can restrict land zoning for agricultural use only, and land prices would thus reflect agricultural use alone. Since this tax would rise as the value of the land increased, or fall as it decreased, there would be no basis for speculation in land. A policy that kept taxes on agricultural lands appropriate to the profits that can be realized from farming might encourage farmers to look favorably on zoning proposals. Shifting taxes away from labor and capital and increasing taxes on land values would help keep farm costs affordable and farming viable. Finance currently invested in site costs will be available for new technologies and practices which could improve agricultural efficiency or soil quality. In areas with particularly high land values, farmers could be granted assessment exemptions that would reduce their tax liability. For instance, they could be granted a land assessment exemption of $500 an acre, which would roughly compensate them for inland improvements such as grading, ponding, fertilizing, or tree-breaking.

Improvements in assessment practices could also reduce farmers' tax liability under this reform. Assessors could exempt not only improvements on the land such as buildings and fences, but also improvements in the land, such as grading, draining, ponding, irrigation, or fertilizing. The assessor could determine in each case how much such improvements increase the selling price of the land, and then, say, for ten years, deduct from the farmer's land tax bill one-tenth of the increase added to interest on the unpaid balance. Thus recompensed for his improvements, which have become part of the taxable land value, the farmer would receive a legitimate reduction in his land-value tax bill. A shift to the split-rate tax might lower the taxes of many farmers.[24]

Yet another way to support and protect farmers for the risks of their occupation would be to make land-value tax payments conditional on crop price and production, in which case they would be insured against occasional failure in the yield.[25] Certain forms of tax abatements could be offered. Any tax increases resulting from the shift to the split-rate tax, for example, could be left unpaid, to accrue against the eventual transfer of the farm by either sale or death; when the transfer is made, then the government can collect its back taxes from the new owner. With these concessions to the farmer, any inconvenience caused by a more effective property tax system would seem very minor indeed.

In implementing zoning policies and other contracts between government and landowners, principles of justice and fairness must be uppermost. The "agricultural reserves" prevalent in areas of California, such as Orange County, which went into bankruptcy a few years ago, have something to teach us in this regard. Many thousands of acres of this rich county placed in such reserves means that they are taxed only for being used as farmland, although oil refining, food processing, and vacant land were also approved as "agricultural uses." These agricultural preserve contracts between Orange County and a few gigantic landowners clearly benefited the few at the expense of the many.

The Impact of Urban Sprawl on Farmland Prices

Low-density, discontinuous land development, known as "sprawl," contributes to many of the ills that plague our society.[26] Sprawl negates the purpose of cities, which is to let people live and work close together so as to utilize and enjoy the greatest efficiency of community facilities and enterprises.

Surburban sprawl results from owners who hold out for high capital gains on acreage cheaply obtained years ago. Evidence suggests that the split-rate property tax reform can create economic incentives to reverse this trend, thereby conserving open space and decreasing the pressures of development that absorb agricultural land.

Sprawl inhibits the use of transit, which thus necessitates auto travel, and that in turn contributes to air pollution. Energy and time are wasted in traffic jams that reduce productivity and increase stress. Health is endangered by pollution and automobile accidents.

Infrastructure costs per capita are high because roads, sewers, and other public utilities must be extended through sparsely occupied areas. Pockets of undeveloped areas are often too small and too scattered to support meaningful conservation uses or agriculture.

Sprawl penalizes farmers who want to raise crops rather than speculate and it discourages farm improvements on fringe land around cities. Sprawl drives up the price of land in rural areas. It also fuels land speculation while making it increasingly difficult to secure access to affordable land for farming operations.

The economic incentives promoting sprawl can be partially explained by the unproductive way in which landowners earn money. Either a landowner can make money by developing a site and renting or selling it to someone who will use that development; or the owner can wait for population increases, wage increases, or improvements in public infrastructure to impart value to a site, which he can appropriate through a higher rent or sales price.

All too often, land near public infrastructure such as a subway station or major road intersection remains vacant or grossly underutilized because a landowner is waiting for a price in excess of what space users will pay today. This phenomenon forces developers to seek cheaper sites that are farther away from public infrastructure.

Once this cheaper land is developed and inhabited, the occupants of this area create political pressure to extend the infrastructure to it. When this process occurs, land prices rise, choking off development there, even though additional capacity exists, and again driving developers and users even farther into the hinterland.

Landowners who underutilize valuable land sites with speculative intent thus contribute to sprawl and the costly, inefficient use of infrastructure. Perhaps the most effective way to counteract the harmful effects of sprawl is to implement policies that encourage the development of housing in close proximity to jobs, schools, recreation, and shopping.

A significant amount of vacant and underutilized land exists within most urban areas. *By encouraging development within the existing urbanized areas, the two-rate property tax counteracts sprawl and land speculation, and thereby decreases development pressures and escalation of land prices on nearby farmlands and other rural areas.*

All this suggests that to minimize any possible harmful impact on efficiently managed farms located in the path of urban development, the two-rate tax should probably be implemented within boroughs and cities that are near these farms before it is extended to the rural areas. The resultant decrease in development and speculative pressures on rural lands should keep farmland prices affordable for working farmers while their tax liabilities would in most cases be at or below what is currently the case when the two-rate tax will be implemented rurally.

Once farmlands are no longer plagued by sprawl and land speculation, the resultant inflation in land price would be minimized. The two-rate property tax reform could then be extended to townships and school districts that include farms, without concern that it would harm genuine farming operations.

Land Speculation and Land Tenure

A "Berry's World" cartoon shows a politician, in a suit and tie, a briefcase at his side, sitting in a barn alongside a dejected-looking farmer. With his hand on the farmer's shoulder, the politician says: "We in Washington see prosperity just around the corner for the family farm. All you have to do is survive until the suburbs reach you, and you'll make a fortune in real estate!"

The average value of each acre, including land and buildings, of Pennsylvania farmland was $373 in 1970 but had risen to $2,339 by 1995. Rent for an acre of cropland rose from $15.30 to $38.80 and for pasture from $8.30 to $29.80.[27] Rents and land costs are clearly rising faster than the return farmers receive for their labor.

For the well-being of society as a whole, is it better to reward farmers and other workers and working capitalists for their contributions in providing life's basic necessities, or to permit speculation and profiteering in our land and resource base? A very high LVT rate might lower land prices, but that would benefit young entering farmers; the current property tax benefits land-speculating older farmers who are looking to leave agricultural pursuits. Do we want to encourage land speculation in our farmlands or new farming opportunities?

Taxing farm buildings and farmers' income is a burden on the shoulders of those who labor. Removing such a burden would contribute to the well-being of farmers and their families.

Increasing the tax on land values would curb land speculation, and so maintain affordability of land for viable farming operations. "Land hoarding, another deleterious consequence of land speculation, can be reduced by site-value taxation."[28] To the landowner, taxes are an expense. To the public through government, the tax is a return. Whatever the division between public and private portions of value, the quantity of land and the full value remain unchanged. But the taxation of land values does have a significant effect on market price and the functioning of society as a whole. Lowering the tax on land values raises market price, which means the public gets less in taxes while the individual seeking access to land must pay more. Raising the tax on land values lowers the market price of land. The public thus gets more in tax revenue, and the individual seeking access to land finds that the market price is more affordable.[29]

Urban sprawl and land price escalation turn farmers into land speculators and create arid belts around cities. Land-value taxation, observes Francis Peddle, "would restrain the urbanization of valuable and productive farmland, but would negatively affect those farmers who have more of an eye to land speculation than farming."[30] Eliminating the nonproductive drain of land speculation while farmers are allowed to keep full profits from their labor would establish the economic base on principles of market freedom and efficiency as well as fairness and equity.

There is yet another important reason to eliminate the scourge of land speculation and private profiteering in land-price escalation. Widely dispersed private ownership of land and affordable land access is fundamental to a well-functioning democratic system of governance. When land becomes owned by a relatively few and unaffordable to the many, produced wealth itself becomes concentrated, the gap between rich and poor increases, and the democratic process itself is eventually undermined.

The condition of landownership in the United States is cause for alarm. Overall concentration of landownership is far more extensive than many realize.[31] For example, 1.3 billion acres or about 58 percent of the total land mass is in private hands. The broadest distribution of landownership among individuals is residential but this accounts for only 26.3 million acres, or 2 percent, of private land. Another 3 percent of the American population owns 55 percent of all the land and 95 percent of private land. Furthermore, 568 companies control 301.7 million acres, which is equivalent to 11 percent of the total land area or 23 percent of all private land. These same companies control 2 billion acres worldwide—an area larger than that of Europe.[32] Forty percent of all private farmland in the United States is owned by nonfarmers. Between 1945 and 1970 the amount of farmland remained almost constant but the number of farmers who owned their land decreased by 62 percent.[33] Working farmers who must rent land face an unfair disadvantage. In certain areas, crop shares going to landlords run 50 percent or more. Those who simply own land profit without labor. We who live in American society surely must reverse this alarming trend so that working farmers can afford direct access to land.

The problems of land speculation and land tenure are conjoined and their impact on agriculture is profound. Between 1950 and 1970, for example, New York State lost 5.8 million acres of farmland, but its urban area grew by only about 600,000 acres.[34] "The problem is a land shortage, not in the literal but in the economic sense, and its cause is primarily land speculation," says Peddle.[35]

If we are to reward productive labor rather than land speculation, and efficiencies of scale and careful stewardship rather than impersonal big farm consolidations, then fundamental reforms of our system of taxation are essential.

Tax-Loss Farming

A study in 1996 found that annual farm losses in New York State exceeded farm income. Statistics support the argument for eliminating farm income from the state income tax. As the Senate Minority Finance Committee staff explains, "by exempting farm income, you automatically exempt farm losses, thereby raising tax revenue by about $10 million per year."[36]

How could eliminating farm income tax actually increase the tax base? The answer is in a deeper analysis which distinguishes real farmers from "pseudofarmers." Pseudofarmers include those who lose more money farming than they earn over the long run. Such a list may include:

1. Losers: Bona fide farmers who intend to earn income by farming, but just happen to be failures and will eventually be forced to stop farming.

2. Lifestyle-choice farmers: Those who enjoy farming or living on a farm and are willing to pay for the privilege.
3. Tax-calculating farmers: People who own farms to reap an assortment of tax and other government benefits targeted to farmers.
4. Real-estate farmers: Some of these include real estate speculators who receive special farm tax benefits while waiting to sell the land as building sites.
5. Political farmers: Politicians who own farms to impress their farming constituents.

In 1993, there were about 35,000 taxpayers in New York who reported either positive or negative farm income as reported on federal Schedule F forms. Of these, 14,000 had an income and 21,000 a loss. Total farm income in New York was more than offset by the losses of farms owned by households with over $60,000 in nonfarm income.

The data give some indication of where the pseudofarmers are located on the income distribution. Of households earning over $100,000 a year in nonfarm income, 84 percent had farm losses. Of households earning $25,000 in nonfarm income, only 30 percent had farm losses. Out of the 468 farm households which earned between $100,000 and $200,000 in nonfarm income, every one reported a farm loss in 1993. By contrast, for farm households earning under $5,000 in nonfarm income, only one in five reported a farm loss. While families with $50,000 and less of nonfarm income generated more farm income than loss, families with over $50,000 in nonfarm income had net losses of over $11 million.

The New York study noted that despite their motivation for unprofitable farming, pseudofarmers still competed with real farmers. The extra production might benefit consumers in the short run, by driving down prices of local produce, but in the long run such tax-loss farming operations "may lead to scarcity as real farmers are driven out of business and pseudo-farmers sell off for land development."[37] The study concluded:

> "Real" farmers, i.e., those who have income exceeding losses over the long run, and who farm as their principal occupation, would benefit from the proposal to exempt farm income and loss from the calculation of adjusted gross income under the personal income tax. The provision would increase the financial rewards for farming, yet give the state a

> revenue gain because "pseudo" farmers could no longer use income losses from farming as a way to decrease their tax liabilities from other sources of income.[38]

Similar studies should be conducted in Pennsylvania and elsewhere, where it is likely that the situation resembles that in New York to some degree. That would indicate that an increase in taxes on land values should be combined not only with a reduction or elimination of taxes on buildings and other capital improvements, but also with the exemption of farm income and loss from the calculation of adjusted gross income under the personal income tax. Such a policy approach would:

1. Encourage and support efficient, profitable farming operations.
2. Keep farmland prices at levels affordable for entry-level farmers.
3. Discourage the purchase of farms for real estate speculation and tax shelter opportunities.
4. Enhance the ability of the state and local tax base to provide necessary community services and infrastructure maintenance.

Considerations Concerning Subsidies

The number of American farms decreased 45 percent from 1960 to 1989; average farm size increased 54 percent during the same period. In 1990, farmers received 16 percent of their total income from direct federal payments; 62 percent of that money went to only 15 percent of the farmers—those whose sales exceeded $100,000 a year![39]

Since then farm subsidy programs have continued to benefit relatively few recipients. In 1994 the USDA spent $15 billion on farm programs, $10.3 billion of which covered subsidies, export, and related programs (an additional $37 billion was spent on nonfarm food programs, such as school lunches, food stamps, and child nutrition). Nearly one-third of the $472 million funneled to Pennsylvanians from 1985 to 1994 went to just 2 percent of the recipients.[40] Michael Mihalke, a spokesman for Richard Santorum of the Senate Agriculture Committee, said that these data are "a resounding confirmation of our philosophy that the current farm system is actually working against small and midsized farmers in Pennsylvania and across the nation."[41]

In Pennsylvania's Franklin County, farmers received $3,340,223 in federal farm subsidies from 1985 to 1994. The top 2 percent of those recipients received 21.9 percent of the government money. The county's Consolidated Farm Service Agency handles four subsidy programs and paid $664,315 in 1994. That money went to about a quarter of the county's farms, a total of 336.

While some might argue that larger farms get more money because they have larger operations, other farmers believe subsidies keep inefficient farmers in business. John Stoner, one of six brothers who own a 1,700-acre dairy farm with 500 milking cows in Franklin County, says that even though his farm has benefited from subsidies, he supports gradually cutting the programs: "We ought to allow the chips to fall where they may."[42]

But other commodities receiving federal support, such as wheat at $1,730.5 million and cotton at $1,539.5 million per annum, receive considerably more than other major Pennsylvania agricultural commodities, among which corn gets $692.7 million and dairy $158.1 million.

Instead of wasting subsidies, it might make more sense and be more equitable if the federal or state government could make low-cost loans available to farmers to provide them with the necessary capital to develop their farms properly, and to exempt from taxes all farm improvements.

Pennsylvania Studies

Research on the potential effect of the split-rate tax on farmers in Pennsylvania has not been extensive. The studies that have been conducted indicate that a shift to property taxes based on land value would not injure most farmers.

Since boroughs may soon receive permission from the state to use the split-rate tax, let us first explore the possible effect on farms within boroughs.

A 1995 study of Dauphin County shows that the actual impact of a two-rate property tax on agriculturally assessed property is small when the percentage share of assessed value in a borough is analyzed.[43] In Dauphin County there are sixteen boroughs. Agricultural activity, while strong across the county, is rare or absent in boroughs. Analysis of the sixteen boroughs showed that eight had no "assessed agricultural value" (AAV). Of the eight that had farms, only two had an AAV over 5 percent of the total borough assessment. Among these eight boroughs, four had an AAV of less than 1 percent of the total borough assessment. The study concludes that farmland exists, as a general rule, outside the limits of cities and boroughs. Since farmland already enjoys protections that do not exist for other types of property in both zoning and tax policy (see Farmland Protection Policies), unwarranted concern for farmland within boroughs would deny the vast majority of citizens the many benefits of the two-rate property tax option. If citizens of a borough should want to preserve farmland within their jurisdiction, voter referenda could establish special urban agriculture land assessment districts or tax rebates.

Dauphin County—which contains Pennsylvania's capital of Harrisburg, a city that taxes land values four times more than buildings—has a mix of urban, suburban, and rural land. Another 1995 study prepared by the Center for the Study of Economics for the Dauphin County board of commissioners found that farmers and clearly defined rural segments made up only 4.88 percent of the total taxable assessed value of the county. The average tax bill for a farm with buildings was $610 for that year. The usual two-rate shift—the tax on buildings is 80 percent of current property tax rate—would have the farmer pay $729, a difference of $119.[44] The overall benefits to society of this tax shift—and future taxation of farm improvements would be taxed at a lower rate while land speculation and thus land-price inflation would be curbed—should ensure that this small tax increase in rapidly developing Dauphin County will not be prohibitive to viable farming operations. There is a lot of dispersed urban value in fast-growing counties like Dauphin. More purely rural counties would have much less land value per acre and thus the land-value tax would be that much less. This study as well requires a consideration of the boost in land values created by farm subsidies. The absence of artificial price supports, combined with a decrease in speculative pressures, would bring down agricultural land values and thus the land-value tax would most likely be lighter on working farmers than this study indicates.

A 1973 study of rural Indiana County, which is about fifty-five miles northeast of Pittsburgh with a population of 75,000 (Indiana, the largest city, has 13,000 residents), shows that the impact of the split-rate tax would vary according to the level of development of the individual tract or parcel.[45] The county had considerable coal mining, while about 55 percent of the area was in woodland, and 33 percent in crop and pasture. Dairying was the chief farm activity. The research took a representative sample of sixty farms out of the approximately 1,200 on the tax books. It determined how each of them would be affected by a 25 percent reduction in the building tax rate and a corresponding increase in the land-tax rate, which would be necessary to yield the same revenue to the county's school districts as under the present uniform rate system. The research also determined the possible effects if all improvements were exempted.

The study found that only two properties would receive considerable tax changes. One farm, quite near to town and fronting a main highway, had been developed to include a motel, rest home, apartments, and dairy store. This property would receive a reduction of $681.90 if its buildings were tax exempt 25 percent, or $2,727.60 if they were totally untaxed. The other property in Indiana County that would be significantly affected was a multimillion-dollar corporation with holdings estimated at $7 million. This corporation used some of its land for growing Christmas trees and landscaping shrubbery, but most of it was waste, woodland, or brush. A 25 percent tax exemption for buildings would bring a tax increase of $2,988.40 under the split-rate system, and total exemptions of buildings would increase taxes to $11,953.60. While Christmas tree farms in Indiana County would tend to pay more taxes under this system, properties experiencing tax decreases would be the more highly developed ones; dairy farms tended to be in this group. A tax exemption of 25 percent for buildings would impose on half the sample of sixty farms tax increases of less than $50 at the end of the first year, or $200 if improvements were completely exempted. The exemption of 25 percent for improvements would bring to another quarter of the sample tax increases or decreases ranging from $50 to $100, or from $200 to $400 if improvements were altogether exempt. Tax changes of this magnitude are generally considered quite moderate.

The study concludes that the majority of Indiana farms would not pay substantially higher taxes as a result of a shift to split-rate and would be benefited by improvements in the county's total economy most likely stimulated by the change.

> The economic growth thus encouraged could create opportunities not only for the farmer himself, but could create jobs for his children who might otherwise have to migrate to distant cities in search for them, as an increasing number of farmers' children are forced to do these days.

> This might be of far greater importance to the farmer than small changes in his property tax.[46]

If particular properties have ratios of buildings to land higher than the citywide average, then a split-rate property tax would impose a lower tax on them. In other words, with a revenue-neutral shift to split-rate, they would save more than the usual one-rate property tax would provide them. If they have a lower ratio, they would pay more; if the same, then there will be no change.

A survey in 1988 of Altoona assessments found only a handful of agricultural properties on the books. These parcels would save money because it was determined that their assessment ratios of building to land (7.6467 : 1) were higher than the citywide average (6.8084 : 1).[47] A similar study in Coatesville determined that the ratio of buildings to land was 4.3 : 1, while the ratio for agricultural properties was 5.9 : 1. Farmers most decidedly had saved money.[48]

Other States

California's Wright Act of 1887 allowed communities to vote to create irrigation districts for the building of dams and canals, and to pay for them by taxing the increase in land value. Once irrigated, land was too valuable for grazing and too costly for hoarding. So cattlemen sold fields to farmers at prices the farmers could afford. In ten years the Central Valley was transformed into more than 7,000 independent farmsteads. Over the next few decades, vast tracts of treeless, semiarid plains became the "breadbasket of America" and one of the most productive areas on earth. It is a prime example of how land-value taxation can promote and enhance the viability of both an efficient and an equitable agricultural base.

In a study in 1987 of farms in Ohio County, which is located in the northern panhandle of West Virginia, researchers asked a farmland assessor to pick three average farms, three excellent farms, and three poor ones. The study clearly indicated that the best farms (the ones with the highest value amount in buildings and improvements) would benefit from this tax reform; average farms paid a somewhat but modest higher percentage of taxes; while the highest percentage in changes, still moderate, fell on poorer farms.[49] This split-rate policy would be an incentive for good land use not only to urban but also to rural areas.

On further consideration, the researchers also concluded that a broad application of the land-value tax that would include nonfarm properties and the much greater land values in urban areas would automatically effect a significant reduction of tax burdens throughout the entire farm sector.

While land-value taxation would inhibit agricultural land speculation and promote more efficient and intensive use of farmland, it is not necessarily detrimental to large-scale agricultural pursuits if carried out efficiently.

A 1995 report on property-tax valuation in the state of Hawaii showed that 65 percent of the property tax revenue came from land assessments. Since 1990 the island of Kauai has been shifting its taxes toward land. For example, in 1990 agricultural land was taxed at 1.05 times the improvement rate. In 1995 it was taxed at 1.87 times the improvement rate.[50] For Kauai agricultural and conservation properties, assessment appeals were only 6.6 percent of the total number, but in Maui, which maintains the same property-tax rate on buildings as on land values, they were 9.6 percent. Thus, it would seem that a two-rate property tax reduces, not increases, assessment appeals.[51]

Other Countries

Farmers have been a prime force behind the use of the split-rate tax in Australia, New Zealand, Denmark, and other countries, which indicates that they benefit from it financially.

"Site rating," as land-value taxation is called in Australia, was applied first to farming districts. This policy was extended to towns and cities only after its suitability for farmers and their receptivity to it had been demonstrated. Site rating was first applied to the shires of Queensland in 1887, specifically to ease the position of genuine farmers,[52] who were finding that under the system of the time they were paying more than their own share of municipal costs to make up for the token payments from other owners of vast, undeveloped property. The situation was the same in New South Wales, where site rating was also applied first to the shires, then later on to the urban areas.

In Western Australia, site rating was first used in the rural districts in 1902. Only in 1948 were the twenty-one urban councils given optional powers to use it. Site rating has since become the dominant system in Australia, where it is used by approximately two-thirds of all local government councils. The councils using site-value constitute more than 92 percent of the municipalized area of Australia. The fact that the remaining 8 percent have not changed shows that site rating's appeal has been primarily for the farmers. The rural parts of Victoria that still tax buildings and farm improvements are among the 8 percent. There is no public demand in other states to change back to what they now regard as an outdated system of taxing buildings.

The states of Queensland, New South Wales, and Western Australia apply site rating universally to farming properties. In South Australia, Victoria, and Tasmania, its application is not universal. In comparisons of development, it was shown that farmers generally have been in a sounder position in the states that have taxed potential land value, rather than the actual development itself.

In the depression years 1930 to 1939 the total acreage farmed in the site-rated states increased by 21 percent. Acreage in states not rating site value decreased by 8 percent. In the postwar years from 1947 to 1959, acreage cultivated in the site-rated areas increased by 35 percent. Other areas not site rated decreased by 1 percent.

Australian farmers pay less with LVT than under other tax systems. For example, 81 percent in Keilor Shire paid less. The figures are 77 percent in Eltham Shire, and 55 percent in Frankston and Hastings shires, all in Victoria. The rural shires of Rosedale and Yea have used site rating since 1921. Reversion polls were taken in 1953 and 1959 to determine whether farmers wanted to retain site value or go back to taxing improvements. The vote left no doubt that after experiencing both systems, farmers prefer site value. In Rosedale Shire 84 percent of the registered voters voted for site rating in 1953. In Yea Shire 68 percent voted in favor. While the voters in the town areas of Rosedale and Yea strongly favored site rating, the farmers did so even more.

In most cases, resident farmers benefit under site value by lower rates, just as householders do in the towns. This was found to be true for farmers in the old Keilor, Eltham, Frankston, and Mulgrave shires. These areas, now mostly suburban, changed to site rating when the shires were once regarded as rural. This principle still holds for today's farming districts closest to Melbourne.

It is in the interests of all Victorians to assure farmers that they have every incentive to produce, and rating land value does exactly that. Genuine farmers understand this, and once given the opportunity have always chosen site rating. Genuine farmers have recognized the better balance of development for rural areas that site rating brings: more opportunities for their children in industry, building, transport, and trade. Site rating enabled better educational facilities and a whole host of other amenities to help stop, at least to some extent, the drift to the city.

The Danes, by tradition, believe that the land belongs to the people.[53] The rapid industrialization and land enclosures of the eighteenth and nineteenth centuries brought this tradition under attack. Farmers in Denmark were hard-pressed in the second half of the nineteenth century. Many of them found support in the ideas contained in *Progress and Poverty*. As the economic situation became even tougher for small farmers, the Henry George Union was founded in 1902 and cooperated with other philosophic groups and public leaders to work for land-value taxation in place of taxes on income and capital as the basis of government revenue.

Eventually the Justice Party was formed on this platform. Its economic policy was simple—to collect the economic rent of land and abolish all taxes on labor and capital. For a new political party, its success was astonishing. Progress was quick, and in 1952 it won twelve seats out of a possible 179. It was instrumental in the creation of a government commission for ground rent in Denmark, which wrote a report clearly advocating the benefits of site revenue. In 1957 the Justice Party, together with other political groups, formed what was to become the most prosperous Danish government, basing itself on the principles of ground-rent collection (land-value taxation), liberalization of trade, and a tax freeze.

It was generally expected that after the formation of the government, some kind of land-value taxation would be introduced, so land speculation ceased immediately. Legislation taxing increased land value was prepared, presented to parliament, and subsequently passed. The economic effects of the cessation of land speculation were astounding and aroused much attention. On October 2, 1960, the *New York Times* headlined, "Big Lesson from a Small Nation" and noted the many improvements in Denmark's economic situation.

Prior to the election of 1957, Denmark had a sizable deficit on her balance of payments, was considerably in debt abroad, and was burdened with a relatively high interest rate, widespread unemployment, and an annual rate of inflation of approximately 5 percent. From 1957 to 1960, however, these improvements took place:

1. The enormous deficit on the balance of payments was turned into a surplus.
2. Denmark's total foreign debts of 1,600 million krone were reduced to one-fourth, or about 400 million krone.
3. The rate of interest, and hence mortgage levels, went down.
4. Unemployment was soon replaced by almost full employment, together with considerable increases in production and wages.
5. Inflation was brought to a standstill. All wage increases were real wage increases, the highest in Denmark's history.
6. The time was free of strikes, industrial production went up 32 percent, and investment rose 135 percent.
7. Savings increased immensely, since it again became profitable to accumulate money.

After three years with a land-value tax in force, Denmark had no foreign debt, no inflation, and an unemployment level of 1 percent, considered full employment.

So why is this not continuing? A number of factors were at play, too complex to document for the purposes of this chapter. Essentially, public understanding of the basic principles of this policy was not broad enough to prevent its demise after 1964 and Denmark again experienced a number of social and economic problems to the detriment of most farmers, other workers, and business owners.

Reflections on the Potential Revival of Sustainable Agriculture for Pennsylvania

The high price of land means that the modern food and agriculture system provides no options for those who cannot find a paying job other than subsistence on charity or government supports. People with minimum wage incomes are finding it increasingly difficult to afford decent housing. These social problems and pressures are bound to increase with the cut-off of welfare and other government subsidies to the poor.

In Pennsylvania in 1991, 6.9 percent of the children were living in severely distressed neighborhoods;[54] the state ranked twenty-third in a study of the fifty states (the national average is 6.2 percent). Lancaster County, known for its lush farmland, has some of the state's poorest areas. "When people think of Lancaster County . . . it's an idyllic scene," said Ronald Sell, executive director of Pennsylvania Partnerships for Children. But "there is the same poverty . . . and unemployment happening within the city of Lancaster as [in] the city of Philadelphia."[55]

Now more than ever before, there is the need to optimize the use of land resources to meet the food, fiber, and livelihood needs of people in an environmentally sustainable way.

The effects of the split-rate tax on future land use can only be conjectured, but it is likely that the selling price of currently marginal waste, wooded, and brush land would fall noticeably because they would be taxed at a higher rate. These rural lands, now more affordably priced, could become magnets for land reclamation and new sustainable farming projects. Intensively managed small farms producing a diverse range of food, fiber, livestock, and energy products for local markets are the order of the day. Biointensive farming methods depending on renewable energy sources (including animal power and biogas) can yield both social and environmental stability.[56] The establishment of small farming operations biointensive and intensive in labor can be greatly furthered by land-value tax policies that remove taxes on labor and productive capital while promoting affordable land access.

Conclusions

While determining the potential impact of a shift from the traditional property tax to the split-rate tax on Pennsylvania farmers is a complex subject, there is a basis, in both theory and practice, for these conclusions:

1. Overall, as currently administered in most states, the property tax appears to be regressive since farm owners with larger amounts of land value pay disproportionately less in taxes than those with less valuable holdings.
2. The excessive complexity of the property tax is an administrative shortcoming and must be remedied before the real property tax can become an effective instrument of land use policy.
3. Smaller farms tend to have more buildings than larger ones but under the current system pay more because of these improvements.
4. Overtaxing buildings and undertaxing land favor large farming operations that are not necessarily the most efficient.
5. Lower property-tax rates coincide with greater concentration of

farm ownership and higher land costs, which is a barrier to entry-level farmers.

6. The property tax would be more progressive if changed to a pure land tax which exempts buildings.
7. The greater the shift of property taxes from buildings and onto land values, the more likely that the surplus land of larger, less efficient farms or speculative holdings would be released for affordable purchase by entry-level farmers.
8. While preferential assessments and farm subsidies may not be helpful in preserving farmland and, as currently administered, may be inequitable, zoning, tax abatements, and improvements in assessment practices could work in tandem with the split-rate tax shift, especially in urbanizing areas with high land values.
9. Urban sprawl and land speculation contribute to land-price inflation, which is a major barrier to entry-level farming. By encouraging infill-development and redevelopment within areas already urbanized, the split-rate tax could decrease pressures of land cost on farmers.
10. Concentration in farm ownership, proceeding at an alarming pace for the past several decades, makes it essential to reform our system of taxation—then we can reward productive labor rather than land speculation, efficiencies of scale and careful stewardship rather than impersonal big farm consolidations.
11. Most farmers in rural areas of the state and particularly those with proportionately higher ratios of buildings to land will save with a shift to the split-rate tax.
12. Although this tax reform will make some farms near urban areas pay more, it may not be significantly more, and the overall improvements in the economic climate of the locality would be of benefit to the farming sector as well.
13. Substantially shifting taxes from buildings and productivity and onto land values could be a major stimulus for the revival of sustainable agriculture in Pennsylvania and thus could help to alleviate poverty and other social problems.
14. Property taxes based on land value have been actively supported by farmers in other parts of the world.

The split-rate tax is likely to have an impact on Pennsylvania farmers and farmland because it discourages speculation in land; reduces the price of land to equate with its value for production; enables entrants more easily to obtain land; limits farm sizes to the most productive units; enables the reduction of taxation on earnings and capital; reduces interest rates as land becomes more affordable; prevents rural depopulation; discourages urban sprawl on farmland; encourages occupation by owners rather than absentee ownership; and promotes more responsible use of land.

Our evidence thus suggests that the split-rate tax policy, especially with a heavy reduction of millage rate on building values, would significantly enhance incentives for the continuation and expansion of a viable, efficient, and sustainable agriculture in Pennsylvania and anywhere else.

Notes

1. C. Lowell Harriss, "The Economic Effects of Today's Property Tax," *Encyclopaedia Britannica,* 15th ed. (1974).
2. Alanna Hartzok, "Pennsylvania's Success with Local Property Tax Reform: The Split Rate Tax," *American Journal of Economics and Sociology* 56, no. 2 (April 1997): 205.
3. United States Department of Agriculture, Economic Research Service, *Major Land Uses in the United States* (1992).
4. USDA, Economic Research Service, *Agricultural Real Estate Taxes,* AREI Update No. 9 (1995).
5. "Town revenue" is taxes, fees, and charges generated within the fiscal unit, that is, no funds transferred from other jurisdictions. See: Advisory Commission on Intergovernmental Relations, *Significant Features of Fiscal Federalism,* vol. 2 (1994): 66 and 67.
6. Gene Wunderlich, "Land Taxes in Agriculture: Preferential Rates and Assessment Effects," *The American Journal of Economics and Sociology* 56, no. 2 (April 1997): 220.
7. Gene Wunderlich and John Blackledge, "Taxing Farmland in the United States," *USDA Economic Research Service Agriculture Economic Report,* no. 679 (March 1994).
8. Gene Wunderlich, "Land Taxes in Agriculture," 218–219.
9. Mason Gaffney, "Rising Inequality and Falling Property Tax Rates," in *Land Ownership and Taxation in American Agriculture,* Gene Wunderlich, ed. (San Francisco: Westview Press, 1992), 119.
10. Ibid.,120.
11. Ibid.,123.
12. Ibid.,125.
13. Ibid.,128.
14. Ibid.,131.

15. Ibid.
16. See David Aiken, "State Farmland Preferential Assessment Statutes," *University of Nebraska Research Bulletin,* no. 310 (September 1989).
17. Title 16, Section 11941, ff., Pennsylvania Statutes.
18. Title 72, Section 5490.1, ff., Pennsylvania Statutes.
19. USDA, *Agricultural Real Estate Taxes.*
20. Jane Malme, *Preferential Property Tax Treatment of Land* (Cambridge: Lincoln Institute of Land Policy, 1993), 22.
21. Wunderlich, "Land Taxes in Agriculture," 5.
22. Justin R. Ward, F. Kaid Benfield, and Anne E. Kinsinger, "Reaping the Revenue Code: Why We Need Sensible Tax Reform for Sustainable Agriculture" (New York: Natural Resources Defense Council, 1989): 73–74.
23. Ibid., 7.
24. Steven Cord, "Impact of a Graded Tax on a Rural Area," *American Journal of Economics and Sociology* 35, no. 1 (January 1976): 74.
25. "Incentive Taxation," October 1994, Henry George Foundation of America (HGFA), 2000 Century Plaza, Suite #238, Columbia, MD 21044.
26. Rick Rybeck, "Tax Reform Motivates Sustainable Development," *American Institute of Architects/DC News* (December 1995/January 1996): 4–5.
27. USDA/Pennsylvania Department of Agriculture, National Agricultural Statistics Service, *Statistical Summary Annual Report,* PASS-119 (1995–1996), 88.
28. Francis K. Peddle, *Cities and Greed: Taxes, Inflation and Land Speculation* (Ottawa: Canadian Research Committee on Taxation, 1994), 180.
29. For a discussion of "market price" as distinct from "full value," consult Gene Wunderlich, "Land Taxes in Agriculture," 6.
30. Peddle, *Cities and Greed,* 223.
31. Peter Meyer, "Land Rush—A Survey of America's Land," *Harper's,* January 1979, 49.
32. Ibid., 50.
33. Peddle, *Cities and Greed,* 57.
34. Meyer, "Land Rush," 63.
35. Peddle, *Cities and Greed,* 58.
36. As reported in a June 5, 1996, memorandum to the Senate Minority Finance Committee staff with data from *Tax Free Farm Income,* March 20, 1996, 2.
37. Ibid.
38. Ibid.
39. *US News and World Report,* March 25, 1991, 19, citing the USDA.
40. As reported in "Farm Subsidies Fair?," *Public Opinion,* September 9, 1995, 3A, Chambersburg, PA.
41. Ibid.
42. Ibid.
43. Available from the Center for the Study of Economics (CSE), 2000 Center Plaza, #238, Columbia, MD 21044.
44. Ibid.
45. Cord, "Impact of a Graded Tax on a Rural Area," 71–75.
46. Ibid., 4.
47. Steven Cord, "Survey of Altoona Assessments," October 1988, available from the CSE.

48. The Coatesville study was also conducted by Steven Cord and is available from the CSE.

49. Walter Rybeck, Center for Public Dialogue, 10615 Brunswick Ave., Kensington, MD 20895.

50. SRD Group, *Property Taxation in Hawaii,* 247 Flinders Lane, Melbourne, 3000, Australia, 995.

51. "Incentive Taxation Bulletin," May 1995, Henry George Foundation of America. Tax information provided by Gary Kiyota, tax administrator for the County of Hawaii.

52. The term "farmer" is often used loosely to describe anyone who owns rural property. It is necessary, however, to distinguish between the genuine farmer, who lives and works on the farm, and the owner who holds rural property underdeveloped as an investment. The effects upon the two, as far as rating is concerned, are not the same. It is the interests of resident farmers that are more important for the development of Australian agriculture.

53. Information concerning Denmark has been extracted from Viggo Starcke, *Triumph or Fiasco* (Copenhagen: Stig Vendelkaen, 1972). Starcke was leader of the Justice Party for many years.

54. *Kids Count Data Book,* in "A Rough Go for Pa. Kids," *Public Opinion,* April 5, 1994, Chambersburg, PA. From a study funded by the Annie E. Casey Foundation.

55. Ibid.

56. David C. Korten, *Civic Engagement to Create Just and Sustainable Societies for the 21st Century* (New York: The People-Centered Development Forum, January 10, 1996), 25.

18

Vernon I. Saunders

In Defense of the Two-Rate Property Tax

Abstract

The real property tax as a source of financing for government services is much maligned because it is not generally realized that it is a two-pronged tax. The part that falls on land values has a favorable effect on the economy and is the more just tax; that falling on improvements is the bane of the economy and should be abolished. The property tax should not be summarily abandoned, but should be a tax on land values only. The efficacy of this reform has been demonstrated in communities as nearby as Pennsylvania and as distant as Australia.

Introduction

The property tax as a source of public revenue has come to be scorned almost to the point of hysteria. For example, in the summer of 1993, the Michigan legislature passed a bill to eliminate local property taxes

---

This article originally appeared in the *Journal of the Institute of Assessing Officers* 38, no. 1 (January 1996): 10–16. This journal is published by the New York State Assessors Association, and the article was originally entitled "In Defense of the Property Tax." It is reprinted here with permission of the editor, Nathaniel A. Jackson.

as a source of funding for public schools with no plan for replacement revenue. This problem was resolved, however, in March 1995, when voters passed a referendum to raise the state sales tax from 4 percent to 6 percent. Wisconsin followed suit by rejecting property-tax revenue for education and even proposed that a tax give-back be phased in. A commission was to report in September 1995, on the revenue-source question.[1]

On the assumption that the property tax must be abolished, officials are groping wildly for a replacement that they can only hope will prove to be more acceptable, whether or not it will be a more easily administered or more equitable tax. It might be wiser to examine the present property-tax system to discern why it is not working. A careful look at land-value taxation (LVT) is in order.

Economic Effects of the Real Property Tax

Real property, or real estate, is "land, including the buildings or improvements on it and its natural assets such as minerals, water, etc."[2] The simpler definition, "land and the structures that are permanently attached to it,"[3] will be used here, although the importance of natural assets cannot be ignored in establishing the value of land. The word "tax" may mean the rate of taxation on an assessed valuation or the revenue resulting from taxing it.

A crucial feature of the property tax as it is administered in New York State and many other parts of the world is its heavy incidence on the value of improvements, which is the component of the property that represents the owner's contribution to its value. Thus, of two homeowners living on comparable lots, the one who has invested more income and industry in his or her home pays the higher tax, which is probably not commensurate with the difference in governmental and educational costs associated with the sites. This situation inhibits the improvement and maintenance of properties.

At the same time, the relatively light tax on vacant and underused land encourages the holding of land off the market, which permits increased land prices, a stagnant tax base and attendant economic problems, and an unearned reward for the owner when the land is sold. In urban areas, deterioration of properties and inefficiencies in the use of government services ensue. Development takes place horizontally instead of vertically and surrounding farmlands and natural areas are invaded.

Reason tells us that the deleterious effects of the present system will be largely eliminated by moving the tax burden off improvement values and onto land. The increased tax on vacant and underused land will drastically reduce the profit in land speculation. Interest in this pursuit will decline, land prices will fall, and the tax on a property will be of more concern to the buyer than its price.

Reforming the Property Tax

Although many localities in Australia have converted in one step to land-value taxation without repercussion, most advocates propose a gradual reform. The approach taken may be influenced by particulars of the taxing jurisdiction and will depend upon existing laws. Several methods have been described by Steven Cord.[4]

One of these is the selection of a lower assessment ratio for improvements than for land. At the same tax rate, the tax burden will be shifted toward land. Recently, Peoria, Illinois, considered adopting a ratio of 62.5 percent for land and 25 percent for buildings. Of course, a split-tax rate applied to assessments at the same percentage of value would accomplish the same thing and would probably be more understandable to the public than an assessment roll using two different assessment levels. Assessment practices are not disturbed, but tax rates are gradually lowered on improvements and increased on land.

The use of exemptions on the assessments of improvements may be attractive to some jurisdictions. This exemption could be a percentage or a dollar amount that is increased each year. With the former, all properties would attain complete relief from the tax on improvements at the same time. The dollar-amount exemption might appeal to less affluent property owners because they would be the first to be freed of the tax. The use of tax abatements on new construction (at the expense of established properties) to lure new enterprises is an admission that municipal officials recognize the adverse effects of the tax. Still, they continue to shun the reform that would preclude the use of abatements of this type.[5]

The Two-Rate Tax and Land-Value Taxation in Practice

There is no lack of experience with either the two-rate tax or other forms of LVT. Some of the results in only two countries should be considered. In the state of Victoria, Australia, outside the city of Melbourne, 7 percent of the municipalities taxed only land during the period from 1921 to 1923, but they accounted for 46 percent of the newly constructed homes. From 1954 to 1958, the 19 percent of municipalities that used LVT accounted for 62 percent of new home construction. Five areas that adopted LVT for the period 1958 to 1962 had an increase in construction activity 34 percent greater than that for neighboring areas that also taxed improvements. Especially significant is that LVT was not phased in but always adopted by one plebiscite of the property owners. It should also be noted that there is a large farming population in these communities. By 1979, two-thirds of Australian jurisdictions taxed only land as their sole source of revenue.[6]

Although some cities in Pennsylvania have had permission to use a two-rate tax since 1913 and other classes have been added to the list since then, the conversion to LVT has been less dramatic than in Australia and in no case has it been complete. Fifteen cities now have a two-rate system. In 1993, third-class school districts coterminous with third-class cities were given two-rate home rule, and Aliquippa School District immediately prepared to introduce a 16.3 percent tax on land assessments and 1.1 percent on buildings to replace the single rate of 5.3 percent.[7]

Upon lowering the tax on improvements, these Pennsylvania cities consistently experienced increases in construction activity. For example, the value in permits issued in the first three years after Oil City adopted a two-rate tax in 1989 indicates that new construction was 58 percent greater than in the prior three-year period, whereas for nearby Franklin, which held to a one-rate tax during this period, there was a 12 percent decrease in construction.[8]

New York State and the Two-Rate Tax

In states whose constitutions and laws permit little home rule with respect to administration of the local property tax, a formidable barrier is presented to tax reformers. The constitution of New York State, although it does not dictate the tax rate, requires that the same rate be applied against land and improvements, and limits the amount of revenue that can be raised.

Only recently has any locality been given permission to test the two-rate tax. After a long struggle by proponents and their allies in the legislature, the city of Amsterdam, reeling with financial problems, was persuaded to petition for home rule with respect to the two-rate tax. In August 1993, enabling legislation was passed. The city then prepared to convert to a mill rate of 130 on land and 61 on buildings. A study had shown that if the land tax were doubled to yield 25 percent of the total revenue and the tax on improvements lowered accordingly, 80 percent of homeowners would enjoy a lower total tax and owners of vacant land would experience a tax increase.[9]

Fairness and the Land Tax

There is no lack of written material both for and against land-value taxation.[10] In the foregoing, I have indicated economic and social effects that might be considered support for its adoption. I have touched on the subject of fairness with respect to the larger tax that the more affluent landowner pays, which is based not on a greater use of government services, but on the greater private investment put into the property. Thus, for developed property, most of the tax can be considered to be in accord with the principle of "ability to pay," which seems to receive much approval. That this principle also applies to the land-value tax is attributable to the likelihood that wealthy people own large amounts of very valuable land. In Vancouver, British Columbia, in 1975, the richest 1 percent of landowners held 62 percent of the total land value and the richest 10 percent owned 73 percent. In the United States, 5 percent of the landowners own 75 percent of the privately held land.[11] Drawing on data like these compared with the distribution of income, Cord argues that the land tax is more progressive than the income tax.[12] In any case, it is not so blatantly a tax on productivity as are sales and income taxes, and therefore should not be replaced by either of these.

A tax on improvements is a tax on personal property in which the owner has invested income that has survived sales and income and perhaps other taxes, and the property is no less "personal" because it is attached to the land. The tax, because it is an annual levy on a one-time investment, is tantamount to a rent. The tax on land can also be construed as a rent. The concept of rent is charged with the sense of nonpossession, but in urban areas in particular, the value of a site is rooted in intangibles rather than in anything intrinsic to the land. Thus, thinking of the land tax as payment for continuing services takes the bite out of the word "rent." Even in rural areas, as the Australian experience illustrates, there can be strong support for LVT.

The land tax is therefore fairer than a tax on both land and improvements. But the free-market principle, "payment for value received," as a measure of fairness, goes against the land tax. It does not take into account, for example, the number of persons, schoolchildren, and automobiles resident at a site. These data could be taken into consideration in levying taxes, but such a modification would also raise the issue of the social philosophy of public education. For the present, let us say that the first step in replacing the conventional property tax as a source of local public revenue should not be to jump into the untested waters of income or sales taxes, which are both taxes on productivity, but to take the gentler, tested path of the land-value tax, which is a fee for local services.

In an area where roads and other government services are to be introduced and development is anticipated, land speculation waits in the wings and the feebleness of the tax on land encourages it. Under LVT, the municipality would assess land according to a potential market value instead of waiting for development to be completed so that a tax on improvements could be applied. Undeveloped land could not then be kept off the market for long and still reward the owner with a profit. The unrealized profit would be retained by the community and help to defray the cost of governmental investment. Land prices would be lower, real property sold more readily, and the community rather than the speculator be the beneficiary.

The argument that LVT is a more desirable tax can be extended to the problem of the encroachment of development on the natural environment such as farmland that is not being farmed but held off the market as a speculation. A higher land tax would promote compact development close to urban areas. At the same time, to be sure, changing lifestyles and population growth seem bound to contribute to the shrinking of the natural environment.

Another advantage of LVT is that it would diminish the workload of assessors. Neither assessors nor property owners like revaluations, and it is not surprising that some assessments are not in line or up-to-date and that grievances are all too common. Taxing of land values only would make assessments fairer and less open to challenge. Because much less inventory data would need to be collected and recorded, the tax could be administered with less effort and expense. Once land-value profiles are established for a locality, assessments can be kept current and taxes can be easily adjusted for changes in assessed value to meet budgetary requirements.

Endorsements

An extensive and yet partial list of eminent persons who have endorsed Henry George's single tax or the two-rate form of land-value taxation is provided in Steven Cord's *Catalyst.*[13] Cord avers that it is very difficult to find experts in taxation and land use who oppose LVT.

Chinese statesman Sun Yat-sen: "The reasons for the heavy burdens upon the poor are the unjust system of taxation practiced by the government and the unequal distribution of land power. . . . If we can put the land tax completely into effect, the land problem will be solved and the common people will not have to endure such suffering."[14] Sir Winston Churchill: "unearned increments in land are not the only form of unearned profit . . . but it is the principal form . . . which is derived from processes . . . positively detrimental to the general public."[15] Economist Lester Thurow: "You have rediscovered the Henry George argument for the tax on land and it is as valid today as it was then."[16] Economist and Nobel Prize winner Milton Friedman: "The least bad tax is the property tax on the unimproved value of the land."[17] David Nolan (one of the founders of the Libertarian Party): "in a less-than-ideal world, some services will be force-financed for the foreseeable future, . . . the worst form of taxation is a tax on productivity. . . . My own preference is for a single tax on land, with land holders doing their own valuation."[18] Lawyer Clarence Darrow (when asked about Henry George's single tax): "Well, you either come to it or go broke."[19]

Summary

The real property tax, as it is constituted today, has become the scapegoat for economic problems in localities and has been attacked without consideration of its nature and economic effects. Its malevolence comes of the partition of its burden with respect to the portioning of its assessments between land and improvements. A low tax on land encourages land speculation, leads to land hoarding, and increases land prices; and a high tax on buildings discourages the construction of new buildings and the maintenance and improvement of existing structures.

The results are growth of slums and horizontal rather than vertical development in urban areas. Development thus tends to encroach upon farm and wildlife areas.

Notes

1. Penelope Lemov, *Journal of the Institute of Assessing Officers* 37, no. 1 (January 1995): 15–21. See also a paper by Robert W. Wassmer and Ronald C. Fisher presented at the conference "Land, Wealth, and Poverty" sponsored by the Jerome Levy Economics Institute, Bard College, November 2–4, 1995.

2. *Webster's New Universal Unabridged Dictionary,* 2d ed. (New World Dictionaries/Simon and Schuster, 1979), 1501.

3. Nathaniel A. Jackson, "Understanding Assessments and Property Taxes," *Journal of the Institute of Assessing Officers* (1988): 5.

4. Steven Cord, *5 Pathways to Land Value Taxation* (Columbia, MD: The Center for the Study of Economics, 1993).

5. New York State Law 704 (1993) allows localities such as towns and schools to exempt construction projects until completed.

6. Steven Cord, *Catalyst* (Columbia, MD: Henry George Foundation of America, 1979), 89.

7. Steven Cord, ed., *Incentive Taxation* 19, no. 4 (September 1993): 2. This newsletter is published by the Henry George Foundation of America, Columbia, MD.

8. *Incentive Taxation* 20, no. 6 (November 1994): 1–2.

9. Nadine Stoner, ed., *GroundSwell* 6, no. 3 (July–August 1993), 1, 3, and 4 (Common Ground-USA, Evanston, IL).

10. Henry George, *Progress and Poverty,* Centenary Edition (New York: Robert Schalkenbach Foundation, 1979); Murray N. Rothbard, *Power and Market* (Kansas City, KS: Sheed Andrews and McMeel, 1970), see especially pages 122–135; and Robert V. Andelson, ed., *Critics of Henry George* (Cranbury, NJ: Associated University Presses, 1979).

11. *Incentive Taxation* 20, no. 2 (June 1994): 3–4.

12. Cord, *Catalyst,* 29–31.

13. Ibid., 101.

14. As quoted in *Incentive Taxation* 19, no. 3 (July 1993): 3.

15. Ibid., 20, no. 4 (August 1994): 4.

16. Ibid.

17. Ibid., 19, no. 6 (December 1993): 3.

18. *Libertarian Party News* (March 1995).

19. *Incentive Taxation* 20, no. 4 (August 1994): 4.

19

Godfrey R.A. Dunkley

Why Tax Land?

There is an old saying:
Income: one pound; expenditure: nineteen shillings and sixpence—Happiness.
Income: one pound, expenditure: one pound and six-pence—Misery!

Introduction

There is no lack of evidence to the effect that the greatest justice in society should be linked to a system of taxation that encourages a more equitable distribution of landownership and land usage. In modern jargon people speak of leveling the playing fields.

Much has been written on the subject of a land-value tax as conforming best to Adam Smith's canons of taxation. There is a wealth of information on the subject in "ancient scriptures" and contemporary literature. Selective libraries contain hundreds of related works. The present need is not more writings, lectures, and erudite papers but better methods of marketing the concepts that are most urgently needed by societies throughout the world. There is enough evidence to show plainly that modern economic theories and advice have been an abysmal failure. The poverty and unemployment that stem from such bad advice are visible. Some old sayings apply:

"There are none so deaf as those who will not hear" and "Hearing, they do not understand."

In today's world people are swamped by literature and the media; they have learned to switch off mentally, they bar and lock the front door of the mind against new ideas, but the back door often stands open. Is the time not ripe for Georgists to stop banging on the front door and instead walk in through the back? Stop preaching the single tax and two-rate variations of land-value taxation (LVT), which only results in the audience's becoming deaf. Instead, Georgists need to listen to the people and understand the causes of their plight and misery, then talk to their agenda.

The time has come to relate every social evil and distress to the economic causes from which these problems arise—the underlying errors of modern economics and bad taxation. When enough people realize that modern taxation and bad legislation are gripping society in unemployment, poverty, crime, and violence, they may be prepared to open the front door of their minds to reasonable ideas that would help restore the stability and dignity of individuals and society.

The Method

The first step would be to pick the most destructive taxes and show how they create a wedge between labor and employment. They could be studied individually or collectively to show their effects on both marginal land and marginal labor. Georgists have tended to confine their discussion and argument to marginal land and the collection of rent or LVT on all better land. What has gained little attention are the effects of present taxes on marginal labor.

Marginal labor could be defined as that type or quality of labor which, when employed under existing conditions, brings returns equal only to the total cost of employing such labor. Any increase in the cost of employing such labor, or decrease in the value of its production, will render that labor unemployable. Most unemployment is the direct result of conditions that have gone beyond this point of balance. They have also gone beyond the margin of production.

The two major causes of rendering labor submarginal are the combined effect of bad taxation and mandatory contributions to unemployment, usually in the form of Social Security Contributions (SSC).

These two factors combine to create a vicious circle since taxes produce unemployment at the original margin of production, and then that unemployment combines with the resultant SSC to contribute to spreading this joblessness like a cancer in society. Both causes must be stopped. Bad taxes breed unemployment and this joblessness further breeds still more for its increasing need for Social Security.

Consider whether you have heard of a modern politician, economist, or economic analyst warning about the bad effects of the budget at the economic margin of production. Why do they not address the main issue? Why do they dodge reading the main pulse of society?

Henry George, in the opening chapters of *Social Problems,* states that big business is in league with government, since both fear change. The same applies to economists and economic lecturers; they have a vested interest in the present system which outweighs the truth. Even if they have fully understood the destructive effects of modern taxes at the margin of production, most of them fear to speak out or admit the truth. They would be scorned by their peers or even made redundant. Together with landowners, land speculators, and some big business, they must support the present system.

The Primary Cause of Unemployment

Most but not all taxes form part of the wedge between labor and employment. Among the most undesirable taxes are a general sales tax (GST) and a value added tax (VAT), which both fit into the same category; they do *not* reduce to zero at the margin of production.

In many countries the VAT is between 10 percent and 25 percent, sometimes even higher. It is generally considered as a tax on the consumer but is in fact a tax on the producer or employer. Workers normally receive the least for which they are prepared to work. When VAT is introduced or increased, labor demands, and usually receives, an equivalent increase in salaries and wages. The burden of this tax is then passed on to the employer. As a direct result of VAT, the cost of production is increased on the labor content of production. If the market can afford it, the increase is passed on to the consumer but frequently this is not possible, and the industry or business is driven closer to the margin of production. If the operation is already at the margin of production, then it soon goes out of business, or that section of production is closed down. This condition results in unemployment.

Where it is possible to pass the increased cost on to the consumer, the result is spiraling inflation. In the Republic of South Africa, inflation stood at about 3 to 4 percent before GST was introduced. Soon after its implementation, inflation rose rapidly. The GST was replaced by VAT, which steadily increased, and without an exact analysis, inflation appeared to follow a graph that was ahead of the value of the VAT. When the VAT rose to 14 percent, inflation increased to around 17 percent.[1]

There is another way of looking at the effects of VAT. In the various stages of production, the VAT paid out is offset against VAT received. The difference is paid over to the receiver of revenue (receiver) or tax collector. In effect, each stage of production, distribution, and marketing is collecting and paying over to the receiver the VAT on that portion which the operation has contributed to the final selling price. When all the parts are added together, the receiver collects VAT on the final selling price.

For ease of calculation, let us assume VAT at 16 percent, which the consumer has to pay at the final point of sale. But it is only half the story. Assume further that salaries and wages account for half of the selling price at each stage of production before paying VAT, and that materials and services are brought into account for the other half. At the final stage of primary production, salaries and wages are inflated by VAT to the tune of 16 percent: an increase of 16 percent on half the cost of production, and 8 percent on the cost of production. At the second stage of production, wages again result in an increase of 8 percent on production. To this is added an increase of 8 percent on materials and services, or 4 percent on the total cost, which gives a total increase of 12 percent. It is passed on to the next stage of production. By the same reasoning this third stage experiences a cost increase of 8 percent plus 6 percent, which totals 14 percent. The fourth stage rises to 15 percent, and so it progresses toward 16 percent in the final cost of production.

Normally the consumer has to pay this increased price of 16 percent in addition to 16 percent on 116 percent, to which the selling price has risen. The consumer is thus paying 34.5 percent more than the original price before a VAT of 16 percent was introduced. A 34.5 percent wedge between labor and employment is brought about only by VAT. Many other taxes can be treated in a similar manner.

Pay as you earn (PAYE), which is paid directly to the receiver or tax collector by all employers on an official scale that increases with rising wages or salaries, can vary in time and place, but in general it exempts those at the bottom end of the wage scale. It would thus have little or no impact on unemployment of unskilled labor. At the other end of the scale PAYE, a personal income tax, or both could be an additional cause of unemployment among the highly skilled in times of economic downturn. It could also have a bad side effect on unskilled labor.

A company tax is hardly a factor at the economic margin of production because if there are no profits there would be no taxes, but it could have an adverse effect on financial investment decisions. High company taxes can persuade international concerns to invest in other countries, again reducing the potential of employment.

Secondary Causes of Unemployment

A major secondary cause of unemployment is the social security system now so common in many countries. A large portion of the cost of social security goes toward supporting those people who are initially unemployed because of bad taxation. In time, the cost of unemployment adds fuel to the fire.

At first, the idea of supporting the unemployed seems rational and humane: the need to alleviate the suffering of those who lose their jobs because of bad taxation. In discussions with a variety of officials and businessmen in Ireland, Belgium, the Czech Republic, and Hungary, the same story is repeated time and again, varying only in the amount paid to social security, which is based on wages.

Some years ago in Ireland, the contribution to social security was 12 percent of wages paid by the worker and an additional 7.5 percent paid by the employer, a total of 19.5 percent. This system too would have a multiplier effect, which would take it up to well over 30 percent, depending on how it is applied. Naturally, the workers cannot afford to pay the 12 percent, so they would accordingly demand a pay increase. Negotiation would determine what they receive, whatever it is, and would then add to the cost of employment and shift the employer closer to the margin of production, if not beyond it.

In 1995, according to my available sources, the figures for VAT and social security contributions in both Prague and Budapest were found to be far higher than anywhere else in the world; in all cases in excess of 25 percent, if memory serves me. The exact amount is not pertinent to this discussion but is most certainly the underlying principle. Both cities cried out for ameliorative work to be implemented, but the effective cost of labor was too high, while men were almost begging for employment in spite of social security. Unemployment, needless to say, was extremely high.

In many countries the combined cost of VAT and unemployment benefit contributions or social security amounts to between 25 percent and 65 percent even without the multiplier effect discussed above. The multiplier effect would push many taxes above 70 percent, not an unrealistic figure. Some twelve years ago a gentleman in Brussels told me that if his company paid him an extra one thousand units on his salary, he would have an increased spending power of about four hundred units, and it would cost the company approximately 1,600 units. This is a wedge of some 75 percent created between labor and employment. The workers' effective pay package—that is, three times the workers' effective purchasing power—is telling the employer to replace the worker with some machine or labor-saving device.

The system is rotten through and through, but the experts seem to have no rational answers.

Another secondary cause of unemployment, not to be overlooked, is generated by many trade unions. These unions, like some big business, are for the most part not in the least concerned with the welfare of society or the plight of the unemployed and the resultant hardship and misery. While looking after the welfare of their own members, they often impose conditions that reduce the demand for labor or make it nearly impossible for unskilled labor to gain an entry into the economy. In addition, many officials are concerned only with power and their personal agenda.

It seems likely that, were it not for the hardship caused by bad taxation and poor legislation, the trade unions would not have developed the power they now command; so the restricting rules and regulations that now have a further bad effect on employment would not exist. If the trade union officials understood the harm of present taxation, they would be fighting for tax reform instead of increased wages and restraining regulations on employment.

Two aspects of regulations that detract from employment are minimum wages and conditions on retrenchment. A minimum wage that is too high could put most domestic servants and gardeners out of a job. Young and inexperienced job seekers would have nowhere to gain the experience that would make them worthy of the minimum wage; nowhere to start climbing the ladder of success or to develop dignity. Imposition of a high minimum wage could also result in a surge of unemployment. Regulations regarding retrenchment or the dismissal of redundant or ineffective staff and unskilled labor seriously affect the incentive to employ. Fear of the cost of retrenchment, which deprives workers of the benefits of full employment, leads some companies to keep staff on a temporary or short-term contract basis for many years. My experience in a brief venture into small business with a partner, employing a number of semiskilled workers, provides a great incentive never to employ again. That attitude is common in South Africa.

Strategy

To recapitulate, the time has come for Georgists to stop actively promoting the single tax or LVT and thereby allowing the experts to place us on trial to defend ourselves. It is time to place them on trial and make them defend themselves against the harm that they have caused society—unemployment, poverty, and misery with the resultant crime and violence. Leave them struggling for answers and the fear that their pseudoknowledge will become redundant.

Georgists know and have proof that the present system does not work and that most politicians and economists are not to be trusted with the welfare of the people. Place them on trial and "grill" them until they admit that they have no effective answers. Eventually some may be able to open the front door of their minds. When they truly start looking for answers, then and only then should Georgists start to discuss the alternative solution: to eliminate most if not all of the present taxation, and replace it with the natural source of revenue—collection of the entire or partial land rent through land-value taxation.

There is another important reason for not discussing or even considering various aspects of a single tax or other LVT variation. Promoting them should not exclude the possible need for an additional form of taxation to cater to the changing conditions in society that did not exist during Henry George's lifetime. It may become necessary to help reduce the vast accumulation of personal and company wealth that may not be directly related to landownership. Under the LVT form of revenue collection, many forms of speculation and international money and futures dealing could conceivably escape the receiver. Such taxes may include a small amount on money transactions not directly related to normal trade.

Fortunes are made at the expense of nations and communities without the speculators' adding one grain of wealth to the national total. In many cases, the dealing is a highly respectable form of legalized theft. Redistribution by some other form of taxation is becoming more necessary.[2]

At this stage the issue should be kept simple. The immediate need is to expose the weaknesses of the present systems of taxation and to press for tax reform that would encourage full employment.

Notes

1. This is a subject that deserves further investigation.
2. Such a subject also warrants a separate study.

20

Jerome F. Heavey

The Single-Tax Fiscal System

Introduction

The purpose of this article is not to explain the "What?" and the "Why?" of the single tax, but to attempt some answers to the "How?" and the "When?" "How would government administer a single tax?" "When might a single tax be adopted?" This discussion assumes that the single tax is to be the only tax levied by governments, an assumption that allows us to explore many of the issues involved in the operation of the single tax.

We would not bother to talk about the single tax at length if we thought that it would be a minor tax. Unless it is to be a major tax, why talk about it at all? Once we recognize the single tax as a major tax, many of the questions discussed here immediately come to the fore, questions such as: "Which level or levels of government shall levy the single tax?" and "If more than one level of government levies a single tax, how are their tax rates to be coordinated?" Although much of the analysis in this paper would be relevant even if there were other taxes, the discussion is in the context of the polar case, where the single tax is not only a major tax; it is the only tax.

I assume the continuance of the basic social and political arrangements currently existing in the United States: a federal system of government, involving the constitutional degrees of sovereignty presently possessed by the federal and state levels, as well as the practical sovereignty possessed by local governments; the institutional arrangements for private property and markets that currently exist in the United States; and expenditure patterns at all three levels of government essentially unchanged from what they are at present. Although this discussion takes place in the context of the nation's fiscal and economic system, similar constitutional structures and property rights arrangements are to be found in the economic and fiscal systems of many countries, and so the conclusions of this investigation have applicability in other countries.

It may be true, as single-tax proponents argue, that the beneficial effects of the single tax would greatly alter the nature and perhaps the scale of government expenditures. At the beginning, however, when the single tax is first introduced, these beneficial effects would not have had their effect, and it would be required to finance government as it exists today.

The Nature of the Single Tax

There is no doubt that a tax on land is possible: 80,000 jurisdictions in the United States now do so as part of the real-estate tax. Nor can there be any argument that it is possible to remove the taxes on improvements. The measurement process is, to be sure, somewhat more difficult for the single tax than for a real-estate tax. This is because transactions in real estate normally involve the sale of land and improvements together. The single tax requires that the value of land be measured separately from the value of improvements. The experiences of a number of jurisdictions that have levied tax rates on land different from taxes on buildings demonstrate that it is practical to separate the value of land from the value of improvements. If the single tax were to be more widely used, then it is likely that real-estate markets would develop superior mechanisms for pricing land separately from the value of improvements.

All taxes on value, as opposed to taxes on existence, rely ultimately on a market determination of value.[1] The liability for a flow tax, such as an income tax or a sales tax, arises simultaneously with the transaction that establishes the value of the flow. The liability for a stock tax, such as the real-estate tax, arises even when there is no transaction. The single tax as it currently exists is a stock tax. The owner of real estate is liable for a tax on the value of that real estate every year, even though it may have been many years since that parcel of real estate was involved in a market transaction. The assessment process for a real-estate tax depends on comparable sales, and this method has been shown to operate quite satisfactorily.

Although the implementation of the single tax might involve increased administrative costs initially, these costs are not such as to discourage the use of the tax. As a proportion of revenue collected, administrative cost can be expected to decrease as the single tax is more widely used. To the extent that the single tax replaces other taxes, the administrative costs of those taxes would be reduced. Most important is that the single tax distorts economic decision-making less than do other taxes, and this greater economic efficiency is a reduction of the total burden of taxes on society. The single tax is also more equitable than other taxes, and the improvement of equity can justify an increase in administrative costs, especially if that increase is expected to be only temporary.

Governments have three major ways of obtaining revenues: taxes, user charges, and borrowing.[2] User charges are a consequence of government ownership of real assets, such as water treatment plants and toll bridges. Other assets owned by the government, such as the national Capitol and the local town hall, do not generate user charges, but there is an implicit income to government, no different in nature from the implicit income of housing occupied by the owner that is included in the estimation of gross domestic product. The implementation of the single tax would not directly affect government ownership of resources, though it may affect the responsibilities of governments for the resources that they do own.

The adoption of the single tax would not eliminate user charges and government borrowing, for reasons that we discuss later.

Constitutional Questions

If the single tax is to be the only tax, and if it is to provide revenue to all three levels of government, they must agree that the total tax collected will not exceed the annual rent of the land, and therefore must agree on how much of the rent each level of government would collect. It is not immediately apparent how this agreement is to be reached, but an amendment to the Constitution must be part of it. One reason a constitutional amendment would be necessary is that Article I, Section 8, gives Congress power to levy a variety of taxes, and Amendment XVI adds the power to levy taxes on income. If the single tax is to be the only tax, then the Constitution must be amended to remove the power of Congress to levy other taxes.

A hypothetical constitutional amendment might take the form shown in Figure 20.1. The first four sections limit the taxing powers of Congress and the states to the use of the single tax. The fifth section apportions the land rent among the federal and state levels. It would be left to each state to determine, perhaps by amendment to its own constitution, how the state's half of the rental value would be apportioned between state and local governments. A state might decide that it would collect no more than one-fourth of the annual rental value from any piece of land, allowing the local government in which the land is situated to collect as much of the remaining one-fourth as it chose.

Such an amendment will settle what otherwise would be insurmountable constitutional problems. One is the question of whether the federal government can prohibit state governments from levying particular taxes. If an amendment such as this were adopted, it would not be the federal government that imposes the limitations upon state governments. That limitation would be imposed by the Constitution, just as the Constitution has from the beginning prohibited states from levying taxes on the exports of other states. Another question is whether the federal government can dictate the fiscal relationship between a state and its local governments. Again, if the amendment described here were adopted, each of the states would be left to decide that relationship, and a long-established rule is that local governments are the creatures of the state governments, which already determine what taxes their local governments will be allowed to employ.

Determination of the Tax Base

When three levels of government are taxing the same parcel of land, and the sum of the taxes raised by them is not to exceed the annual rental value of the land, all three governments must agree on what that annual rent is. A model for this is currently operative in a number of states, and the main features of that model could be adapted to the single tax in a federal system.

In its current form the real-estate tax is the principal source of local

Figure 20.1 **A Hypothetical Constitutional Amendment**

Section 1. Congress shall have power to levy and collect taxes on the rent of land wherever situated.

Section 2. Congress shall have no other powers of taxation.

Section 3. Each of the several states shall have power to levy and collect taxes on the rent of land wherever situated within the borders of the state.[3]

Section 4. No state shall have any other powers of taxation.

Section 5. On any piece of land Congress may collect in tax no more than one-half of the annual rental value.[4]

Section 6. This Article shall become effective on the first day of January in the tenth year following ratification.

tax revenue to support public education at the primary and secondary levels. Even before *Serrano v. Priest,* however, a number of state governments recognized that this method of financing education made elementary and secondary education inferior in poorer school districts to that in wealthy districts. To reduce the degree of inequality, state governments provide funding to local school districts, using revenues generated from statewide sales and income taxes. The amount of funding that a school district will receive from its state government is determined by a formula established by each state, and the formulas frequently are structured to provide greater state aid to districts with lower market values for a student.

Such formulas create a moral hazard for the local school district. It is in the district's self-interest to understate the value of its taxable property. One way to eliminate this evasion is to make assessment a function on the state level. Instead, assessment has remained at the local level. But a state office reviews the assessments in local districts and compares them with values established by sales of real estate in that district each year. This provides a relatively inexpensive way of equalizing assessments across the state, and effectively removes the moral hazard.

If the single tax were to be adopted for the nation as a whole, a similar moral hazard would exist for the state governments. Each state could lower the federal tax burden on its citizens by understating the value of land in the state. There are several correctives to this perverse incentive. One is self-corrective: The state government that did understate the value of land within its borders would thereby lower the amount of revenue that it could raise from its own share of the single tax. The other corrective would be to establish a federal office similar to the existing state offices described here. Its function would be to sample the actual sales of land in each state and use this sample to equalize assessments nationwide. Thus, the assessment function would remain as a function of local government, just as it is now.

Intergovernmental Revenues

Just as state governments provide substantial transfers to local governments, so the federal government provides substantial transfers to state governments. The amount of transfers from a government of the higher level is partially dependent upon the fiscal resources and fiscal needs at the lower level. In a fiscal system based upon the single tax, the total rental value available to any state would be a factor in determining the size of federal transfers to that state.

User Charges

In addition to taxes, governments generate revenue from user charges. The strict definition of a tax is a compulsory payment to government for which there is no direct return of goods or services. The amount of tax that an individual pays bears no direct relationship to the services provided to that individual by government. The amount of real-estate tax that a household must pay to the local school district, for example, is independent of whether any members of the household attend, have ever attended, or will ever attend the local public schools. Likewise, the household's access to the services financed by taxes is independent of the amount of taxes that the household pays. User charges are payments to government for benefits received directly by the household. All true taxes are levied on the principle of ability to pay, while all true user charges are levied on the principle of benefit. Examples of user charges are bridge tolls and water and sewerage fees. User charges finance what are essentially private goods, in which the recipient of the benefit and the amount of benefit received can be clearly identified.[5]

User charges arise in connection with government ownership of productive assets, such as toll roads and, in some cases, public utilities. User charges are collected in the course of market transactions, the government often being the monopoly provider of the good or service. If the user charges are set properly, then the quantity of the good or service that is provided will be the economically efficient quantity.

Should the adoption of the single tax be the occasion for the abolition of user charges? A prior question is whether government ownership of such assets should continue at all. The services financed by user charges are not public goods such as national defense, environmental quality, and city streets. They are instead private goods such as drinking water and toll bridges.

This chapter will not address the question of whether such goods and services should be provided by the public as opposed to private sectors. We assume that the division between the two sectors will continue as it is. It is the charges for these goods and services that are of interest here.

Most of the goods and services financed by user charges are provided by local governments, and the benefits of those goods and services manifest themselves in increased land values. User charges are a price mechanism, and they carry with them the benefits of the pricing mechanism, particularly the promotion of efficient use of resources. A philosophical implication of the single tax is that the role of government should be limited. The primary means of allocating resources should be decentralized, individual decision making, commonly called the market system. It is only when goods cannot be provided through the market that government has an allocative role. Those goods and services that are currently financed by user charges could be provided through the market. When the government instead provides them, as much as possible of the benefits of the market mechanism should be preserved, and this is a major reason for continuing to finance goods through user charges rather than through the single tax.

It is important that user charges not be higher than is adequate to cover the full cost of providing the goods or services in question. If they are, then the user charge contains a hidden excise tax. Our hypothetical constitutional amendment would forbid excise taxes, but they might be slipped in under the guise of net revenues of a government enterprise.

A notorious example of such a disguised excise tax can be found in state lotteries. A lottery is a good of a private character, and states operating lotteries generally speak of the lottery as a government enterprise. The price of a lottery ticket is the sum of three components: the prize fund, administrative costs, and the hidden excise tax. Consider a typical state lottery, with a ticket price of one dollar. On average, states return as prize money 45 percent of the ticket price. Roughly 10 percent of the ticket price pays for administrative costs, including the commissions of sellers. The remainder, averaging about 45 percent, goes to the state government. States operating a lottery may choose to speak of this remainder as the profits of a state enterprise, but it is indistinguishable from an excise tax on lottery tickets.

A similar argument applies to a user charge for any good or service provided by government. If government were providing such goods in a competitive market, the pressure of competition would tend to drive the price to the level of the average total cost, so that there would be no excise tax markup. But, of course, government provision of a good or service is invariably a monopoly provision.

Excise taxes are regressive, particularly when levied on the kinds of goods and services that government finances with user charges. Regressivity is a strong argument against excise taxes, and therefore it is a strong argument against user charges that are set above the level of cost.

Government Borrowing

In addition to employing taxes and user charges, governments acquire funds through borrowing. Governments borrow to finance capital projects, to smooth out the flow of revenues, and to finance budget deficits. These motivations differ primarily by their time horizons.

The costs of capital-construction projects are front-loaded, while the increase in revenues is distributed over the years of the useful life of the new facility. The cost of the project may consequently exceed the revenue available during the time of construction, so that the project could not be financed on the basis of "pay as you go." Some capital projects, such as water-treatment plants and toll bridges, provide a private type of good or service and therefore generate a stream of user charges over the life of the physical plant. Other capital projects, such as city streets and environmental programs, provide a good or service of a public nature. Although no stream of user charges issues from these goods and services, land rents go up in the area served by the new facility. It is appropriate that the cost of the project be spread out over the same span of years that the user charges or increased land rents will exist. This points toward long-term financing through borrowing.

An example of borrowing to coordinate the timing of revenues and expenditures would be by a city government that must pay its police officers and firefighters every two weeks, beginning in January, while most of the real-estate tax may come due in June. Short-term borrowing that anticipates taxes smooths the government's cash flow, adjusting the timing of income to the timing of expenditures.

Borrowing for financing of budget deficits is similar, though looking to a longer time horizon. Governments are able to borrow money only if they can convince lenders that they will be able to pay it back according to a schedule agreed upon. Although expenditures currently exceed revenues, the situation will be reversed in the future, when repayment of the debt is due. Like the other two types of borrowing, this is fully consistent with a single tax.

A Last Comment

Section 6 of the hypothetical constitutional amendment stated that the single tax would go into effect ten years after ratification of the amendment. Whether the necessary lead time is ten years, or twenty, or eight, I do not know, but surely a long lead time for implementation is necessary. The implementation of the single tax requires the establishment of the mechanisms for assessment and collection at all three levels of government. It also requires that all existing taxpayers adjust to the new tax structure. Unavoidable windfall gains and losses will fall to individual persons and firms. Albeit that society as a whole will be better off, the burden on individuals would be intolerable if the transition were carried out too quickly. A long lead time is the opportunity for individuals and firms to adjust to the change in tax regimes.

Notes

1. Levies on value are also called "ad valorem taxes"; taxes on existence are termed "unit taxes."

2. A national government has also the printing press, using inflation to generate revenue by monetizing some part of the budget deficit and to reduce the real value of its debt. It may be that only unanticipated inflation should be included here, because anticipated inflation will be reflected in higher interest costs that the national government will pay on its borrowing.

3. Section 3, taken by itself, is not necessary, for state governments already have the power to tax the rent of land. But Section 3 together with Section 4 spells out the extent and the limitations of state taxing power.

4. As was stated earlier, much of the discussion in this paper would be relevant even if the single tax were not the only tax imposed by government. If other taxes were to be allowed, then, of course, Sections 2 and 4 would be deleted from the amendment.

5. Economists define private goods as those that have the following two characteristics. First, exclusion is feasible; those who do not pay for the good can be excluded from the consumption of it. Second, consumption is rival; as one person consumes the good, less remains for everyone else. Only the first characteristic need exist in order for user charges, or prices, to be practicable.

About the Contributors

Robert V. Andelson is professor emeritus of philosophy, Auburn University. He is also president of the International Union for Land-Value Taxation and Free Trade, and Distinguished Research Fellow of the American Institute for Economic Research.

Herbert Barry III is a professor at the University of Pittsburgh. He received his Ph.D. in psychology from Yale University in 1957. Topics of his publications include personality development, psychobiography, political science, psychiatry, and psychopharmacology.

Hanno T. Beck is founder and president of the Benjamin Banneker Center for Economic Justice, Columbia, Maryland. He is the publisher of a family of Web sites.

Harry Gunnison Brown was a distinguished economist who lived from 1880 until 1975. He received his Ph.D. from Yale in 1904. He taught economics there from 1909 to 1915 and subsequently, until 1947, at the University of Missouri, where he became chairman. After retirement he continued his role of educator at The New School, the University of Mississipi, and Franklin and Marshall. He wrote extensively and was a staunch advocate of land-value taxation.

Roy Douglas is emeritus reader at the University of Surrey, England. He is author of a number of books, mostly on historical subjects, including a study of the land question in United Kingdom politics. He has been a Liberal parliamentary candidate on five occasions and is chairman of the Land Value Taxation Campaign.

Godfrey R. A. Dunkley has studied and tutored economics at the School of Economic Science in South Africa and served two terms as the president of the International Union for Land Value Taxation and Free Trade. He carried out two RSA surveys on municipal rating, and is the author of the 1990 book *That All May Live—Guidelines: Towards a Better Society* and the pamphlet "Land Tenure: A Time Bomb Ticking in South Africa."

Fred E. Foldvary teaches economics at John F. Kennedy University, California State University at Hayward, and the University of California at Berkeley Extension. He is the author of *The Soul of Liberty* and *Public Goods and Private Communities,* and has edited *Beyond Neoclassical Economics.* His *Dictionary of Free-Market Economics* was published at the end of 1998.

Mason Gaffney is professor of economics at the University of California at Riverside. He received his Ph.D. in economics at the University of California, Berkeley. He has served as a consultant for many jurisdictions both here and abroad. He has been the organizer of conferences and author of numerous books, articles, speeches, and essays on economics.

Damon J. Gross received his Ph.D. in philosophy in 1978 at the University of Iowa. He has spent most of his working life in the computer industry. He has taught part-time at a number of universities and is published in the fields of social and political philosophy.

C. Lowell Harriss is professor emeritus of political science, Columbia University; chairman of the Robert Schalkenbach Foundation; and faculty associate, Lincoln Institute of Land Policy.

Alanna Hartzok is state coordinator for the Pennsylvania Fair Tax Coalition.

Jerome F. Heavey received his Ph.D. from Penn State. He was a visiting scholar at University College, Dublin. He is currently chairman of the Department of Economics and Business at Lafayette College and a senior adviser for the Fiscal Reform Project to the Russian Federation.

Vernon I. Saunders received his M.Sc. from the University of Western Ontario in 1946 and worked for the Eastman Kodak Company for thirty-five years. He has been an advocate of land-value taxation for twenty years.

T. Nicolaus Tideman is professor of economics, Virginia Polytechnic Institute and State University. He received his Ph.D. in economics from the University of Chicago in 1969. He has taught at Harvard University and the University of Buckingham and has served as a senior staff economist for the President's Council of Economic Advisors. He is the author of more than forty articles, mainly on topics in public finance and efficient public decision-making.

William Vickrey was a professor of economics at Columbia University. He was a Nobel laureate for economics in 1996 in sharing the honors with James Mirrless. He died shortly thereafter .

Kenneth C. Wenzer is a historian. He received his Ph.D in history from the Catholic University of America in 1992. He is the author of *Anarchists Adrift* and a number of articles and essays, and he is the editor of *The Henry George Centennial Trilogy,* which appeared in 1997. He is also an inventor who holds several patents.

Thomas R. West is associate professor of history at the Catholic University of America. He is the author of *Flesh of Steel; Nature, Community, and Will;* and *The Ambiguous Sin of Property.* He is also the coauthor of *The Torch Is Passed:The Kennedy Brothers and American Liberalism; Column Right;* and *To Redeem a Nation: A History and Anthology of the Civil Rights Movement.*

Index

E

F

G

H

I

J

K

L

Q

R

S

T

U

V

W

Z